Wise-Minded Parenting

7 Essentials for Raising Successful Tweens + Teens

Laura S. Kaster, Ph.D.

with Kristen A. Russell

FOREWORD BY DANIEL J. SIEGEL, M.D.

Praise for *Wise-Minded Parenting*

"*Wise-Minded Parenting* is such a welcome resource for parents who want to understand what really works to build success in teens. The authors go way beyond the usual parenting tips to describe cutting-edge research on such topics as self-control, academic performance, and mindsets. And they provide simple, down-to-earth strategies. How rewarding to see scientifically-proven practices given to parents where it can do so much good!"

—CAROL S. DWECK, PH. D.
Lewis and Virginia Eaton Professor of Psychology, Stanford University
Author, *Mindset: How You Can Fulfill Your Potential*

"This book is a guideline for how to stay in wise mind with your child—a difficult task indeed. When parenting, staying out of extreme emotion mind is both of the essence and extremely difficult. Thank heaven for this book, which gives step-by-step instructions on how to get into and stay in wise mind."

—MARSHA LINEHAN, PH.D.
Professor of psychology and adjunct professor of psychiatry
and behavioral sciences at the University of Washington

"It's very easy as a parent to lose your mind just when you need it the most. This wonderfully thoughtful, wise, and comprehensive guide maps out the latest research and knowledge about what our tweens and teens need to thrive, and, most importantly, offers us much-needed practical strategies for acting and responding more mindfully and effectively throughout this rich and challenging period, helping us to maintain our deep threads of connection with our children as they come to build trust in themselves."

—MYLA AND JON KABAT-ZINN
Authors, *Everyday Blessings: The Inner Work of Mindful Parenting*

"This is such an amazingly useful book for parents of teenagers. It gives you realistic dialogue that fails, and the retakes that make these dialogues work. First of all, what defines a great conversation with a teen may surprise many parents. Second of all, Kastner teaches you the specific skills and the general wisdom to guide your teen through adolescence, and stay emotionally connected throughout. This is a great book—a must-read for all parents."

—JOHN M. GOTTMAN, PH.D.
Author, *Raising an Emotionally Intelligent Child*

"*Wise-Minded Parenting* is one of those rarities in the world of parenting guides: a thoughtful and practical resource that is grounded in the scientific study of child development and parent-child relationships. I recommend it enthusiastically."

—LAURENCE STEINBERG, PH.D.
Professor of psychology at Temple University
Author, *The 10 Basic Principles of Good Parenting* and *You and Your Adolescent*

"Do I contradict myself?
Very well then I contradict myself,
(I am large, I contain multitudes.)"
—*Walt Whitman, "Song of Myself"*

Printed in the United States of America
Published by ParentMap
Distributed by Ingram Publisher Services

01 24 13 MAL 01 3000 1995

Cover photograph: Will Austin
Cover design: Emily Johnson
Interior design and composition: Emily Johnson
Library of Congress Cataloging-in-Publication Data is available.

ISBN-13: 978-0-9830128-5-6
ISBN-10: 0-9830128-5-7

ParentMap dba Gracie Enterprises
4742 42nd Ave. S.W., #399
Seattle, WA 98116-4553
206-709-9026

ParentMap books are available at special discounts when purchased in bulk for premiums and sales promotions as well as for fundraisers or educational use. Place book orders at *parentmap.com* or 206-709-9026.

SUSTAINABLE FORESTRY INITIATIVE
Label applies to the text stock

Certified Sourcing
www.sfiprogram.org
SFI-00341

Contents

Foreword BY DANIEL J. SIEGEL, M.D.

Parenting is a challenging long-distance course that can also be one of the most rewarding adventures we have in life. The transition from parenting in the early years of childhood to adolescence is huge. This book will make that transition smoother, and the experience of being a parent more effective and enjoyable for you.

The journey of parenting becomes more complex and confusing as our children enter the preteen period, or "tween" years, when transformations in their bodies and changes in their social worlds bring on new requirements for how we approach our parenting role. As these children move on into the teen years, maturation of the body continues with important reconstruction of the brain itself, making teens prone to abrupt emotional shifts that can be confusing for any parent.

What can we do with these new ways our sons and daughters are behaving, thinking, and feeling? Given that research clearly demonstrates that what we do as parents matters greatly in shaping the development of our children's and teens' minds, how can we parent them so that they are equipped with the essential abilities to not only survive this challenging period, but also thrive? In *Wise-Minded Parenting*, you have a magnificent tool kit to help you become the parent you will be proud to be—one who knows what can be known during this beguiling period, and understands how to interact with your adolescent so that they can be given the best opportunity to become resilient in the face of stress, kind and compassionate to themselves and others, and prepared with a lifelong inner strength to face the complex and rapidly changing world. With these skills, your tween and teen will emerge from these years not only able to meet life's demands, but to find meaning and purpose in their lives.

Reading such offerings about a single book, you might think I am the author's brother! But the truth is that I am a parent of two adolescents, as well as a child and adolescent psychiatrist, and an educator in the field of mental health, working within an interdisciplinary approach called interpersonal neurobiology. I am not Dr. Kastner's brother. In her clear and well-planned book, written with Kristen Russell, you will find a rich source of easily understood information that draws on a wide array of sciences to support the question: What is the best thing I can do as a parent for my tween and teen? Science and clinical practice are woven seamlessly together in the chapters ahead to provide you with one of the most articulately expressed, useful sets of research-validated parenting strategies you'll ever find.

In these pages, you will learn the basics of how the parent-child attachment relationship forms the internal foundation that sets the stage for how adolescents move through their important transition from child to adult. You'll explore vital ideas about the brain and how our ability to develop self-control—how we regulate our feelings, thoughts, attention, impulses, and behaviors—is formed by the experiences we have at home and in school. When this self-control is applied to our "work" at school, we learn to become disciplined in our efforts and to realize that how we try shapes how we academically succeed. That is a lesson that can be generalized in everything an adolescent will do later in life, from work settings to interpersonal relationships. Effort is needed for success in life. Parents are the first teachers for this important life lesson.

You'll also discover how research has shown that relationships shape nearly everything in our lives, from our physical health to our mental development. We thrive socially when our connections with others are honored and cultivated.

Wise-minded parents learn to provide the kind of authoritative guidance—filled with warmth, limit setting, and the age-appropriate honoring of the child's growth of autonomy—that research has repeatedly shown, across cultures and socioeconomic status, to be the best approach to helping our offspring grow well in their emotional, social, and intellectual lives. Being authoritative, and not excessively permissive or authoritarian, is a skill that you can learn, if you are not already there. Science has demonstrated that when you bring this authoritative approach to your children, it raises the likelihood that they will flourish emotionally.

And if all of this were not enough, the book goes even further to explore the science of how personality is formed, and what we can do as parents to help our children develop key character elements, such as kindness, honesty, love of learning, optimism, collaboration, and even social and emotional intelligence, that support a healthy life in adolescence and adulthood. We learn how to bring more positive emotions into our family life, filling our inner and interpersonal lives with gratitude, a sense of generosity, and a feeling of connection to others. Character is built on a foundation of solid physical health, and in the final chapter you'll find an excellent overview of the crucial elements of daily life, including sleep, eating, and physical activities, that support a healthy lifestyle.

Throughout the book, you'll come upon sections that help you practice what is taught, learning how to reflect on what things are like in your family, and how to make your approach as a parent more effective and more rewarding. There are numerous immersions in important topics, such as how we can deal with the onslaught of digital media in all our lives and how changes in sexual behavior have been altering the nature of friendships during this important period of life. The authors leave no stone unturned, and we, the readers, are the immediate beneficiaries of this beautifully constructed book. The next in line to reap the wonderful gifts this work offers are our tweens and teens, whose lives will be greatly enhanced by the skills and knowledge we acquire as their parents. What better gift to give to our children—and to ourselves—than this comprehensive and scientifically based set of effective strategies to help our adolescents thrive?

Daniel J. Siegel, M.D.
Executive director, Mindsight Institute
Clinical professor, UCLA School of Medicine
Author, *The Developing Mind* and *Mindsight*
Co-author, *Parenting from the Inside Out* and *The Whole-Brain Child*

Acknowledgments

When we first dreamed up this interactive, multiplatform parenting resource, we knew we need look no further than the visionary, exuberant publisher of *ParentMap*, Alayne Sulkin, to see it through to fruition. Our deep appreciation goes to Alayne and her marvelous team of media innovators, and their commitment to educating, connecting, and delighting parents.

Thanks are also due to our insightful and generous editor, Ingrid Emerick, who kept us on the straight and narrow; our eagle-eyed and patient copy editor, Sunny Parsons; our meticulous research assistant, Shawna Leader; and our designer, Emily Johnson, who made perfect sense of many moving parts.

It's been a tremendous privilege studying and synthesizing the important and ever-growing body of research into child development, family life, and parenting, and inventing ways to make that information accessible and relevant to parents' lives. We offer our appreciation and admiration to the brilliant, dedicated scientists and researchers who continue to elevate our understanding of the inner lives of teens. The parents and teenagers who appear throughout this book are composites based on real-life families from Laura Kastner's clinical experience over decades; their persistence, determination, and love are humbling and inspiring.

Finally, to our own families, the biggest thanks of all: Philip, Cameron, and Lindley; and Aidan, Kayleigh, and John: You are our true essentials.

Introduction

Do seemingly benign interactions with your tween or teen often inexplicably turn nasty? Does a simple, offhanded comment trigger a response dripping with sarcasm or rudeness? Does it sometimes feel as if you are living in a powder keg of pent-up anger? If you answered yes to some or all of the above, take heart; you are probably the parent of a normal teenager. For those parents lucky enough to live in a still-harmonious home, take a deep, appreciative breath and know that someday soon, your child might just change the game, leaving you scratching your head over the complicated—and emotionally loaded—new ground rules.

Navigating the tween and teen years is a challenge for any parent, and even the calmest and wisest among us struggle with this crucial phase of our child's development. Raising a happy, healthy, and successful teenager is a serious undertaking, and doing so requires all sorts of skills that most of us don't naturally possess.

As if that weren't enough, the whole thing seems to sneak up on you. You've made it through the sleep-deprived infant phase, the busy, boundary-testing toddler and pre-school days, and the ever-changing elementary school years. You have a little more freedom, maybe a little more "me" time; you can even squeeze in a date night here and there. Your child is probably more and more independent, but still affectionate and generally does as you ask. This is what you've been waiting for: All that hard work has finally paid off!

And then one day, your family life becomes tumultuous. Your good parenting is no longer enough. Your best efforts meet with failure. You are made to feel that everything you do is intensely annoying, irrelevant, and uncool.

It's a hard landing for most parents, and it can leave many of us feeling defeated, frustrated, and as unsure of ourselves as when we first held our newborns. The good news is that you have far more—and far better—resources to draw upon than ever before; new research in the fields of neuroscience, child development, and psychology offers greater understanding and insight into our children's development. And that's where this book comes in, merging the most recent information on adolescence with a unique framework to help parents navigate this new phase in their child's life—and their own.

Recent research shows that negotiating the inevitable family minefield of the tween and teen years is infinitely easier for parents who develop a certain set of skills. We call these parents "wise-minded," borrowing the term from an emerging system of treatment called dialectical behavior therapy (DBT). In the following pages, you'll learn much more about DBT, and about compelling new research on adolescents, families, and neuroscience, which, along with my thirty years of clinical practice, inform this book.

Simply put, wise-minded parenting is what happens when you balance both sides of your mental equation: rational thought and emotion. You become wise-minded when you combine the power of thinking with a keen understanding of your emotions—and your teen's—to come up with thoughtful and effective ways of handling difficult, upsetting, and emotionally complex situations.

To do this, however, you must first reach a calm physiological state. This allows you to access both cool-headed decision-making (in DBT, this is called "reason mind") and the ability to quell the intense distress of your emotions (or "emotion mind"). Mindful parenting, a popular style of child rearing these days, is a start, because it emphasizes the importance of empathy and emotional awareness. Building on that awareness, wise-minded parenting allows you to nurture your child with a steady hand, informed by a deep understanding of his or her inner emotional landscape and a clear idea of what's reasonable to expect. Learning and utilizing this practice can restore harmony to your home by helping you avoid emotional firefights with your kids. You'll discover how to contain blowups, to respond to them effectively when they do happen, and to develop deeper empathy for your continually evolving—and sometimes downright chaotic—child.

Whether you are feeling increasingly disconnected from your teenager, seeing the first inklings of a troubling trend, or witnessing worrisome and unacceptable behavior, there are practical ways to turn the tide. It takes time and energy—both increasingly spare commodities in our fast-paced, modern lives—so *Wise-Minded Parenting* provides you with easy-to-use techniques, activities, and tips, and even mantras—simple phrases to hold in mind as you work to evaluate and improve your interactions with your kids.

Quizzes, tips, action plans, practice scripts, and real-life vignettes—all grounded in fifty years of parenting research and current evidence-based treatment models—will help you better support your teen as he or she develops the seven essentials for a healthy and successful future: secure attachment, self-control, academic success, social thriving, emotional flourishing, strong character, and physical health. You'll learn *why* these are the seven essentials, and determine which are solidly under construction in your child and which are most important to work on right now.

As you progress through each chapter, feel free to write your answers directly in the book, or keep a notebook or journal handy. The work you do here will help you assess your family situation, prioritize tasks, and plot your course.

Unlike parenting books of the past, *Wise-Minded Parenting* offers vital material across multiple platforms—with companion mobile, online, and interactive elements—making it easy for parents to incorporate new skills into their busy lives. Through the mobile-enabled Wise-Minded Parenting website (*wisemindedparenting.com*), you'll get free access to a program of "Wise-Minded Parenting Skills," which features fifty-two exercises you can use to support your progress. The Wise-Minded Parenting website offers a meeting place where you can interact with other parents and the experts to swap ideas, share successes, and, sometimes, just commiserate. More information about adolescent development can be found in the Parent Resources section at the end of this book.

Our world is moving ever faster, and parents have to fit family life into an ever-narrowing window of time. Most of us are expected to simultaneously hold down a job, maintain a household, raise terrific kids, and uphold community obligations. That's nothing new, but what is new is that in more families than ever, both parents work; in 2010, nearly 65 percent of all families had both parents in the labor force, according to the U.S. Census. That same year, more than nine million families with children younger than eighteen were being maintained by single mothers.

Teens are busier than ever, too, and hyperconnected to each other and to media in unprecedented ways. As a result, peer influences, always a crucial part of shaping self-perception and actions, are even more amped up. As teen-peer connectedness explodes in this technology-saturated world, teen-parent connectedness is taking a beating. We need new tools for addressing our kids' ever-changing social-media worlds, prioritizing family time, and competing for the attention of our already tuned-out teens.

And while we're at it, we need to remember that teenagers are on a thrilling—and often excruciating—ride. Understanding the fundamental social, emotional, and neuro-logical dynamics is key. Why? Because with understanding comes empathy, and, for many of us, an increase in patience and peacefulness—two parenting skills that are so crucial, they inspired the creation of my previous book, *Getting to Calm: Cool-headed Strategies for Parenting Tweens + Teens*, co-written with Dr. Jennifer Wyatt.

Getting to Calm presented management approaches for "hot button" teen behaviors to help parents. In *Wise-Minded Parenting*, I've collaborated with co-author Kristen Russell to bring you the "best practices" of effective parents who help their teens master the seven essentials vital to future happiness and success. After reading this book, you'll better understand the unique experience of being a teenager and develop calmer, more resourceful ways of navigating these challenging years.

Raising successful teenagers is a lofty enough goal for any family. For those struggling with specific problems associated with depression, divorce, abuse, or disability, the skills presented in this book may not be appropriate, or go far enough, and professional assis-tance should be sought. But for most of us coping with the mixed, messy bag that is adolescence, the news is promising: Most teenagers turn out OK, even terrific.

From time immemorial, parents have sought help from any and all sources—friends, family, the experts—as they guide and support their teen. The aim of *Wise-Minded Parenting* is to provide that helping hand in the form of a research-based, user-friendly, multimedia support system as you work to reach the ultimate goal: a warm and loving connection to your happy, thriving, and successful teen.

CHAPTER 1
Secure Attachment

Scene: *It's dinnertime on a school night, and just as a mom is putting food on the table, her teenager hits her with a request.*

> *Kate: I need to go to Jen's after dinner. Can you take me?*
> *Mom: Wait—I thought you had a huge math test tomorrow. You need to stay home and study.*
> *Kate: Mom, I'm ready for the test. Jen's upset. She needs me.*
> *Mom: I'm sorry about Jen, but studying comes first. You're staying home. And you know we have a no-socializing rule on school nights anyway.*
> *Kate: You never liked Jen! I hate your stupid rules! You are such a mean mom!*
> *Mom: Mean? After all I do for you? I'm just trying to keep you from failing math.*
> *Kate: I'll fail it anyway. You're ruining my life.*

Sound extreme? Maybe not, if you've got a full-blown teenager living in your house. Communication breakdowns like this one are all too common during the late-tween and early-teen years, and they can be baffling, frustrating, and even frighteningly explosive at times. Where did this exchange take a wrong turn? How did this mother and daughter, who actually both want the same things—good math scores and a healthy social life— end up so at odds? What strategy could the wise-minded parent employ to reach a more satisfying outcome?

If you live with an older tween or teen, you've probably already noticed: Your darling child is morphing into something new—something strange and wonderful, but also occasionally sullen, self-absorbed, and even downright rude. If your child is still a preteen (or "tween," between nine and fourteen years of age), know that this transformation is probably coming, if it hasn't already arrived. Some days will be fine; on others, you may wonder if the two of you even *like* each other anymore. At those times, it might be hard to imagine how you'll ever again feel a connection to this sulking ball of hormones and attitude. Is all of this frequent conflict—and your mounting frustration with your child's behavior—doing permanent damage to your relationship? How can you keep communication flowing and your once loving connection strong through the turbulent teen years? And does it really matter to your child's future success if you don't?

Why Attachment Matters

Maintaining a warm, loving bond with your child certainly *does* matter, and not just because those glimmers of fond connection provide welcome relief during stormy times. A secure attachment is crucial to your child's future success in all kinds of measurable ways. Tweens and teens who share a strong bond with their parents are better adjusted socially, get better grades, are less likely to use alcohol and drugs . . . the list goes on, and the research backs it up (Cassidy and Shaver 2008). Secure attachment is also associated with other crucial strengths in adulthood: the ability to form trusting romantic relationships, a greater resilience when under stress, and less susceptibility to mental illness, to name just a few.

As a bonus, it's easier to parent securely attached kids: They show more initiative and self-control, and have a greater capacity to make and keep friends than kids with histories of anxious and insecure attachment. These findings hold up in study after study, even after accounting for the effects of socioeconomic disparity, IQ, and temperament. With all of that on the line, it's clear that fostering and maintaining a secure, loving attachment with your teen is essential to your child's success.

HOW ATTACHMENTS ARE FORMED

To understand the nature of your child's attachment to you today, it's helpful to trace the roots of your bond. Back when your tween or teen was just a baby, you formed an attachment with him using a powerful tool: love. Although "love" is the word we use most commonly to describe our feelings for the children we adore, "secure attachment" is the psychological term that describes the optimal emotional, social, and cognitive bond that results from certain parental behaviors.

A child is securely attached when the parent or caregiver is reliable and responsive to his needs and emotions. As a result, the child sees the world as a stable place that is safe to explore. Initially, he explores with his eyes, mouth, and hands, all of which serve to charm and engage his loving parent, forming an even stronger shared bond. The brain of a securely attached child actually converts this sense of security into physical, neural connections, which continue to develop in response to attentive parenting over time.

British psychiatrist John Bowlby and Canadian developmental psychologist Mary Ainsworth were the first to introduce the theory of secure attachment in babies nearly fifty years ago; research done since the introduction of this theory has established secure attachment's importance to child, adolescent, and adult mental health and adjustment. Furthermore, neuroscientists studying brain scans have found that the brain is "wired" to connect; in fact, it connects neurons on the basis of loving interactions. Brain science has finally caught up with what observational research had been showing for several decades: The trust and security established during childhood and adolescence are critical in helping young people successfully launch to adulthood.

Psychiatrist and researcher Daniel Siegel is considered a bridge builder in the study of secure attachment; he has linked the worlds of child development, infant research, psychotherapy, and neuroscience into what he calls the "neurobiology" of attachment (Siegel 2001). Siegel is on a public-health mission to help parents understand that neural growth in a baby's brain isn't merely caused by positive connections; it actually *depends* upon those connections. A secure attachment stimulates neural growth—literally. The loving, encouraging interactions you had with your baby helped to build his sense of security, which in turn built neural connections, which end up predicting all manner of strengths that contribute to success later in life.

> **ESSENTIAL**
> # FACT
> ### The Importance of Bonding
> Neural growth in a baby's brain depends on responsive, attuned interactions, which build a foundation for security in future relationships with others.

If you feel pretty good about the first few years of your parenting life, when the bonds of attachment are first forged, this research will come as a relief. But if you remember those first years as difficult or tumultuous, it may cause concern. You may wonder if your "imperfect" parenting has set your child up for later failure or unhappiness. Here's the good news: In the same way that "genes are not destiny," neither is early life. In fact, a successful person is often the result of a mysterious and messy recipe, of which a solid early childhood is only one ingredient.

The brain continues to remodel itself in response to experiences we have throughout our lives. And thanks to the brain's plasticity, positive interpersonal interactions of all kinds—both within and outside of the family—contribute to the positive emotions and responsive interactions that result in neural growth. It has even been suggested that we can *remove* the legacy of early attachment deficits through therapeutic and loving experiences later on. If your bond with your child is not all that you wish it were—all that it needs to be—there is still time to strengthen this essential attachment.

BEGIN WITH UNDERSTANDING

Whether your bond is solid or in need of some reinforcement, the first step to fostering this secure attachment in the adolescent years is to understand what your child is going through on a physiological and neural level.

Your adolescent is facing a monumental developmental project—identity formation—which is made possible because of all the trust and inner security she's built up over the years. Teens want to trust their parents, and they want to be trusted themselves, so that they can explore, establish their own identities, become independent, and develop their skills. It's a teen-parent dance to negotiate this process, balancing the child's quest for increasing freedom with the parent's desire to keep their child safe. Striking that tricky balance is at the root of many a teen-parent conflict. And it's easy to lose sight of the warm teen-parent connection when you're constantly at odds.

To maintain this connection, parents need to give love and nurturance—*even while being dumped on, neglected, and taken for granted!* (Yes, there are limits, as we'll explain later.) Essentially, parents have to trust that the love connection is still there during the slim-pickings period of adolescence. In the dance of the second decade, there are many other dynamics at play that make the love connection less overtly expressed than it was in the first decade. In fact, the teen's erratic efforts to develop their identity and individuality make it all but certain that there will be a lot of tension and conflict in the dance.

You may not always get along with your teen—in fact, it might seem like you are rarely at peace—but underneath it all, the bond developed in that first decade together remains firmly in place in the vast majority of families.

But here's something to keep in mind: Closeness—and opportunities for becoming closer and strengthening that bond—will be negotiated with the teen (not you!) taking the lead. If it's easy for you to let go of the need for a nonstop positive rapport with your teen, take it as a clue that you're secure, either because of your family-of-origin experience, sunny and resilient temperament, good psychotherapy, or a combination of those factors. If not, be reassured that you'll probably still have a lot of good times with your teen; it's just that needing, insisting on, or pushing for good times *on your schedule* will usually result in a backlash.

Some parents will be lucky: Their kids will disclose openly and welcome their company, even their advice. Other families will suffer a high level of friction due to external circumstances, the parent's temperament, the child's temperament, or a combination of all three. The majority of parents, however, will see an increase in volatility and distancing at around age twelve or thirteen, and then a gradual decrease in later adolescence.

WHY IS MAINTAINING A CLOSE BOND WITH MY TEENAGER SO HARD?

Any one or all of the realities presented below might be at work in your relationship with your child.

You are being set up to fail by your child, who has the difficult developmental task of individuating from you. In the process, you have to become "chopped liver." Your teenager must come to see and assess (and probably helpfully point out!) your many flaws as part of his own self-construction.

You are the safest person for your teenager to dump on. Your teenager is sometimes "self-controlled out." She needs to drop that exhausting effort sometimes and let rip some cathartic palate-cleansing rudeness. Unfortunately, your agenda of having nice family moments is often subverted by her agenda of letting loose emotionally.

You may be dealing with a teen who has a difficult temperament. If your child is very sensitive, anxious, or reactive, he will be more likely to lash out or have bafflingly volatile responses to your most innocuous overtures.

Life is like that. Busy, stressful, demanding, difficult . . . daily life takes a lot of energy to negotiate at the best of times.

You might be expecting too much. It's important—though not always easy—to have realistic expectations. The vast majority of teens are more attached to parents than to anyone else, but their displays of love and appreciation often go underground during this period. They are breaking away and creating space to establish their own unique identities. Teen rudeness is rarely about something egregious the parent has done; instead, it stems from the teen's developmental need for individuation, their compromised impulse control, and general hormonal moodiness. Thus, parents need to do most of the bridge building—and tolerate a lot of friction—in order to foster the bond, despite negative messages from the teen.

YOUR CHILD'S ATTACHMENT

In the face of mounting sarcasm, fits of temper, or total withdrawal, it may seem to you that your teen's attachment to you is somehow at risk, but that's not necessarily so. You can get a sense of the state of your child's attachment by taking the following quiz.

ESSENTIAL
QUIZ

How Secure Is Your Teen's Attachment to You?

Indicate whether you believe your teen would agree or disagree with the following statements regarding his or her relationship with you. Note: For this exercise, what's important are your impressions. Like all of the quizzes in this book, this is not a psychometrically validated assessment—it's a shorthand quiz! Asking these questions of your child, while interesting, may not yield much insight into your relationship, since he may be in a bad mood or just want to bring you down a notch. If you co-parent, you may want to ask your partner to take the quiz separately and then compare notes.

	Agree	Disagree	
1.	☐	☐	My parent respects my feelings.
2.	☐	☐	My parent accepts me just the way I am.
3.	☐	☐	My parent is a reliable source of support for me.
4.	☐	☐	I value my parent's perspectives on issues.
5.	☐	☐	My parent values my opinions on issues.
6.	☐	☐	When I'm upset, my parent shows concern.

If you answered "agree" to all or most of the above, you probably share a strong, stable attachment with your child. But even parents who enjoy a strong bond with their kids may check "disagree" on one or more of these statements.

Every parent can benefit from cultivating more empathy for their teen by understanding what he or she is going through developmentally—from significant changes in brain chemistry to an onslaught of hormones, to the stresses and pressures of school and friends, all set against a backdrop of identify formation and individuation. Individuation—the gradual creation of an individual self through the examination and exploration of goals, values, and competencies—is necessary for a healthy launching into the adult world. It's a long haul to build this competent self, and much of it will be somewhat chaotic and fraught with explorative forays into thoughts, feelings, and actions—some of which will be uncomfortable for the parent. But this important work of building a robust self is best accomplished by teens whose parents encourage the individuation process despite that discomfort. In the pages that follow, you'll learn how to better cope with some of the normal messiness of teen individuation.

Wise-Minded Parenting 101

For help with handling the tough and emotionally laden times with teens, parents can utilize some of the concepts and techniques of an evidence-based treatment approach called dialectical behavior therapy (DBT). Developed by University of Washington psychology researcher Marsha M. Linehan for individuals who have problems with emotional control, DBT combines common cognitive-behavioral techniques for emotional regulation with elements drawn from the Buddhist traditions of acceptance, tolerance, and mindfulness (Linehan 1993). While Linehan developed DBT in research with adults, other clinicians have translated its principles for working with children, especially for kids who experience intense emotions (Harvey and Penzo 2009).

The word "dialectical" refers to the crucial process by which we examine opposing truths in an effort to reach a deep understanding of a principle, a feeling, or a dynamic. For instance, we love our family members, but they often frustrate us or make us mad. To understand the truth of intimacy, we need to examine the ways in which we love and cherish our families, even as we can be made to feel furious, exasperated, or trapped by them. Remember the ancient philosophers Socrates and Plato? Dialectics is what they were engaging in during all those amazing dialogues—and what happens in the best class-rooms and dinner conversations! We want our kids to become critical thinkers, and this is one of the ways it can be developed. (Learn about the "Socratic method" in chapter 4.)

One of the most important dialectical principles to understand and embrace is the "acceptance/change" principle: In order for you to help your children change, you must first accept them unconditionally. Think how often we react to our child (in mind, mood, or words) with "I love you, but…" Even though children need to mature, learn new behaviors, and change old ones, they first need to feel they are accepted. Change evolves from the bedrock of acceptance.

Here are some important DBT principles that can help parents learn to practice acceptance:

- **Your child is doing the best he can at this moment in time.** Parents who accept this truth can move the child along toward change in the future.

- **Your child needs to do better, try harder, and be more motivated to change**, but that will result from your skillful handling of his extreme emotions and behavior.

- **Your child wants to make things better.** Children naturally seek approval from their parents and are happier when they master challenges.

- **Your child must learn new behaviors and take responsibility for coping in difficult situations.** And she will, as she matures and you skillfully work with her.

- **Family members should take things in a well-meaning way and not assume the worst.** Negative reactions are normal, but they're not usually helpful.

- **There is no absolute truth.** Think about how often you argue over the truth with your child. He may say, "You never let me do anything." Or maybe, "You always take my brother's side." You have a choice: You can argue—and have a power struggle—or avoid an argument and say nothing. Even better would be saying something that validates his intense feelings and opinions right now. Arguing over the truth usually exacerbates conflicts when people are extremely upset.

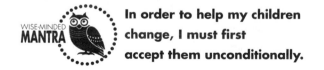

In order to help my children change, I must first accept them unconditionally.

The "wise mind" is a concept Linehan developed to emphasize the effectiveness of combining thinking processes (the "reason mind") with emotional regulation (the "emotion mind") to produce intuitive, effective ways of handling distressing situations.

To be wise-minded, you harness the quiet empathy that comes with a deep understanding and acceptance of emotions, both yours and your child's, and then integrate that empathy with reason for a balanced response. This dynamic combination allows parents to come up with wise, discerning, and—best of all—effective strategies for handling any given conflict or situation with their child.

The wise-minded parent moves beyond reason mind, which processes and responds to the mere facts of a situation. For example, the facts of the scenario at the beginning of the chapter are: Kate has a math test. The parents have a no-socializing rule for school nights. Kate is being extremely rude. If she goes to Jen's, she won't study as much. The mother also knows, or should know, that kids have intense feelings about their friends at this age. Basing her response on the facts alone—accurate though they are—discounts how Kate feels, hinders empathy, and significantly reduces Mom's effectiveness as a parent.

Before deciding on a way to handle hot situations, the wise-minded parent also knows to calm her emotion mind, which is what we are feeling when we are deeply distressed. This mother is no doubt feeling angry about being treated rudely, anxious about her daughter's math test, uneasy about her daughter's rage over the no-socializing rule, panicked about the night ending up in a big fight, and worried about the state of her relationship with her daughter.

The wise-minded mother knows she must first settle her emotion mind so that she can be empathic, prevent making the situation worse, and set her priorities. She might ask herself: "I *feel* entitled to hold my daughter accountable for her infuriating comments, but will that make me most effective?" The wise-minded mom calms herself first and reflects on how normal this behavior is for a tween or teen, so that she can approach her daughter *without contempt or judgment*. She resolves to be understanding and to focus on the most important goal for right now: Ensuring that her daughter properly prepares for the math test while finding a way for her to support her friend.

Once this mom quiets her emotion mind and reason mind, she knows intuitively that the most important thing right now is to not react to her daughter's emotions ("Jen needs me! I hate rules and math! Mom is a horrible obstacle to everything I want!") and instead, find a way to negotiate a truce between the competing agendas. Mom resists the urge to guilt-trip Kate about how bratty and irresponsible she is acting. She may choose to bring up the rude behavior later, when her daughter isn't flooded with emotion.

Let's revisit our opening vignette and see what wise-minded parenting can bring to the exchange.

Take Two:

> Kate: *I need to go to Jen's after dinner. Can you take me?*
>
> Mom: *I thought you had a huge math test tomorrow. And you know we don't usually do social stuff on school nights.*
>
> Kate: *Mom, I'm ready for the test. And I hate that stupid rule! Jen's upset! She needs me! You are such a control freak!*
>
> Mom: *You're a good friend to Jen. It's one of your greatest strengths. Look, honey, I'm reluctant to veer from our policy, but I can see you're upset and that this is really important. Why don't you put in one hour of study time, and then we'll figure out how you can help Jen? I can see that is a huge priority for you.*
>
> Kate: *This is an emergency! Aren't you listening?! You are so mean!*
>
> Mom: *I'm listening, but I'm not agreeing to drive you over there right now. If the next hour goes well with your math studies, I'm open to some problem solving.*
>
> Kate: *Fine. But it makes me so mad that you won't take me right now!*

Why is this dialogue a "win," despite the fact that Kate is still fuming? Because Mom did not add grease to the fire, but instead offered Kate an incentive to buckle down for an hour; she did not make things worse by fighting about rudeness, the importance of academics, or drama with friends.

How did things go after that? Kate actually did some studying, and while Mom held firm on not driving over to Jen's, she allowed a later bedtime so that they could make cookies to take to Jen at school the next day. As a bonus, Mom and Kate got a little connecting time—eating cookie dough is one of the best bonding milieus on the planet! And the truth is that sometimes math *is* less important than responding to friends' emergencies, resolving blowups, and building connections.

Getting away from the irritated, knee-jerk reaction that's so common—especially when being called names at the end of a busy day—takes practice, but it's well worth the work. Before learning and practicing some more wise-minded tools, take the following simple quiz to get a sense of your own starting point.

How Wise-Minded Are You?

True **False**

1. ☐ ☐ My teen needs to be confronted directly when she dumps her bad moods on me.

2. ☐ ☐ I trust my gut reaction when I'm mad about my child's behavior.

3. ☐ ☐ I think it is helpful to tell my child when he is being irrational.

4. ☐ ☐ My child will not understand how disappointed I am with her if I just keep my criticisms to myself.

5. ☐ ☐ When my teen makes a sweeping statement ("You never listen to my side!" "I don't have any real friends at school!"), I point out the exaggeration.

6. ☐ ☐ When my child expresses views that are offensive to me, I tell him straight away.

7. ☐ ☐ I think my perspectives on most topics are more valid than my child's because I am so much more experienced.

If you answered "false" to all of these questions, congratulations! You are probably pretty adept at staying wise-minded in the heat of the moment. But many—perhaps even most—parents have work to do in this area. What follows are some tools to help you get started.

The Importance of Attunement

One of the key wise-minded skills to master in the quest for secure attachment is attunement. An attuned parent "tunes into" the signals of the child and then attends to the child's needs. When the sensitive mom or dad coos, touches, soothes, revs up (or down), and feeds the baby *according to her needs*, the baby's neurons grow and sync up, establishing a whole neural network that associates mom and dad with a sense of security.

Cooing doesn't often work with teens, but attuned parents will still need to pick up on, correctly interpret, and attend to the verbal and nonverbal messages they receive from their kids. With teens, reading these messages, or "cues," can be especially tricky. Those who say "Leave me alone" may actually need to be: (1) left alone; (2) given some space initially, but then approached later on so that they know you care; (3) talked to about their feelings then and there; or (4) some combination of these options. Figuring out a teen's mixed signals and feelings is like entering an emotional matrix.

When your adolescent is irritable or despairing, you need to figure out the best course of action by considering a whole host of factors—a task complicated by the fact that teenagers often can't even tell you exactly what's wrong, or what they want you to do about it.

ESSENTIAL
TOOL

The Wise-Minded Parent Filter

The next time you're in a difficult parenting situation (your child is yelling at you, having a meltdown, or you are facing flagrant disobedience), pause and run it through your wise-minded parent filter. Ask yourself these questions before reacting:

- Am I calm and nonjudgmental?
- Am I sending any messages that negative emotions are bad?
- Can I separate my response to my child's behavior from my response to his/her emotions?
- Do I have empathy for what my child is going through right now?
- What's my goal right now?
- Is my goal realistic given my child's emotional state, age, and stage?
- Will what I'm about to say have a good chance of getting me closer to or farther from my goal?

Stopping time in the middle of a conflict for this kind of self-assessment may seem impossible, but with practice, the wise-minded parent learns to do it—because it works! The answers to those seven questions become instinctive if time is taken for calming and reflection, and that's why wise-minded parenting is so very effective.

THE ART OF MINDFULNESS

So, how do you sort through conflicting messages to get to the essence of what's going on with your teen? Start with the practice of mindfulness, the art of staying focused on the present moment without passing judgment. It is through mindfulness that you quiet the jumbled-up feelings and judgments that prevent an attuned response. In parenting, refraining from passing judgment requires you to accept your teen or tween completely—in all his messy glory—with a clear understanding of the realities of his particular age and stage. Parents who practice mindfulness know that their child (despite occasional evidence to the contrary!) is doing the best that he can, given his physical and emotional states. He's literally "under construction," learning many things all at once: how to behave, be empathetic, reach goals and meet expectations, and master a huge host of other critical life skills. He needs a lot of patience and guidance, both of which are most effectively delivered in the context of acceptance. It sounds simple, but it's certainly not, and for the vast majority of parents, there is plenty of room for improvement.

But even as a parent is being mindful and mining that deep well of understanding, she must also summon a big-picture perspective of a given situation, and then construct a realistic and positive plan that improves the situation, or at least doesn't make it any worse! This, in a nutshell, is the art of wise-minded parenting.

Mindful parenting is a beautiful foundation for wise-minded parenting, because it involves tuning into—and feeling compassion and empathy for—your own emotions and those of your child (Duncan et al. 2009). It provides crucial insights and empathy, which the wise-minded parent then combines with knowledge and reason.

Here are the five dimensions of mindful parenting:
- listening with full attention
- nonjudgmental acceptance of self and child
- emotional awareness of self and child
- parental self-regulation (self-control)
- compassion for self and child

How do you begin to work toward mindful parenting? The first writers on the subject, Myla and Jon Kabat-Zinn (Kabat-Zinn and Kabat-Zinn 1997), recommend eight practices. We've paraphrased them below in an activity that can offer valuable insight into your child's emotional world. Remember as you work in this book or your own journal that there are no "right" answers, and that your answers will probably evolve over time.

ESSENTIAL
ACTIVITY

Mindful Parenting in Practice

Answer the following questions as best you can.

1. Imagine the world from your child's point of view.
   My child sees the world as:

   _____

   _____

   _____

   _____

2. Imagine how you appear and sound from your child's point of view.
   My child sees me as:

   _____

   _____

   _____

   _____

3. Practice accepting your child just the way she is in this present moment.
   I can live with my child's:

   _____

   _____

   _____

   _____

4. Consider whether your expectations for your child right now are realistic and in his best interest.
Note and reflect on a few of your expectations:

_____
_____
_____
_____

5. Practice putting the emotional needs of your child above your own and looking for common ground.
A few goals I share with my child are:

_____
_____
_____
_____

6. If you don't know what to do about a dilemma, sit quietly and your intuition may guide you. If not, remain silent.
List a technique—breathing, journaling, a brisk walk—that you can use to calm yourself for reflection:

_____
_____
_____
_____

7. If you are laying down a unilateral mandate for your child, make sure it is prompted by awareness, generosity, and discernment, not from an automatic negative reaction or a need for control.
Sometimes when I lay down the law when I'm upset with my child, I am motivated by:

_____
_____
_____
_____

8. The greatest gift you can give is yourself—your time, focused attention, and awareness.
This week, I promise to do these three things with/for my child:

_____
_____
_____
_____

Mindful parenting means striving to understand your child, and being attuned to his needs and current life dilemmas, so that you can interpret his "Leave me alone" refrain effectively. Remember that teens can give contradictory signals and have mixed, confusing, or changing feelings. Despite the mess—and despite "go away" signals—many teens will benefit from their parents' skillful attempts at connection.

Making a Connection

A key component of secure attachment—and an important tool for the wise-minded parent—is effective communication. But as the parent of any teenager will tell you, communication is not always easy. Sometimes, families make connections effortlessly: Parent and child are both in good moods, open for conversation, and enjoying the relationship. At other times, especially with tweens and teens, it feels like a conversational wasteland, with the parent doing all the work. See if you recognize your family in this vignette, which illustrates an all-too-common teen exchange.

Scene: *It's late afternoon, and you're in the school pickup line. You know your fifteen-year-old had a huge presentation in class today and you want to hear how it went, but you are feeling a bit distracted from dealing with a load of your own stressors all day. Still, you want to connect with your teen for the brief time you have together, so you make the usual bid for information, with predictable results.*

> You: *How did your presentation go?*
> Teen: *Fine.*
> You: *Did your classmates like it?*
> Teen: *How do I know?*
> You: *Did you remember your speech?*
> Teen: *Yeah, whatever.*
> You: *Thanks for the attitude!*

You get the bare minimum of information, delivered in a tone dripping with rudeness. Why? It could be that you are falling back on a default script, riddled with yes-or-no questions. I call this the "brisk interview about school" and know from working with hundreds of teens that they detest this perfunctory questioning about what is usually their least favorite subject: school (unless something spectacular happened, and then they will let you know). Parents are earnestly attempting connection, but teens often see it as a cheap, short-cut way by which parents seek reassurance that everything is great so that they can feel good, even though the teens feel exhausted from the detritus of the day. This perception of parents is why so many teens respond with rude "whatevers" or even just a grunt. Teens frequently tell me: "Parents can't possibly understand what we've been through in a day at school. We can't possibly explain it because it's so overwhelming, and we would never want all their reactions to it, anyway! So we just say 'Whatever.'" The rote but innocent approach of asking "How's it going?" may work with your friends or coworkers—who will usually meet you halfway to connect—but not with a grumpy adolescent. Take a hint from the annals of teen gruntology: Those grunts mean the "interview" approach isn't working.

ESSENTIAL
FACT

Making a Connection
To a teenager, "How was school?" is one of the single most annoying ways to open a conversation.

For most of us, snippy retorts from a teen can easily prompt snippy responses back, and before you know it, you're saying something "reasonable" about all the things you do for him or making a snide remark about attitude. Ask yourself, is this wise and effective for getting a good connection going? Probably not. When you find yourself in this predicament, try this simple technique to help you refocus on the present moment and the task at hand: Start by giving your full attention to the current moment and refrain from judging your child or yourself. In other words, be "mindful." If you tend to be judgmental (understandable, given the roller-coaster ride of child-rearing), take a deep breath and let the moment pass. Focus instead on finding empathy for your teen, despite his sullen or rude behavior.

Being wise-minded doesn't mean you approve of or agree with everything your teen is doing or saying. It means you are being respectful of your teen, not trying to control his thoughts and feelings. (Note: There are limits. If his response to you includes profanity or over-the-line behavior, you may want to deliver a consequence later.) Wise-minded parents accept that children have negative emotions, and they don't try to change them.

Let's go back to the school pickup line, but this time, you'll prepare in advance to give yourself the best chance of being the mindful, nonjudgmental, nonreactive parent you want to be. Ten minutes before your child gets into the car, turn off the radio, turn off your cell phone, and shut down the "files" spooling in your head; they can wait. Take deep, slow breaths, using the 4-7-8 breathing technique (see next page). Engage your brain's strategic side by making a plan of action. Think about timing and specific questions you will ask (not yes-or-no questions!).

Take Two:

> *You:* You were worried about including the maps and graphs in your presentation. How do you think it came off?
> *Teen:* Fine, I guess.
> *You:* What part of the presentation made you the proudest?
> *Teen:* The spreadsheet. No one else bothered to do anything like that.
> *You:* I was impressed that you figured out how to pull that off. How did you do that?
> *Teen:* It was right on the "nav bar," Mom. It wasn't that big of a deal.

Despite the put-down at the end, count this exchange as a success. Just because you give your kid focused attention and praise doesn't mean he's going to get mushy, as he did when he was eight years old. Still, the little connections—and the specific and authentic praise—do sink in and are squirreled away deep inside your teen. Wait a decade or so; he may one day tell you what it meant to him!

ESSENTIAL
TOOL

The 4-7-8 Breathing Technique

Try calming and centering yourself with this simple technique.

- Exhale completely through your mouth, allowing your stomach to relax.
- Close your mouth and inhale through your nose while mentally counting to four ("one one thousand, two one thousand . . .").
- Hold your breath for a count of seven.
- Open your lips partway and exhale slowly while counting to eight.
- Repeat the preceding steps three more times.

Note: Check with your doctor first if you have any heart or lung conditions.

THE 'SWIRL IN' TECHNIQUE

Getting some children to open up often requires stealthier methods. Here's one that's tried and true: the "swirl in" technique. During the coming week, look for a moment to connect with your child. Instead of barreling in and asking, "How are you?" or the dreaded "How was school?" think about something your child has told you is important to him, such as competing in an online video game, taking a test, or going to a school dance. Then, watch for an opening.

The "swirl in" technique is a communication strategy that I've used for decades with tight-lipped tweens or teens who don't want to open up. I have encouraged parents to try it, and it works for them, too, because it feels less intrusive and personal than more pointed questions, such as "How do you feel about [school, friends, soccer, the upcoming dance]?" To swirl in, you kick-start a conversation on the outer edges of a topic and then circle in gradually. Do this casually, without applying any pressure. Teens shut their parents down when they sense an interrogation coming—and for them, just about anything can feel like an interrogation.

Getting kids to talk about school or friends or other potentially touchy subjects can be tough, so start with something they enjoy discussing. For instance, if your teen is into online gaming, you might do some research on the game and then ask your teen for help understanding the characters, levels, and point system. If you're curious about the upcoming dance, ask about the DJ who's been hired, and who selects and screens the music. Ask your teen how he would decide on a playlist. What songs would he include? Would he be nervous about satisfying his classmates' tastes and preferences? Would he get input from friends? To hone in on a school topic, start by asking what your child thinks of a particular teacher's lecture style. Do kids ever nod off in class? If so, what happens? What part of the reading was interesting? Remember: Don't ask about studying or test performance unless you want to be quickly shut down—this conversation is supposed to be about connecting, not evaluating.

The idea is not to toss out twenty questions, just a few thoughtful ones. If you're lucky enough to get a response, try to stay innocuous enough to keep your teen chatting. Think of yourself as engaged in artful and respectful anthropological research: You make contact with your subject by first educating yourself about what interests them and then engaging with them using their "cultural" norms. If you do your research well, he'll forget how irritated he is, generally speaking, with the usual slog of life and become motivated to at least *complain* about something (the lame test, dance, etc.). *Et voila!* He's talking.

The most important thing to remember: *Do not be judgmental.* You are there to connect with your teen and maybe even learn a thing or two about his world. Ask too many questions and you'll stress your kid out and turn him off.

> ESSENTIAL
> ## TOOL
>
> ### The 'Swirl In' Technique
> Instead of tackling a topic head on, kick-start a conversation on the outer edges of the topic and "swirl in" to the main issue.

Many parents complain that, even though they are ready and willing to listen without judging or reacting, their kids just won't talk. For those parents, timing is everything; it's a bit like "hunt and peck." You hunt for a moment and ask a random (but specific and nonthreatening) question about music, school, or another topic of interest, and if your teen is in the mood or feeling a little generous, she might throw you some chickenfeed. Then, if you've aroused a smidgen of interest on her part (and haven't been too hungry while gobbling it up), she may give you some more. Also, the "side by side" technique outlined on the next page sometimes gets reluctant teens to open up more easily.

The whole thing takes some finesse and can leave you feeling miffed at your beggar-like status, but take heart: This sometimes tedious, frustrating, and often rejection-filled process will eventually pay off in dividends with a deeper connection.

Some parents have the opposite problem: Their teens happily and regularly spout off—with views that are at best, naïve; at worst, in complete disagreement with cherished family values. What to do? The best approach is to listen and let the child explore their perspectives on controversial issues. Research shows that secure attachment during adolescence is associated with allowing kids to explore independence in thought and speech (Allen et al. 2003). Furthermore, it is positively linked to outcomes ranging from good peer relationships to higher self-esteem, and inversely related to outcomes ranging from depression to delinquency (Allen et al. 1998). Exploring and discussing independent thoughts and feelings are related to a close parent-child bond and great outcomes, even though they may offend in the short run.

TOOL

The 'Side by Side' Technique

Some parents find that the "side by side" technique of chatting while driving helps open up communication, because it cuts down on the dreaded "over-intimacy." Because your teen's big developmental task is identity formation (more on this in chapter 4), she creates space for her private forging of her new self by giving you the cold shoulder, resisting conversation about her personal life, and making fun of you if you try to seek excessive (according to her!) closeness. Bonding to you can feel like bondage to her. If your teen discovers you exploiting the car's "no escape" feature, get ready for the ear buds to be popped in. Music is better than interrogation, any day.

By practicing wise-minded communication techniques, you are sending a clear message to your child that you value and respect her, which further fosters your shared bond. In the important bank account of secure attachment, you won't make unnecessary withdrawals by making needless criticisms or nasty remarks. And while your teen may "hate" you at times for imposing discipline and limits, commit to charting a steady course through the inevitable storms. Your teen will draw crucial self-confidence from your carefully nurtured store of understanding and acceptance, and that self-confidence provides a solid foundation from which to strike out and explore the world.

KEEPING REJECTION IN PERSPECTIVE

Every parent has their own special overture that signals to the teen, "I'm available to offer support and won't overstay my welcome." Sometimes it's a back rub, an invitation to watch funny YouTube videos together, or a comfort food. But even if the teen rejects these attempts at bonding, she knows that her parents are sending loving bids for connection. When she stops idolizing you, it's a sign of *more* attachment security, not less. Because she is secure enough to throw you off the throne and call out your flaws, she feels a little less vulnerable about her own as she moves into the big, expanded world of adolescence.

Even though teens often reject them, parental overtures of support mean more to them than they'll admit until years later. Earnest love messages cross over into the emotional brain of the teen and soothe, even if the teen can't resist expressing disgust or irritation. Your child, like all humans, can feel a bundle of emotions all at the same time. She may want comfort, but also privacy, space for pondering her complex dilemmas, and the power to make you feel miserable when she feels that way.

Walt Whitman said it best when he wrote: "Do I contradict myself? Very well then I contradict myself. (I am large, I contain multitudes.)"

Teens, with their kaleidoscope of feelings, stressors, pressures, questions, and dilemmas, contain a multitude of contradictions. When they give us all those mixed messages about

needing us while hating us, and wanting comfort while thinking we can't possibly understand or help them, they are actually being honest.

These contradictions make the sacred art of attunement with teens a tough order
of business. When you're frustrated in your attempts at closeness or by their persistent
rejections, you need to consider:

- their needs;
- whether your appraisal of their needs is colored by your own needs; and
- their mixed-up feelings.

Keeping a healthy perspective on what might be fueling their rejection of closeness
with you is important for you and your relationship.

WISE-MINDED
MANTRA

**My love messages really matter,
even if my teen can't resist
expressing disgust or irritation.**

TOLERATING TEEN EXPLORATION

Wise-minded, attuned parenting during adolescence happens when parents have a sense
of their teen's internal world and convey empathy and understanding—even when it's
difficult. As in infancy, children in their teenage years use their parents as a secure base
from which to explore the world, but instead of crawling around the living room, they're
investigating new language idioms, dress codes, music, politics, religious thought, and
dreams of the future. Believe it or not, sometimes what may seem like "threatening" explo-
rations (to parents, anyway) are part of what produces a successful and well-adjusted young
adult. Tolerating, even *encouraging* teen exploration, even if it makes us uncomfortable, is
an important aspect of attunement.

Here's evidence: Researchers in a landmark developmental study of the relationship
between parenting behaviors and teens' psychological adjustment and competence
observed family discussions of controversial topics (Grotevant and Cooper 1985). They
found that teens whose parents were accepting of their independent perspectives,
even when dissonant with their own values, were more psychologically healthy and highly
functioning than the teens whose parents corrected or criticized them.

If your teen occasionally horrifies you with his outlandish views on political, religious,
or social issues, take it as a sign that you're doing a good job. Research has associated independence in thought and speech with close parent-child relationships and healthy
adjustment, so we can chalk much of that exasperating free thinking up to the healthy
exploration of the adolescent self. And if your teen is quick to point out your flaws, consider
that a victory, too! Research has even established that securely attached teens *do not*
idealize their parents. Secure teens see their parents as fallible human beings and that
allows them to strike out on their own, emotionally and mentally (Allen et al. 2003).

ATTUNED VERSUS OVERINDULGENT

Does "attuned" mean going along with teens when they tell you to leave them alone or to stop nagging them? The answer is sometimes yes, and sometimes no. If your baby smiled when you picked him up, there's a good chance that his pleasure was due to your "attuned" response to his cues. But when your teenage son smiles when you give him unlimited ATM or screen access, it's probably more of a reflection of your overindulgence than of your attuned or responsive parenting.

Even as you allow your teen to explore, remember that parenting that promotes security is not just made up of acceptance, mutual enjoyment, and connections. In fact, it can often look and feel like "mean" parenting, because it involves saying no a lot, monitoring activities, and insisting on chores and rule compliance. This is where the wise-mindedness comes into play. As you look at the situation with a wide angle, whose long-term needs are you serving if you give in to that ATM smile? Can you back it up with a wise analysis about why it's a good idea?

For some parents, the desire to express love and maintain closeness gets mixed up with trying to make their children happy. An instrumental part of good parenting is figuring out *what is in the best interest of the child*. If you bend to your teen's desires, there should be a good reason—not laziness, desire for affection, conflict avoidance, or fear of falling out of the teen's good graces. Since children and teens are happiest when you give them stuff and make their lives as easy as possible, a child's approving smiles are not good measures of your parenting. You should only go so far for those smiles.

The Art of Making Necessary But Unpopular Rules

Wise-minded parents know that with love and connection as their drivers, it is up to them to do all sorts of difficult (and unpopular) things to keep their kids on the right track. The following scenario is a very common parenting challenge, the limiting of screen time, followed by some practical tools.

Scene: *It's 8 p.m. on a work night, and you're hammering away on your laptop. You do a mental inventory and realize that every family member is on at least one—if not two— screens. You've noticed that this is a nightly ritual. You tell yourself it is legitimate since everyone has homework, e-mail, and relaxing to do, but what about "face time"? These days, family dinners only last about ten minutes. That's better than no dinners, but still—ten minutes? You don't want your kids to hate you (they will), but you know something has to be done. You've been thinking that it would be a good idea to have the whole family go offline on Sunday evenings.*

Most parents—especially those of tweens and teens—have the lurking, uneasy feeling that video games, social media, and screens in general are too prevalent in their children's lives. We know that emotionally close relationships can't develop without "face time"— conversations and shared experiences—but there has been a screen invasion in most households, one that has endangered our most precious of family values: closeness.

The majority of us would love to limit the amount of time spent on screens every day, knowing that it hampers familial communication, but to pull that plug is to invite instant and vicious reaction. For today's teens, social media is practically a lifeline; it's the venue in which they do much of the social sorting and interacting that their parents used to do hanging out in person with one another. Chances are if your preteen doesn't love Facebook (yet), she adores Minecraft, Skyrim, or Webkinz. And parents can be even more tied to their online activities than their teens. It's a tough battle to fight, but anyone who studies family health knows that we need time together—without screens—to nurture our relationships.

Let's say your solution is to mandate a screen-free Sunday night. You know the kids need their computers to complete homework assignments, but you're ready to draw the line and make a bid for a better family connection. How do you go about it?

A common strategy is to call a family meeting, but that can backfire. The term "family meeting" carries with it the implication that discussion will run both ways; that you'll take your teen's input into account. Unless you have reason to believe that they will be open to screen limitations and you will be satisfied with incorporating their ideas, don't lead them on. Sometimes parents just have to lay down a new rule, knowing full well that the kids will hate it. Good parents pick their battles, and this is one worth fighting.

THE FOUR C'S FOR PRESENTING PARENT POLICIES

So, how to go about making a family announcement about a new policy that is surely going to be met with animosity? With a nod to poet Robert Frost, the only way around is through. Forge ahead, but make sure to have at least the first three C's in the following list going for you. If you have the fourth, lucky you!

Calm—Say whatever you need to say briefly and without emotion, and ideally with compassion for how hard the policy will be for kids to tolerate.

Confidence—Let the kids know that you are resolute and that, although you can re-evaluate the new policy in X time (a week or a month, perhaps), you are moving forward with the plan, no matter what. Teens can tell when you feel uncertain or worried, and they have tremendous power to push you back on your heels. If you show any ambivalence, they will take full advantage.

Coparent unity—If you are coparenting, talk it through with your partner first, so you know you both are on the same page, then make it clear to your teen that you have made the decision together and are undivided about the intention to follow through with the policy. If you are a single parent, make it clear that you are not ambivalent, and that you will stand steady in the face of a tsunami of teen emotional backlash. If one or both parents feel wobbly about the policy, wait until you've reached an agreement. Picking off the parent with the weaker resolve is another effective strategy kids use to sabotage unpopular policies. Before you know it, the policy is out the window and parents are fighting with each other rather than implementing the policy.

Collaboration with your teens—If you can incorporate input from your teen, all the better. People almost always cooperate better when they have choices—especially teens. If the teen wants to negotiate for certain perks that you can live with (certain activities, guest invitations, etc.), it might be worth it to get them on board. But parents need to be ready for the kids to go for broke, with a flat-out "No deal!" If this happens, implement the policy anyway. Perhaps the kids will go on strike and not participate in family time, but if you sweeten the deal initially with interesting options (a favorite restaurant, a new game), you may lure them out of their den. Positive interaction can't be forced, but at least you are creating a context for face time.

Parents dread making new policies that they know their kids will hate. It's understandable. As long as the kids are going to suffer the consequences of losing something they love (their gadgets! their lifeline to their peers! their crafted and cool identities on Facebook!), they might as well make their parents suffer, too. Teens feel like their mean parents need to be punished—with a rude comment, with yelling, with stonewalling—whatever they think might make parents rethink their decision. You should steel yourself for some of this, but there are things you can do to minimize the blowup. One idea is to deliver the news via "drive-by."

THE 'DRIVE-BY' TECHNIQUE

The "drive-by" is a technique in which you introduce unpopular news in passing. This could be done as the children leave the house in the morning on their way to the bus stop or the carpool, or later to a social occasion. Announce that, starting this week, you'll be turning off the wireless router on Sunday nights when dinner is served. For that one night a week, cell phones will be parked in a basket. Tell the kids, "I've put a lot of thought into this, and I know you aren't going to like it, but I'm going to do it anyway. We all like our electronics—me included—but starting this Sunday, we are going to have a no-screen rule after dinner. We'll hang out as a family. You'll have to plan to have your homework done before dinner on Sunday."

The advantage of a drive-by announcement, delivered when the teen is on their way out the door, is that they have the day to cool off. Yes, they may use the time to plot their attack (and most likely get a lot of sympathy from their peers!), but at least everyone gets a breather first. You can anticipate that they will tell you this plan won't work or that their homework will suffer, or that they will refuse to talk to you on Sunday nights. But over time, if a leisurely Sunday family dinner—perhaps followed by some board games—is the only fun available on a screen-free night, they will likely warm to it. A small percentage of teenagers actually like family time; these kids will probably take to the new routine more easily, despite the crushing cruelty of screen deprivation. You'll probably make some exceptions with a family movie or offline homework once in a while, but think twice before you turn the router back on.

With one brilliant plan, you solve three problems:
- You are creating vital time and space for family conversations and connections to happen (albeit possibly somewhat sullen time at first).
- You are showing that you value your family relationships.
- And, as a bonus, you are doing away with that all-too-common Sunday-night bugaboo, the last-minute homework meltdown, because homework must be completed before the router and smartphones are switched off.

ESSENTIAL
TOOL

The 'Drive-By' Technique
Deliver unpleasant news about new rules in passing, perhaps as your child leaves for school. This allows processing time before your child reacts.

Coping with Rudeness

Laying down unpopular rules will usually subject you to a good deal of rudeness from your put-upon teen, but rudeness is a fact of teen life, whether you provoke it or not. It's important to understand where it's coming from and to stay above the fray. Most teen rudeness is expressed in the form of a nasty attitude ("I don't need your opinion"), critical insults ("You always repeat yourself"), or by giving the cold shoulder. While retorts can certainly be hurtful, they should be ignored as often as possible. Why? Because responding negatively adds more bad feelings to an already moody state—and turns the focus of the bad mood onto you!

In addition, giving attention of any kind to undesirable behavior is a form of reward. The parent who can successfully stay wise and clear-headed in this classic teenage moment—rather than attempt to dissipate or discipline the attitudes and emotions—is going to come out ahead, by avoiding a negative battle that whittles away at the parent-child relationship. The parent is also showing that they accept their teen's desire to remain private, have a moody moment, and not put effort into the parental bonding agenda. If it all seems too much to keep in mind, just remember this wise-minded mantra: Don't just do something, stand there! Hot emotional reactions can be damaging. When in doubt, bite your tongue.

Scene: *It's laundry day, and this dad is delivering a basketful of clothes to his son's room. He knocks once, then opens the door to a blast of attitude.*

> Brian: *Get out of here! God! I have no privacy!*
>
> Dad: *Hey, I knocked! And excuse me for washing and folding all your clothes. I only wanted to put them away.*
>
> Brian: *Yeah, right. You are spying on me to see if I'm doing my homework instead of being on Facebook.*
>
> Dad: *(backing out of the room) You watch your attitude! You are so disrespectful. And you'd better be doing your homework or you're in serious trouble!*

Why did this simple interaction go so horribly wrong? Because when this dad entered Brian's room after only one knock and without waiting for a response, he was not paying full attention to the moment. He was focused on his mission (getting the chores done) and not receptive to Brian's mental state. Then Dad made the tempting mistake of responding to the offensive content of his son's message, instead of addressing the underlying, bigger picture. Of course a parent would be offended by aggressive remarks like these, but a teen's moodiness about homework—not to mention room territoriality— is natural and normal, even if his response was disproportionate. The good news is that the average teen will develop empathy someday, but first we need to set an example for them. Remember, for a teenager, self-centeredness is as normal as tripping and falling are for a toddler. It's part of development. First they form a self and then they can crawl outside of it for a little perspective on the world. And just as you held your tongue during all those toddler tantrums, you have to exercise similar self-control during teen tantrums as well.

WISE-MINDED **MANTRA**

Don't just do something, stand there!

EXERCISING SELF-CONTROL

Self-control comes naturally for parents who keep the big picture in mind. Don't take teenage rudeness personally. It's a by-product of a critical piece of self-building under way with your teen. Instead, when faced with abject rudeness, leave the room without saying a word. Override the temptation to refer to his ungratefulness, rudeness, and disrespect. When you give in and harp on these, you might be right, but you probably won't be effective. Remember your goal: maintaining positive rapport and connectedness, and limiting the power struggles over little things.

When you are really mad at your teen after a negative exchange or blowup, center yourself by practicing one of the breathing exercises (on pages 15 and 28), or by working through the steps of the CALM technique (explained on page 26). Return later to offer a small, nonverbal connection—perhaps a cup of hot chocolate or a favorite snack. Even if you are rebuffed, the effort will register.

Take Two

Brian: *Dad, I said leave me alone!*

Dad: *Thought you might like a foot rub. What do you say?*

Brian: *Not right now. I really am trying to do homework.*

Dad: *Rain check, then! See you later.*

Brian *(who can't resist): Get a life.*

Why is this a good outcome? Because the dad didn't subtract from his bank account of good feelings by reacting to Brian's bad mood, and Brian was not left with a narrative in his head about how his dad was mean and critical. Not only do those mental narratives deteriorate good relationships, they detract from good studying.

CULTIVATING EMPATHY BY UNDERSTANDING TEEN RUDENESS

If you find it difficult to stay wise-minded when your teen is rude, it's no surprise. The deck is stacked against you because of several inescapable facts of normal teenage behavior.

For one thing, teens often try to pick a fight. That's because, in the chaos and uncertainty of adolescence, parents are a secure base—sort of like the eye of a storm. Lucky you! Teens want to discharge the garbage of their day onto someone who will take it and love them anyway, sticking with them through thick and thin. If it becomes evident that everything you say is "wrong" (even though you know you're right), you can stop the merry-go-round whenever you like by simply withdrawing. Don't walk out with a huffy refrain like "Well, I was just trying to be nice and look at how you treat me!" Instead, say something humble (and accurate), such as, "I can see that you aren't in the mood for chatting. Oh, well, maybe later." Unless their nastiness is persistent, assume that the interaction is more about an opportunity for dumping the garbage than a reflection of your overall relationship.

Teens also pick fights to get some space, and it's a strategy that works. Nothing clears a room faster than a moody teen on a rudeness rampage. Want to be left alone? Pick a fight and presto! This serves a secondary, but equally important, function for teenagers: The fight gives them something new to brood over (how mean you are!), rather than the real daily problems of being a teen.

It's almost impossible to avoid thinking, "I should not let her get away with this"; that by tolerating rudeness, you are teaching your teen that it is acceptable to treat people badly, instead of reining in that impulse and learning to treat people respectfully. Isn't self-control one of the most important goals of child-rearing?

Yes! (See chapter 2.) But here's a little secret: Most teens treat *other* adults well, even as they treat their own parents like they were dung heaps. Ask around and find out how your teen treats coaches, teachers, adult relatives, and neighbors. If the feedback is positive, you can be fairly sure that the rudeness is reserved just for you. You are the secure base, and also the power-wielder (the rule-maker, the resource-controller), as well as the one with whom she feels safe to be herself—especially the worst parts of herself.

When teens are rude, it's easy to think about all the things we do for them and why their behavior is unacceptable. The reason mind can dredge up plenty of facts that legitimize our rage ("How dare you treat me this way when I spend half my life serving you in a zillion ways! A parent needs to teach kids respect. There has to be limit!" or even just "Can't you just throw me a bone?"). Indeed, there are moments when teens smile, show appreciation, and maybe even enjoy their parents, but these moments are exceedingly scarce compared to the first decade of life. And if your teen has a moody temperament or is going through a rough patch, these occurrences can seem as rare as Halley's Comet.

Your saving grace? The rudeness is temporary; it usually peaks between thirteen and sixteen years of age. In the meantime, instead of looking back at the good old times when you were on the pedestal, or looking forward to better times when they will once again acknowledge your magnificence, try to just be present. And savor the smiles and good times when they do come. In the meantime, remember that your teen is doing the best she can, given her age and stage, even though they she needs to mature—a lot.

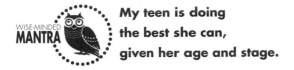

WISE-MINDED
MANTRA

My teen is doing the best she can, given her age and stage.

Remember, the rude behavior is temporary. The goal is acceptance, not change, and to "do no harm" to your secure bond with your child while you ride out the storm.

Here are some more things to try if the rudeness quotient is getting you down.

- Enjoy an evening off from sarcasm by inviting a friend or relative to dinner. Teens rarely express rudeness in front of other respected adults.
- When you start to slip into the same nastiness that your teen is dishing out, stop as soon as you notice it and say, "I'm sorry! I'm trying to be more conscious about slips like that. Excuse me while I reset and reboot." Then do some jumping jacks or yoga stretches, take the dog for a walk, or go somewhere for ten minutes of music, meditation, or reading. Sure, you may look strange, but at least you won't be continuing a negative cycle, and you are setting a good example for dealing with negative emotions. If your teen gets a laugh out of it, even better!
- Tell your teen that you are working on the Zen Buddhist practice of acceptance and not being attached to constant loving kindness from children (insert smile here). However, tomorrow you will need a break. Could she "up her game" for a day and try to be extra nice to you? Ask for only one day (or, depending on your teen, maybe just a couple of hours). Then it is important that she go back to being herself. If she chooses to try it, great. If not, try more breathing and repeat the wise-minded mantra: "She's doing the best she can, given her age and stage . . . and so am I."

ESSENTIAL
FACT

Negative Emotions

It's OK for children to have negative emotions. The parent's goal is to accept emotions and not focus on getting rid of them, but instead to understand what is going on with their teen emotionally. That empathy sets the stage for a possible connection.

THE 'CALM' TECHNIQUE FOR COPING WITH MELTDOWNS (YOURS AND THEIRS)

On occasion, we all "lose it." If a parent or child is emotionally volatile or reactive by nature, these episodes can be frequent and intense. Parents are often caught off guard, astonished that their previously sweet tween can morph into such a disrespectful and loathsome adolescent. How strange it is to tell parents, "Don't take it personally!"— especially when it is personal. Why *wouldn't* someone have a meltdown when their teen screams, "I hate you!" "You are the worst parent!" or "All of my friends feel sorry for me!"

When we become "dysregulated" (the technical term for losing our cool), we might yell, criticize, shame, blame, humiliate, or otherwise lash out at our child. It is the kind of parental behavior you'd pay a lot of money to keep off YouTube. You might be defensive about it ("He made me do it! Look what he said to me!"), but in the end, you know that you are always responsible for your own behavior. After all, you're the adult here.

But we adults are still human, and when our teen yells at or criticizes us, the attack registers in the deep, emotional parts of our brain. This part of the brain fires neurons much more rapidly than the thinking part of the brain, which means we react—often nastily—before we've thought through the implications and possible consequences. And teens, who are undergoing major structural changes in their brains and hormonal changes throughout their bodies, are triggered even more rapidly than adults.

When you have said something awful to your child, the best you can do is damage control. Stop talking immediately and focus on calming down. You want the neurons to fire in the slower, conscious parts of your brain, upping your odds for coming up with a wise next step. But you can't do that until you "get to calm."

When you've said something you regret, try this strategy from *Getting to Calm* (Kastner and Wyatt 2009), which emphasizes the role of emotional regulation in parenting tweens and teens:

C Cool down. Remove yourself; breathe deeply; do not think about the bad interaction or you will stay agitated; get your heart rate down with a distraction or breathing exercise.

A Assess your options. What are the strengths and weaknesses of various approaches you might take for patching up the spat and solving the problem? Should you talk to your child now or later? This evaluative step automatically engages the prefrontal cortex of the brain, facilitating good judgment.

L Listen with empathy. When reengaging your child, acknowledge your child's feelings first, without any "buts." Empathy doesn't mean approval or agreement, but it does open up communication channels.

M Make a plan. Use your calm and wise mind to figure out realistic goals and how to reach them.

ESSENTIAL
TIP

Damage Control
When you have said something awful to your child, the best you can do is damage control. Stop talking immediately and focus on calming down.

LOVING DETACHMENT: THE ART OF DISENGAGING

Sometimes a wound-up teenager's pain, confusion, and emotional flooding lead to an exchange that blows out of proportion, becoming exponentially nastier than it needs to be.

> *You: It's a school night, and you can't go out.*
>
> *Teen: I hate you!*
>
> *You: I'm sticking with our house rules. You don't have to get so surly.*
>
> *Teen: (yelling) I can't wait to leave home and never come back. None of my friends can stand you! You suck!*
>
> *You: I know you're mad, but that language…*
>
> *Teen: You are the worst parent who ever lived!!!*

What to say next? Insults like these can seem so extreme—so hurtful and so out of left field—that we imagine it's bad parenting to not do something about them. But it is exactly times like these that call for a calm extrication—*with a closed mouth*. For the average parent, no good can come from reprimanding a teen in the heat of the moment; often, something bad actually happens: We resort to yelling or lobbing insults ourselves.

When we are really worked up, we tend to recite in our heads the teen's offensive behaviors that justified our bad reactions ("He used profanity!" "I can't let him get away with that!" "There's got to be a limit!"). This is precisely when parents need to stop and ask themselves the wise-minded question: "I may be right, but am I effective?"

All of those appraisals may be quite valid, but does yelling or criticizing really help teens learn? Even sarcasm can have unintentionally hurtful effects: What if you fired off a comment like "Remind me of why I wanted to be a parent!" Before you know it, he'd be telling everyone that you said you wished you had never *had* him. Teens often actually like it when parents talk trash—it gives them the moral high ground, as they can throw your comments back in your face. Most importantly, interactions like this one give teens the message that they can be less accountable for reining in their own impulses. And that's the best reason to stay out of the mud: Never model behavior you don't want to see in your teen.

WISE-MINDED
MANTRA
I may be right, but am I effective?

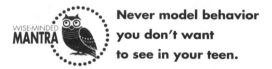

WISE-MINDED MANTRA

Never model behavior you don't want to see in your teen.

Since our brains register and respond to the emotions of others, we need tools for coping with hateful, out-of-control, or scary emotions in our children. Our children know us so well that if we are even *thinking* negative or critical thoughts in their presence, they will sense our emotions and intensify their reactions toward us, creating a cycle that quickly gets ugly.

For help in handling your teen's most intense and out-of-control outbursts, we can draw on skills extrapolated from DBT. These practices will keep exchanges from escalating and help you keep the focus on controlling yourself, not your teen (which is impossible, anyway!).

- **Think about your teen's outburst without judgment.** Regard it with interest. Describe it objectively in your mind. Do not evaluate it. Your inner dialogue might sound something like this: "My child is doing the best he can. He struggles with frustration. I was triggered and now I need to calm down. My teen is having a tough time. His immature brain and hormones are giving him impulse-control problems."
- **Do a breathing exercise,** such as the 4-7-8 method outlined on page 15, or try this simple exercise: Inhale over five seconds, and exhale over five seconds; close your eyes and relax your body. Imagine a favorite and beautiful place. This will slow your heart rate and help calm you down.
- **Wait a moment before responding and do so with a wise mind.** Ask yourself, "What is a realistic goal for me?" And remember: You may be right, but are you effective? Telling a child how she was wrong or irrational invalidates emotions and can set off the conflict again. Even if you believe you need to give a consequence or rehash an event or misbehavior, do it later when you have a chance for a calm, heart-to-heart conversation. Discipline is about learning, and learning does not occur during an intensely negative conflict when emotions are running high.
- **Tell yourself, "The only person I can control is myself.** I will sit here quietly and wait out the rise and fall of my child's extreme emotions. By not reacting, at least I won't be making it worse. Outbursts always pass, especially if I don't react and if I behave and think in an accepting manner."

ESSENTIAL FACT

Discipline Wisdom
Discipline is about learning, and learning does not occur when emotions are running high.

REFLECT ON WHAT PUSHES YOUR BUTTONS

It is difficult, if not downright impossible, to tolerate a loved one turning away or criticizing every move you make. Consolation lies in understanding the "method to the madness"; the ways in which this developmental process works to produce an up-and-running, capable, and loving adult.

The most important thing for parents to remember is that love and connection matter immeasurably to teens, and it's crucial that parents persist despite the feedback teens give ("Go away!" "You're annoying" "You are clueless"). Most back talk is the general moodiness of adolescence, but it's always good to get some perspective by consulting with other parents, friends, and relatives. Maybe what you'll find out will lead you to conclude that your teen really is an outlier and has an emotional problem that needs to be addressed. Or, more likely, what you'll learn is that you are actually too sensitive, and your kid is a gem—albeit a teenage one.

Reflection can give you some insight into the factors underpinning your family's particular brand of teen strife, which may help build acceptance and patience with the sometimes-difficult process of growing a teen.

Wise-minded parenting is a work in progress, to be sure, and involves recognizing when your teen's mood (and your own) won't allow for a warm interaction or a loving connection. Because secure attachment is your goal, you'll keep trying for a connection—one small, shared, positive moment at a time—night after night, despite your teen's plentiful rejections. Try to feel empathy for them, keeping in mind all the developmental pressures coming at them from within (their hormones! their brain remodeling!) and without (school! peers! responsibilities!). Don't take these rejections personally and try to understand that life is tough for teens. They need their loving parents to be patient, very patient, indeed.

You might be thinking, "But it's not all about them! Why don't *they* have to be empathic to *me?*" First, it's not a level playing field. They are the children, and as adults, we are expected to exert self-control and seek empathy elsewhere. Second, when you describe your own stressors and feelings about your life (the edited version, of course), they will have some empathy—as much as they can muster with those egocentric minds of theirs. But demanding empathy for your *negative experiences of them* is tricky at this stage, because they can't distinguish much between your disliking them versus disliking their behavior. You will still try to explain your feelings (a lot!) about their unacceptable behaviors, but there is a difference between that and demanding empathy for the burden of raising a teen. Gathering empathy for raising teens is what friends, families, and communities are for!

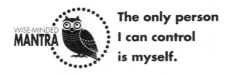 **The only person I can control is myself.**

Managing Yourself When Your Teen Pushes Your Buttons

1. Describe, here or in your journal, what your tween or teen does or says that pushes your buttons the most.

_____

_____

_____

2. List circumstances in your family life or in your teen's life that may make it especially difficult for him or her to deal with the emotions of adolescence right now.

_____

_____

_____

3. Choose one of the exercises in this chapter to help you calm down the next time your tween or teen upsets you.

_____

_____

_____

4. List some things that you are going to tell yourself mentally to help you stay nonjudgmental (of your child and yourself) the next time your teen or tween upsets you.

_____

_____

_____

5. After trying one of these exercises, list some of the results you noticed (e.g., in your body, voice, words, response from your child, feelings about yourself).

_____

_____

_____

6. Once you've responded to a teen conflict or an episode of rudeness with wise-mindedness, reflect on the outcome. How did you feel in the moment and afterward? How did your teen react then and afterward? How was the interaction different than others you've had?

_____

_____

_____

Self-Care

As any good doctor knows, to be a good caregiver you must "heal thyself" first. Parenting is hard work—especially parenting teens. We need to be attuned to ourselves before we can attune to our growing kids. When we are fraught with fatigue or resentment (for our spouses, children, selves, bosses), attempting to strike up a positive interaction with anyone, especially our tetchy teens, will be a challenge. Even with a good grasp of teen development, no amount of knowledge can offset our own frayed emotional state.

How can we expect to read the subtle and confusing cues of our children accurately, and then respond effectively, when we are burned out and irritable? Remember the first time you heard a flight attendant say that parents should put on their own oxygen masks first? The metaphor that we need to be "oxygenated" before attempting to rejuvenate our kids is as good as gold.

A nice, long workout followed by a hot-stone massage would be ideal, of course, but few of us have time for such luxuries in the busy workweek, so try stealing just five minutes for a breathing and visualization exercise (such as the one on page 15) before reconnecting with your teen. Calm and center yourself; as much as you can, try to shake off the stress of the day, or at least put it into perspective. Taking a moment to do this can make a huge difference in the tone of your interactions with your teen.

'Good-Enough' Parenting

The sad fact is, no matter how hard we work and how effective we are, teens are usually not as interested as parents are in creating bonding moments. In fact, even if we understand that a teen's negativity is rarely about us, parenting teens can be an awfully long slog, rife with delayed gratification and thankless days and nights.

Here's a well-kept secret, though: You only need to be "good enough" at this parenting job. Going for perfection will make a head case of you—and your kid. Maintaining secure attachment is a dynamic process. It's a little like tandem bungee-jumping: Sometimes you're close, sometimes far away, sometimes suspended in midair, wondering if you're going to smack into each other, and sometimes just in a breathless, stomach-dropping state of wonder about it all.

ESSENTIAL
FACT

The Parent-Teen Bond
Staying connected to your kids is like tandem bungee-jumping: Sometimes you're close, sometimes far away, sometimes suspended in midair, wondering if you're going to smack into each other, and sometimes just in a breathless, stomach-dropping state of wonder about it all.

Intimate moments and rollicking good times usually happen *on the teen's schedule.* In fact, parents are often amazed at how these moments crop up late at night. Parents, usually hungry for closeness from their chilled-out teen during the rest of the day, may be busy getting ready for bed, sending last-minute e-mail, or vegging out. Suddenly, their teen pops up ready to talk. A coincidence? Probably not. When we are not salivating for closeness, we probably seem safer to bond with.

The reality is that connecting happens during the daily chaos of raising kids, while also going to work, volunteering, cooking meals, and answering e-mail. It's little wonder that we often disappoint our children. But even our failures are an important lesson: Coping with disappointment and an imperfect world helps children develop competence, as does the realization that the other humans in their lives are flawed, and that the world is not "all about them."

For most parents and teens, love and adoration go underground during adolescence. But don't be mistaken—it's there. Ask teens whom they rely on for support, and they will tell you in overwhelming numbers: their parents (Offer 1981). It's just that most teens prefer to spend time with their friends, adopting their customs and tastes (hair styles, musical preferences, lingo, etc.), and parents take this as a signal that they are losing ground in the attachment battle. But usually that's not the case.

Peer attachment actually works *with* parental attachment to foster adolescent adjustment and security. Original research on the subject suggested that both teen and peer attachment were related to well-being and adjustment (Armsden and Greenberg 1987); the current thinking is that parents and peers exert influences in complex ways that are almost impossible to tease out (Collins et al. 2000). For instance, academically oriented families often have teens who are academically driven and who associate with friends who are also academically focused. Does this mean that the friends influenced the achievement, or the parents? It's impossible to know.

Although parents often feel like their relationships with their teens have worsened (and who wouldn't, with all that conflict?), a diverse national sampling of thousands of teens, which replicated the findings of other research on the subject, found that around 80 percent of teens think highly of and enjoy spending time with their mothers and fathers (Moore et al. 2004). Parents may take a beating when in conflict with their teens, but from the teen's perspective, the fights may be more about the irritation they are feeling in the moment than a reflection of the overall quality of the relationship.

The trusting experiences and security with which you provided your child during the first decade of his life is safely tucked inside him. This foundation allows him the ability to claim some psychological distance now. And he needs to do that in order to explore the big "Who am I?" question without constant direction or input from a parental editor, arbiter, and judge. In the meantime, we parents need to keep nurturing our teens in myriad ways—with love, acceptance, and discipline—so that they can develop all the competencies they need for adulthood.

Promoting and maintaining secure attachment with teens—right up until their brains mature in their early twenties—is a tall order. The second decade of childhood challenges parents to practice a kind of acceptance that tests the limits of human empathy, wisdom, and compassion. It's worth it. Investing in building the parent-child bond not only creates the most successful human beings, it gives you a master class in "human being." The growth and understanding that parents themselves experience during this decade is something that few would trade.

ESSENTIAL
FACT

The Parenting Challenge
The second decade of childhood challenges parents to practice a kind of acceptance that tests the limits of human empathy, wisdom, and compassion. It's a growth experience!

Difficulties in Forming Attachment

Creating secure attachment doesn't happen in a vacuum; even very good parents will struggle mightily if their child has a challenging temperament. Temperament is a complex issue for attachment experts, and a good case has been made for the role that extremely sensitive babies may play in their own attachment history (Kagan 2010). There is no question that kids who are high-energy and aggressively impulsive are harder to parent, as are children who are anxious and reactive, or avoidant, withdrawn, and hard to reach. Let's face it: It's easier to parent a child who isn't screaming at the top of her lungs or hitting his sibling every other minute. (We'll go much deeper into temperament in chapter 2.)

Nearly forty years ago, developmental psychologist Mary Ainsworth initiated the original research that measured secure attachment (Ainsworth et al. 1978). Numerous studies conducted all over the world since then have found that about one-third of kids are categorized as "insecurely attached." They probably got that way as a result of many factors, including parent and child temperaments, a lack of support systems, and plain old rotten circumstances. More research is needed on the chicken-egg question of how child temperament and parental variables interact to cause insecure attachment, but in most cases, it's probably a combination of many factors.

In any case, those "insecure" children tend to grow into teens who face more challenges, and parenting them through the adolescent years can take incredible effort. If you find yourself in this situation, seek help. You need backup and support, and so does your teen. Remember that it is never too late. Loving, positive interactions with parents, other family members, friends, teachers—anyone in your "village"—helps to build these connections in your child's brain throughout her life, creating trust, security, and attachment.

It's a Symphony

Secure attachment starts with a symphony of neurons that connect through attuned and responsive parenting. As tweens and teens mature, the parent-child interactions that compose the symphony may become downright screechy at times, or sometimes so quiet that you strain to hear the notes in the score. However, the interpersonal history of love and acceptance is established in both our explicit memory (what we actually remember consciously) and in our implicit memory (early childhood experiences encoded in the memory part of the brain, beneath our conscious awareness). If your child formed a secure attachment during early childhood, chances are good that they will have the inner security to grow into a successful and happy adult.

The symphony of adolescence is best conducted with mindful parenting, which means being "present" and nonjudgmental. When faced with emotional outbursts or tough parenting moments, the wise-minded parent will reflect on the big picture of what's going on emotionally for their child and themselves, and feel empathy for their teen. They will move beyond the facts (reason mind) and personal reactivity (emotion mind), and make a discerning choice about how to proceed in a way that is most likely to a yield positive— or at least benign—outcome.

Parents of teens often marvel that the skills they learn for coping with teens' moods and behaviors help them in many aspects of their lives. Think about all these wise maxims: "The only person I can control is myself." "Breathe through moments of extreme emotion." "She's flooded with emotions, so don't take it personally." Don't these pearls of wisdom also apply to close relationships with spouses, coworkers, relatives, and friends? An "emotional roller coaster" may describe life with teens, but it also describes life in general.

Connection and independence may look like polar opposites in a parent/child relationship, but really, they fuel each other. Trust and connection with parents allow teens the security to explore the world. Feeling competent and strong in the world allows teens to enjoy life, their newly minted identities and . . . their parents! With a little luck, the love connections created in the first decade, and developed in the second, will endure for many years to come.

CHAPTER 2
Self-Control

Scene: *It's Saturday afternoon, and a mother and her teenage daughter hit the athletic shop to buy a new pair of cleats. Mom just wants to finish this one last errand before running home to shower and prep for a big dinner party she's hosting that evening.*

Mom: *OK, let's make this quick. Find cleats you like for less than $100.*

Hayley: *Mom! You can't get good cleats for $100! These are hideous!*

Mom: *I'm sorry, but that's the budget. Hurry up. I have a thousand things to do.*

Hayley: *(voice rising) These shoes are crap! My coach told us to get Nike Vapors. Everyone has Nikes! I'll never score a goal in these cheap shoes.*

Mom: *You sound like a spoiled brat! I've had it with you. Let's get out of here.*

Hayley: *(yelling) God, Mom! You are so cheap and stupid! You don't care if I look like an idiot! You don't care if we lose the game! It's like you hate me. I hate you!*

We all know that acute discomfort of being around an out-of-control child. Whether it's a toddler in full tantrum mode in the grocery store or a raging, insult-hurling teenager at the mall, these emotional outbursts can make us withdraw or attack—or both, like the mom above—depending on our own temperament and frame of mind at the time.

Loss of control is most common among children who have not yet developed self-control. But self-control, sometimes called self-discipline, means more than just keeping a handle on emotions and behaving well in public. When your child does his homework without being reminded, logs off of Facebook to study for a test on his own accord, says "No, thanks" to freely offered beer, and follows through on his weekly chores, he is exercising self-control. It's easy to see why parents consider self-control to be one of life's essentials. As it turns out, scientists do, too.

Why Self-Control Matters

Many parents believe that a high IQ and great test scores are the best indicators of how successful their children will be at realizing ambitious goals. But new research reveals that there is more to that equation. If you want your child to be truly successful in life, you need to help them cultivate strong self-control. In fact, compared to IQ and SAT scores, self-control is *twice* as predictive of health, income levels, and relationship stability in adulthood (Moffitt et al. 2011).

> ESSENTIAL
> ## FACT
>
> ### Self-Control
> Compared to IQ and SAT scores, self-control is *twice* as predictive of health, income levels, and relationship stability in adulthood.

Self-control helps children succeed in virtually every aspect of life, including academic success, romantic happiness, physical health, and financial stability. Kids with self-control stay focused and follow through on all manner of important tasks. They set goals, make a plan to achieve those goals, and persist in the face of difficulty. And these kids are also able to take a hard look at their own progress, and evaluate and adjust as needed.

Self-control is not something we can expect our kids to have fully mastered by age fifteen or even age twenty; for most of us, true self-control remains a lifelong challenge. Even for adults, complicated and deep-seated emotions often weaken our resolve, and a plethora of life issues compete for our attention. It's more challenging for kids, who have less-refined coping skills and a more tenuous understanding of consequences. Imagine what they are up against in terms of frustration, anger, and fatigue!

Yet parents often complain of being frustrated with the lack of self-control their children demonstrate on a regular basis. The reality is that, in terms of the "norms" of adolescent development, it is just not realistic to expect kids to show consistent good judgment and self-control until they reach their early twenties.

There are six major factors that influence how much self-control your kids will exhibit along the way to adulthood:

- Their temperament and yours
- The way emotions and thinking work in the brain
- The changes in the brain (and hormones!) during adolescence
- Your parenting style
- Your family's routines and habits
- Your child's opportunities to practice willpower and self-regulation

These factors also influence whether the task of cultivating self-control will be relatively easy or more challenging. Yet cultivate it we must. Not only is strong self-control a major predictor of adult success, it paves the way for more successful teen years, too. It helps your child think before acting, use time efficiently, and push past distractions and fatigue. If you're very lucky, you're nodding your head right now, thinking, "That's my kid!" Most of us, though, experience a messier mix of teen competencies related to self-control.

Wondering where your child might land on the self-control continuum? Take the quiz on the next page to get a sense of your starting point.

How Much Self-Control Does Your Child Have?

True False

1. ☐ ☐ My child usually does her homework without being asked.
2. ☐ ☐ When my child is working on a project and sees that plan A isn't working, he will invent a plan B.
3. ☐ ☐ My child would not sneak a cookie that's intended for the school bake sale.
4. ☐ ☐ My child often leaves major school projects until the night before they're due.
5. ☐ ☐ If my child were to get an unfair penalty during a game, he would shake it off and continue to play.
6. ☐ ☐ My child very rarely throws tantrums or has meltdowns.
7. ☐ ☐ My child is disorganized for someone of his age.

If you answered "true" to all but 4 and 7, congratulations, you're one of the lucky few! Self-control appears to be well-established in your tween or teen. For most of the rest of us, however, there's probably some work to do in helping our children develop and strengthen this essential skill.

External Controls

Self-control begins with socialization, which is the process of learning what society expects and then finding ways to self-govern accordingly. Whether you realize it or not, you are teaching your child the important lessons of socialization from the moment he is born. By establishing consistent rules and structures ("external controls") in the first few years of life, and then reinforcing and building on those foundations as your child grows, you are not only helping to keep your child safe, you are teaching him how to be socially acceptable, as well.

This learning process continues throughout adolescence, as your child develops the ability to self-regulate (yet another term for self-control), and in response, you gradually loosen the external controls you put into place years before. Your child's particular path to socialization may be straightforward and intuitive, or it could be more of a struggle, depending on multiple factors: environmental influences; cultural background; your child's innate, genetic predispositions; and your personality, parenting style, and parenting philosophy.

Parents who are highly self-controlled are likely to embrace a more authoritative parenting style when it comes to establishing external controls (we'll explain why this is important a little farther on). They are also likely to have a child born with a predisposition to self-regulate. The opposite is also true: Parents who don't like routines, are inconsistent with rules and policies, and pursue pleasures and/or self-gratifying activities (even work) with abandon are less likely to establish the structure that promotes self-discipline in their child. But even these parents can choose to implement parenting practices that promote the essential skill of self-control, and that is the focus of this chapter.

Executive Functioning

Self-control is a component of what psychologists call "executive functioning" (Cox 2007). If self-esteem was the hot parenting topic in the 1980s, then executive functioning and self-control are the hot topics now. While it may be all the rage, executive functioning is by no means a new concept. In fact, this uniquely human capacity is what helped transform early hunter-gatherer societies into more complex civilizations based on agriculture, trade, and technology. Brain scans, psychological testing, and longitudinal research in recent years have proven the integral role executive functioning plays in helping children and adults succeed (Barkley 2012).

Executive functioning includes the ability to:
• make goals, plan, and prioritize steps to accomplish the goals;
• adapt the goals to the demands of the environment or cultural expectations;
• organize and manage time;
• persist in spite of competing interests;
• revise a plan in the face of obstacles or setbacks;
• stand back and assess the big picture in order to self-monitor and evaluate one's progress;
• develop the capacity to think before acting;
• hold information in our memory while performing complex tasks ("working memory");
• meet deadlines efficiently;
• manage emotions in order to achieve goals; and
• maintain attention on a task in spite of distractions, fatigue, and boredom.

Considering our country's love affair with IQ scores and achievement-test data, it is astounding that there is not a national conversation about the importance of self-control, since without it, those high test scores aren't going to get students very far. To understand what determines your child's potential for self-control, it is necessary to understand the inborn qualities of temperament and a little about the workings of the adolescent brain.

The Role of Temperament

Why do we find certain experiences and situations enjoyable and rewarding, and others aversive and anxiety provoking? Why do some of us react to distress with aggression, while others simply withdraw? Why is one person's joy—for example, roller coasters, big parties, or a solitary trail in the woods—another person's nightmare? The answer to all of these questions has to do with our individual temperaments (our "personalities").

Through extensive research on infants and children, noted Harvard psychologist Jerome Kagan determined that our temperaments are distinguished by how we experience and express three traits: fear, aggression, and sociability (Kagan 1997). Fear allows us to detect and avoid danger, aggression enables us to fight it, and sociability gives us the capability of coping with it and collaborating with others.

Some of our sensory experiences related to rewards are universal to all humans (e.g., food, sex, warmth, curiosity), and some are particular to our own gene and environment combinations (e.g., parties, Scrabble, dirt bikes). All of these add up to determine our temperament, our particular self-control challenges, and much of our life journey.

The path to developing self-control is different for every kid, and a lot depends on their unique temperament. Some kids are practically fearless, highly impulsive, sensation seeking, and exuberant. Others are fearful of new situations, avoidant of risk, and prefer the comfort of tasks they know over the angst they feel when confronted with new challenges. Most are in between, but kids at either end of this spectrum can be challenging, and will need to work to develop different kinds of self-control.

Children who are especially exuberant need to learn how to inhibit the impulses that compel them to fling themselves at every new and exciting thing that comes along. Highly sensitive and anxious kids need to learn to ignore the false alarms their sensitive brains sound at every unfamiliar situation. Aggressive kids need to learn to self-regulate their impulses to avoid expressing angry feelings in unrestrained physically or verbally hurtful ways.

Kids at either extreme of the high/low fear continuum are lucky if they are also highly sociable; it mitigates some of the challenges of their temperaments. Some kids are naturally sociable—they're "people persons" who like and feel comfortable with others. For these kids, being around pleasant people increases their levels of serotonin, the neurotransmitter most associated with giving us a feeling of well-being. When anxious kids are also sociable and still want at least one or two friends, this can help them deal with stress. And brash, wild kids who also happen to have high sociability will be motivated to listen to negative feedback and adjust accordingly when they are over the top with their exuberant, aggressive, or bossy impulses. Whether kids are high or low on the fear or aggression spectrums, this third axis of sociability is especially important, since the world we live in is a social one.

The resilience and happiness that can come with sociability and a positive mood can be genetic gifts. Mixed with just the right amount of reactivity to deadlines and people's expectations, these folks have really hit the genetic jackpot (and boy, oh boy, do they make their parents look good!). Some kids, however, have the opposite of sociability—irritability and what is called "high negative affectivity," a tendency to proliferate in negative feelings like anger, frustration, discomfort, and to be unresponsive to attempts at soothing (Rothbart et al. 2001).

These kids are easily annoyed and may exhibit aggressiveness, high anxiety, depressive tendencies, or some combination of the three. Highly aggressive kids will strike out when their fear and irritability are triggered. In the same circumstances, kids who are not aggressive may be more likely to withdraw and "internalize" their distress, which can result in depression. Parents of irritable children are tested to their limits as they struggle to offer compassionate and practical strategies to help their kids self-soothe and solve problems (see chapter 5 for more on this). Nonetheless, it should be noted that tempestuous, melancholic, and intense personalities have created some of the world's most brilliant works of art, science, music, and literature. The trick for any parent is determining their child's innate temperament and sociability, and then finding ways to help them thrive as they develop self-control.

It should also be noted that there is such a thing as too much self-control, especially when it is too narrowly focused. At their extreme, the single-minded self-control and dogged persistence common among some intensely goal-oriented kids can result in lower investment in other goals, such as friendships, family relationships, health, or a purposeful life. If your child is exclusively focused on a single goal—whether it's to become a prima ballerina, gain national status in a computer game, or make a million dollars by age twenty-one—it falls to you to help her strike a balance and develop healthful lifestyles and other virtues.

Even if your kid has a high sociability quotient and a mild temperament (lucky you!), landing somewhere in the middle of the spectrum with regard to fear and aggression, she will still sometimes be overwhelmed by emotions; it's part of being a teen (and a person), after all. By helping her to deepen her well of self-control, you'll ensure that she'll be better able to manage her reactions when threatened by those inevitable emotional floods.

CONTROLLING THE BIG EMOTIONS OF FEAR AND DESIRE: A BRAIN TOUR

When you're facing stress or danger, the part of your brain that detects it and fires off warning bells is called the *amygdala* (pronounced "uh MIG duh luh"). The amygdala is found deep in the emotional part of the brain. It has existed for millions of years, helping our pre-human ancestors survive by alerting them to hazards and triggering the "fight or flight" response. When the amygdala is activated, it sends messages to the thinking part of the brain that there is danger afoot. Adrenaline is released, and we either get ready for battle or retreat. When neuroscientists use the term "activation," they are referring to neurons firing in the brain. It can be observed on functional magnetic resonance imaging (fMRI) as a "lighting up" of the amygdala, depicting the activity of neurons sending messages about danger.

The amygdala can send an accurate danger signal, such as the one activated when we realize our teen is not where he is supposed to be and we panic. It also can send a false alarm, perhaps when we freak out about our son not being at the pickup line, because we forgot he had a drama club meeting that day. And it can fail to send an alarm altogether, such as when we missed the clues that he is routinely skipping drama club to smoke weed in the park.

We can assume that a child who steals his friend's trading cards, sells them online, and then tells his classmates about the caper has an "under-reactive" amygdala—he isn't afraid enough for his own good. Another child, who refuses to go to birthday parties, throws fits about attending day camp, and has meltdowns over impending field trips has an "over-reactive" amygdala; he perceives dangers *everywhere* and is overwhelmed by novel situations.

Threats can be real or imagined, life threatening or innocuous. The amygdala and the attendant arousal system set off physiological and psychological "stress" alarms that vary among individuals based on their sensitivity to internal and external triggers. This system is part of our innate temperament; some of us are highly reactive and oversensitive, some of us are naturally resilient and in the midrange for seeking novelty, and some of us are under-reactive and always looking to rev up the arousal factor.

ADDING TEEN BRAIN MATURATION TO THE MIX

All of us are subject to the characteristics of our temperaments and the way our emotions play out in our brain chemistry, but teens get to add another factor to the mix. Around the age of thirteen, kids undergo a massive remodeling of the prefrontal cortex, the analytic, "thinking" part of the brain, which is located behind our foreheads. Like most remodels, the first phase involves a big "teardown," which, in this case, occurs in the prefrontal cortex. Along with the accompanying hormonal changes of adolescence, this teardown helps explain why teens do so many harebrained things.

The prefrontal cortex is the "newest" part of the brain—it's only been around in its modern form for about 50,000 years. It's a lot younger than the emotional part of the brain, which goes back millions of years in evolutionary history. The prefrontal cortex has made possible our most remarkable human thinking abilities, such as language, imagination, empathy, perspective-taking, and reasoning. It also helped us develop those all-important executive functioning skills, which include the ability to plan ahead, weigh costs and benefits (reasoning), and keep impulses under control. It is within this region that the self-control infrastructure resides.

Think of the prefrontal cortex as the brain's CEO. It runs the business of us, allowing us to make a plan for our goals, remove obstacles, adjust our plans, and regulate our emotions, so that we can handle the difficulties that arise in running any complicated enterprise—especially the messy business of being human!

Now imagine that this CEO is taking a sabbatical of sorts, for personal growth and rebuilding. This is essentially how neuroscientist Jay Giedd described what is happening in the teen brain. In the 1990s, Giedd conducted brain scans at the National Institute of Mental Health on a group of children in their second decade of life (Giedd 1999). He discovered that almost half of the gray matter in the prefrontal cortex is "pruned" or eliminated during this time, creating a particularly sensitive period for brain growth. As the gray matter decreases, "white matter" increases proportionally. The white matter is *myelin*, which covers the axons of the neurons and makes them fire much faster (think of them as superconductors). This remodeling is quite a project!

As neural branches are sloughed off, fresh ones grow and form new connections based on your child's learning and experience. Those new connections result in increased gray-matter density—especially if the learning is challenging and rehearsed repeatedly.

Like all humans, what teens do and what they learn—whether it's tennis, social skills, calculus, or painting—determines their brain growth.

In essence, the ratio of gray matter to white matter is about two to one at around age thirteen. Over the next decade, the ratio is reversed and it stays that way ever after. Giedd's research reflected this ratio inversion in brain matter and explained why the massive connectivity of neurons in the prefrontal cortex represents such a sophisticated transition for brain functioning: The white matter (myelin) creates superconductors between highly specialized areas of the brain capable of advanced thinking and functions. This extensive architectural project explains why a teen's brain is not fully mature until his early twenties, when the remodel is finally done.

It's no wonder that risk-taking behavior peaks between the ages of eighteen and twenty-five—teens don't have mature CEOs running their businesses! But they do have the freedom and sensation-seeking tendencies to explore all sorts of enterprises. Young people make spectacular discoveries—and spectacular mistakes.

The area that registers rewarding experiences, the *nucleus accumbens*, is located deep in the emotional (*limbic*) system of the brain. It activates when pleasurable experiences are anticipated or registered. On a brain scan, you'd see this area light up when rewards are perceived. The nucleus accumbens and another region (called the *ventral tegmental area*) are part of the "dopamine pathway," named for the neurotransmitter that is released when pleasure is anticipated.

When dopamine is released, messages are sent to the thinking brain, which convey the command "Go get that!" There are primal rewards that we all seek, such as food, warmth, social interaction, and sex. Starve any of us for two days, put us in a scanner, and show us pictures of delicious food, and I guarantee you will see the "dopamine pathway" light up like a Christmas tree. There are also rewarding experiences that are related to our temperament and learning history, such as a preference for chocolate, video-gaming, or shopping. Present us with an opportunity to get what we crave, and chances are good that dopamine will be released and we will feel terrific.

Since the prefrontal cortex is under construction (i.e. immature) in adolescence, it doesn't always work very well—especially when taxed by arousal and hopped up on dopamine and high emotions. This is why one of the main features of executive functioning, self-control, is often severely lacking during the teen years. Add hormones, such as testosterone and estrogen (which are released during puberty), to the equation and teens can become more aggressive, moody, emotionally reactive, and prone to risk. Research shows that sensation-seeking behavior increases with brain development during puberty (ages ten to fifteen), subsiding or stabilizing after that; impulse control slowly improves from age ten to brain maturity in the early to mid-twenties (Steinberg et al. 2008).

So it's easy to see why a child in his early teens—who is wired to increasingly seek new sensations, but who also is simultaneously grappling with impulse control—can be at risk of making some astonishingly poor choices. Right when we want our kids to "think before they act" and "make good choices," their cognitive equipment takes a nose dive! That's why self-discipline, good decision making, and willpower take practice, practice, practice.

Complicating matters is a teen's increased desire to spend time with friends, which any parent can tell you results in an even more amped-up emotional arousal.

Let's do the math:

arousal + an immature brain's self-control system + hormones + peers = potential risk

This equation is the reason why developmental psychologists refer to adolescence as a period of great opportunity and great risk. Teens have the opportunity to build their brains by creating extensive new neural connections, thanks to their maturing physical and cognitive abilities combined with rich learning experiences. That's the good news! But they also can also get into a lot of trouble. And that's where parents can make a big difference.

ESSENTIAL
FACT

Self-Control
The teen brain is literally under construction: Almost half of the gray matter in the prefrontal cortex is being "pruned" and rebuilt. Teens are wired to seek new sensations even as they struggle with impulse control.

TEMPERAMENT AND THE PARENT'S ROLE

The debate about the "nature versus nurture" theory is alive and well. What factors influence how children will turn out at age eighteen, or better yet, twenty-five? How much is predetermined by genes? How much by parenting behavior? How much by cultural background? How much by environmental experiences? For our purposes, we'll agree that the answer to all of the above is "a lot." A child's reactivity and self-regulation are somewhat inborn, are evident early in life, and show some stability over time, but they are also influenced by parenting, training, and circumstances (Rothbart and Posner 2005).

When people use the terms "challenging" or "difficult" to describe temperaments, they are often referring to such traits as extreme impulsivity, rigidity, negativity, aggression, and emotional sensitivity. If a child is high energy and impulsive, he is prone to behavioral and social problems. At the other end of the continuum, the shy, inhibited child is at risk for developing anxiety-related issues later in life. It takes extra energy and parenting know-how to help children with challenging temperaments achieve the goal of self-control.

In some ways, your child's temperament is simply out of your hands; some characteristics will endure from cradle to grave. But what your child makes of that innate temperament can be greatly affected by your nurturing. The introverted child may become a famous academic or a hermit, and the aggressive extrovert may become a successful entrepreneur or a con artist. Parent navigation plays a big (but not all-determining) role in the equation. Random events, either good or bad, also play a role, as do the kind of neighborhood and community the child grows up in, the psychological services available to her, the school she attends, and the financial resources at her family's disposal.

For children with difficult temperaments, parental behaviors are even more influential, either protecting them or putting them at risk. For instance, firm, restrictive parenting has been linked to reducing behavioral problems among children with high impulsivity and frustration intolerance (Bates et al. 1998). Another recent study shows that these children are particularly vulnerable to negative parenting (Kiff et al. 2011). They just won't thrive in a home where parents are reactive and respond to misbehaviors with harsh punishments, threats, and criticism. Parents with kids on the far ends of the temperament spectrum will want to seek guidance from professionals about how to support their children through adolescence.

When children are impulsive, resistant, irritable, or aggressive, they easily elicit negative reactions from parents. It takes *parental* self-control to make positive headway with difficult children—rewards and consistent structure are a couple of tools these parents can use effectively. For parents who have kids with "middle of the road" temperaments, tips for developing self-control can still be helpful, as these children will also face mood challenges and developmental "hitches," and exhibit their fair share of resistance to rules and limits. For the parents of these less extreme kids, there is much that can be done at home, although that work can be exceptionally demanding, as well.

Since temperament colors every other life experience, parents will want to know where their particular child falls on the spectrum. This is especially important for parents of kids who are either very fearless or very fearful (with under-reactive or over-reactive arousal systems), high irritability, and low sociability. Most child development experts agree that it's important to:

• tailor your parenting style to the temperament of your child;
• avoid thinking you can mold and shape your child as you please; and
• realize that what works for one of your children may not work for another.

For example, some children benefit from regular "time-outs" for misbehaviors to help them learn self-control, while others might be emotionally crushed by such measures, benefiting more from gentler guidance. Highly sensitive children will still need course corrections, but they need softer voices and may learn better with more modest consequences (e.g., losing a privilege) than by being sent to their rooms. Parents learn what works along the way; it's not a one-size-fits-all proposition. The savvy parent of a high-energy, thrill-seeking child knows she enjoys risk and stimulation. That parent will learn to accept the chaos that accompanies his child's personality type and provide opportunities for her to safely explore her sensation-seeking temperament, so she can learn to curb her excessive zest and cope with limits.

Parents of a shy or anxious child know that certain social or novel situations are challenging for him. But they also know that he benefits from firmly established expectations, and that he will participate in some of these activities, if he is not overwhelmed by excessive social expectations. We all know that kids don't learn to swim well by being thrown into the deep end of the pool. Likewise, rather than suddenly being dropped off at an eight-week summer camp, shy or anxious kids do best with consistent nudges toward greater social engagement.

Whatever his temperament, you've known your child for a while now. Maybe you've thought or even said to someone, "He came out of the womb practically working the room with his social skills," or "She couldn't look someone in the eye until she was five years old," or "He has never sat still in his life." These are all clues as to where your child falls on the temperament continuum. You might think, "No matter what his temperament, I need to teach this child some self-discipline!"—and that's probably true, but in order to devise an effective strategy for just how to do that, parents need to start with some quiet insight about what kind of kid they have to begin with. While your parenting can move the dial on temperamental inclinations a lot, as we will learn in this chapter, there are challenging parts of every kid that require mega doses of pure acceptance and mindfulness.

Let's revisit our opening vignette. This time, with some insight into Hayley's particular temperament, the mom reaches deep into her wise mind, sidestepping the attitude and refusing to take the bait.

Take Two:

> *Mom:* OK, let's make this quick. Find cleats you like for less than $100.
>
> *Hayley:* Mom! You can't get good cleats for less than $100! These are hideous! Our coach said to get Nike Vapors.
>
> *Mom:* Whoa, that's out of our league. Why don't you look around for some in our price range? I need to find the ladies room. Then maybe I'll call the coach or another parent to do some recon.
>
> *Hayley:* Mom, that's stupid! I thought we were in a hurry. Why do you have to cheat me out of quality cleats? You want me to be a loser, don't you? I hate you!
>
> *Mom:* I know this is stressful, honey, because you may worry about what cleats are brand-perfect. I'm confident that we'll find cleats that will do the job. See you in a minute. I really have to go.

Using a positive attitude—and sheer momentum—this mom deftly delivers the news and then makes herself unavailable for the verbal abuse sure to follow. She knows that her hormone-laden, sensitive child's temper spikes when she is anxious about something, and Hayley needs time to cool off. But the mom doesn't say that out loud, because that would be patronizing and make her daughter even angrier. Notice that she chooses empathy, not reactivity, when Hayley mentions the "H" word (hate). The wise mind moves to empathy and understanding, as well as strategy. Staying patient and matter of fact, this mom also indicates that she plans to check her teen's facts. She will stick to the plan, and if Hayley still pitches a fit, her mom will quietly take her home and get her some secondhand cleats later. She wants her daughter to learn to cope with things that are less than perfect.

Learning to handle their emotions is crucial to a teen's ability to develop executive functioning skills, successful social relationships, and self-reliance. This is a tall order, certainly. And many parents assume that children are simply misbehaving and need a dose of one-size-fits-all punishment when they repeatedly seek to either jack up their arousal systems by taking risks, or flat out refuse to go to activities and fulfill their commitments. But the situation often calls for deeper understanding, empathy, and patience on the part of the parent. Finding the correct balance of reward, independence, acceptance, empathy, structure, and discipline for building competence and self-control in children with different temperament styles is part of the art and science of parenting.

Merging calm empathy with an understanding of your teen's emotional life will help you come up with ways to handle very complicated episodes. Your teen may look like she's spoiled and entitled when demanding those brand-name cleats, but she's also hormonal, highly sensitive, anxious about her peer status, and subject to a prefrontal cortex under construction and a "flooding"—experiencing high emotions—so severe that there is no way she'll understand that she can cope with cheaper cleats until she cools off.

ESSENTIAL
ACTIVITY

Your Child's Temperament

Think about your child for a moment, and your intuition about the nature of his temperament. Reflect on parent-teacher conferences, report card narratives, and feedback you've gotten over the years from other adults who know your child well. Now, circle where you believe he (or she) falls on the continuum of these common personality traits. Your answers will give you a starting point from which to observe and ultimately understand your child's innate temperament.

	Least								**Most**	
Impulsiveness	1	2	3	4	5	6	7	8	9	10
Aggression	1	2	3	4	5	6	7	8	9	10
Attraction to Novelty	1	2	3	4	5	6	7	8	9	10
Persistence	1	2	3	4	5	6	7	8	9	10
Organization	1	2	3	4	5	6	7	8	9	10
Focus	1	2	3	4	5	6	7	8	9	10
Fearfulness	1	2	3	4	5	6	7	8	9	10
Shyness	1	2	3	4	5	6	7	8	9	10
Aversion to Change	1	2	3	4	5	6	7	8	9	10

If you rated your child highest at the top of the chart, he might be on the high-energy/impulsive end of the spectrum; kids rating the highest at the bottom tend toward an anxious or avoidant temperament. Kids in either of these groups can be quite persistent, organized, and focused when they are comfortable and thoroughly engaged. In the pages that follow, we'll go deeper into the special challenges faced by kids in both groups and offer some important ways to support them while helping to cultivate their self-control.

Obviously, kids at the far ends of the temperament scale are likely to suffer and may need clinical intervention at some point in their adolescence. Further, for some children diagnosed with attention deficit hyperactivity disorder (ADHD), anxiety, depression, or other challenges, the measures described in this chapter will not go far enough, and professional support should be sought to chart a path that honors and accommodates your child's particular needs. However, even kids without these challenges can face significant roadblocks as they develop self-control, and parents have tough calls to make in their management efforts. If you think your child might be on one end of the spectrum or the other, the following sections provide a closer examination of these temperaments and some helpful strategies for working with kids at the extremes.

Wise-Minded Strategies for Parenting Anxious and Avoidant Kids

"I don't want to go to the party."
"I like watching a movie with my parents on Friday nights."
"I have to get an A on that test."

If your child is prone to making comments like the ones above, you have an "easy" teen in one respect—she stays away from trouble and worries about grades. But this temperament can have a dark side, as well:

"I don't want to go to the graduation party."
"I don't have any friends."
"I'm going to die if I don't get an A on that test!"

Many highly sensitive children with a tendency to be anxious and avoidant have been this way their entire lives, and sometimes their behavior doesn't kick parents into "highly concerned" mode until early adolescence. By then, it becomes clear that the child, if left to his own devices, will miss important growth experiences. American teens build their social and emotional "muscles" in camps, volunteer work, sports activities, and exploring their social worlds independently. Increasingly as these children mature, they need to develop self-awareness about their high sensitivity and proclivity for emotional flooding in the face of new experiences. The goal is to self-regulate these bouts of anxiety so that the child can cope with the challenges of life.

Remember, when we are triggered by a very scary experience, the amygdala—the part of the emotional center of our brain that alerts us to danger—is activated. If we see a snake in our path or can't find our kid in the mall, our heart beats rapidly, adrenaline is released, and our bodies get ready for "fight or flight." This triggered response to danger helped us survive when we needed to grab our babies and run. However, in our modern world, where encountering snakes is rare, the amygdala is triggered when we encounter bad traffic, when our kids don't do their chores, and when the wireless is down. Similarly, our anxious or avoidant teen might receive a false alarm when he is dropped off at a birthday party, has to give a speech in class, or is made to try a new sport. And just like bad traffic and a broken wireless connection, the "dangers" that trigger your child's amygdala are not life threatening, though they are very real. Discounting your child's feelings is a mistake. Do you know anybody who benefits from the advice, "Don't worry about it. It's no big deal!" when they are extremely upset?

When the amygdala is activated, whether by real or perceived danger, its neural firings will dominate the superhighways of the brain and take precedence over the more rational, conscious processing that takes place in the prefrontal cortex. Daniel Goleman coined the term "amygdala hijack" to describe the way that fear reactions trump thinking processes (Goleman 1995). Our emotional centers are triggered many times faster than our thinking brains; that's why we "lose it" and have a meltdown. In order to recover, we need to get neurons firing in our thinking brains again, and the only way to start that process is to calm down. In chapter 1, we introduced several tools that you and your child can use to do this, including breathing exercises (see pages 15 and 28) and the CALM technique (see page 26).

Kids and adults with anxious temperaments receive a lot of false alarms. Their amygdalae cause them to see experiences that others might consider benign or merely challenging as tremendously frightening. Anxious kids, like anxious adults, experience amygdala hijacks quite easily (more on this in chapter 5). With false alarms triggered by novelty (not life-threatening events), these kids are at risk of missing out on a lot of good things in life by fearing and avoiding them. Parents need to be especially skilled at helping their child work through emotions, and at knowing when to let an anxious child call the shots and when to nudge them to experience new situations and challenges.

Here are some typical behaviors of anxious and avoidant children and teens, and some strategies for dealing with them.

1. Your child is reluctant to join in.

Forever preferring life on the sidelines and staying close to home, this child takes patience and persistence to parent. Ultimately, you may have to wait a little longer to prod this child along; perhaps she'll be eleven instead of eight the first time she goes to day camp, and that's fine. You should also carefully consider what you ask her to join. Would your child do better participating in an individual sport, such as martial arts or ballet, than as a member of a team? Just getting out and participating with other kids counts as progress for these teens. Teams can be stressful for anxious kids because of all the inherent responsibilities and interconnectedness that come with the territory. It doesn't mean they'll never play on a team, but they'll probably need to work up to it. Kids who are reluctant to join in may ultimately be a little less involved than you'd like, engage in different activities than you expected, and take to them a little more slowly than other kids, but you should always insist that they do (and keep doing) new things that challenge them.

2. Your child is reluctant to try new things; is averse to novelty.

Anxious and avoidant kids need lots of warning before trying something new, and they need to take smaller steps. Let's say your child will soon be going on a field trip, or maybe you and your partner have planned a weekend away. Do your best to mitigate her reaction by providing clear information in advance. Negotiate what you can to help your child succeed. Before the field trip, talk to the teacher to find out who the chaperones are and what exactly to expect, and then explain it clearly to your child. Just knowing this information can help assure and prepare kids who find novelty to be anxiety provoking. For the weekend away, try to get a close friend or family member, not a baby-sitter, to stay with your child. As much as you can, tell your child the plan for the weekend. Do what you can to reassure your child and make it as comfortable as possible for her, but don't cave when faced with high emotions. Your child needs practice being exposed to challenges, and she needs to see that you have faith in her ability to cope. Let her experience some anxiety and then learn to deal with it. Only with emotional challenges like these will she learn self-control and coping strategies for those "false alarms."

WISE-MINDED **MANTRA**

I will not cave when faced with high emotions.

3. Your child reneges at the last minute on things he agreed to do.

For anxious kids, anticipation is almost always worse than reality, and as the moment approaches to try something new, these kids often attempt to get out of their commitments. When this happens, just say to your child, "I have faith that you can do this." Don't lecture him about the importance of commitments or how others will feel disappointed. You may be right and reasonable, but this will not motivate him, and it doesn't address the real problem: the amygdala hijack. Label the feeling "anxiety" so that the child can develop a vocabulary for their emotions. Try to keep the message positive and do the best you can to help him follow through. Do not engage in power struggles ("You *have* to go on the school retreat").

Don't dismiss his emotions by saying, "You'll be fine." Instead, validate the feeling that has been triggered ("New things give you big waves of fear that feel awful"), tell him you have confidence in him, and practice mindful parenting (i.e., being calm and nonjudgmental). Once your child is relaxed enough to talk about it, compliment his courage and negotiate a plan that helps him cope with his anxiety and follow through. Since extrinsic rewards are appropriate for helping kids (and adults) get over any problem that requires self-control and tremendous effort, a small reward for follow-throughs is perfectly legitimate in this situation. Rewards for practicing self-calming techniques in response to the fearful "thought loops" preceding the event are even better.

4. Your child has meltdowns in the face of a challenge.

If you remember one thing when dealing with an out-of-control child or teen, let it be the wise-minded tip for dealing with high emotions: *Don't just do something, stand there.* When your child is "flooding" (experiencing high emotions), your number-one job is to refrain from adding fuel to the fire. Don't threaten, wheedle, or negotiate. Control yourself and wait it out while making a mindful effort to accept the reality of the moment without passing judgment. Engage your wise mind. Try saying something soothing and then see if you can distract him with a new activity: Hand him his iPod, rub his back if he'll allow it, or offer to shoot hoops with him to help him blow off steam. Sometimes, after he's calmed down a bit, a distraction provides a chance to reset and reboot, and cooperation once again becomes an option. Whatever you do, don't be dismissive or attempt to minimize the situation by saying, "Calm down! You're fine!"—it's the biggest mistake parents make in these moments.

If he is truly overwhelmed and refusing to honor a commitment, try compromising on details, such as bringing a friend along. You can offer to go late to the school basketball game and sit unobtrusively near him and his group of friends. It is likely that after his amygdala calms down, he'll send you home. And if all else fails, don't force it. Instead, try to adopt an accepting attitude: You did the best you could. You can't win them all.

WISE-MINDED
MANTRA

My child is doing the best she can, given her innate temperament.

5. Your child regularly expresses negative, fearful, and extreme thoughts and/or emotions.

Everyone, and especially volatile tweens and teens, feels and verbalizes negative, fearful, and extreme thoughts and emotions at one time or another. Anxious or extremely shy children often think that others don't like them, which is a major reason they avoid social situations. If your child does this a lot, it can be emotionally draining, especially if you let yourself get caught up in trying to talk him out of his thoughts with your "reason mind," just because you want him to see things your way, the rational way. When your child has distorted thoughts because his amygdala has been hijacked, take a step back and practice mindful parenting. Validating feelings is the number-one priority. Then, once he is calm enough to engage in conversation, use this as an opportunity to talk to your child about the science of emotions.

It really does feel like a life-threatening situation when anxiety is sky high: Your anxious child's heart is racing, her palms are sweating, and she'll do anything to get out of the situation causing the terrible feelings. Ask your child to identify her emotion (fear, anger, frustration, etc.) and rate it on a scale from 1 to 10. See if the two of you can figure out what triggered the emotion and what your child's negative assumptions are, and check the facts. For example: "What do you think is the worst thing that could happen at your friend's party?" "What evidence do you have that you won't fit in with the other kids in Math Club?" "What is the probability that the business owner will be mean when you ask for a job application?"

When distressed kids are calm enough—the amygdala hijack is over and the thinking brain is reengaged—they should be able to generate a whole list of times that things have not turned out as badly as their anxious brains expected. But let's be clear: This conversation should be with the child in the driver's seat. Parents ask targeted questions or give gentle suggestions; the child comes up with the solutions for coping.

It's embarrassing for parents when anxious tweens and teens back out of commitments, fail to show friendliness, and act like indulged, spoiled brats. Hold your head high and remember that your child is not intentionally trying to make your life miserable. Repeat the wise-minded mantra: "My child is doing the best he can, given his age, stage, and emotional state—and temperament!" Continue to gently encourage them and know that the more social experiences they have, the more they'll begin to be able to handle, with your careful guidance.

While these measures may feel more like temporary bandages than long-term strategies for helping your child develop self-control, rest assured that these tactics are teaching your child plenty. These maneuvers are training them to cope with distress, face waves of emotion and ride them through to a peak and resolution, and accomplish a mission that, without you, they would have avoided. You are a guide through the perilous land of amygdala hijacks. Courage is the medium, competence is the outcome, and self-control is what you and your child practice every day to get there.

ESSENTIAL
TIP

Wise-Minded Strategies for Anxious and Avoidant Kids
• At whatever pace works, insist that your child do new things that challenge them.
• Provide plenty of warning, but let them experience—and then manage—anxiety.
• Do not engage in power struggles, and don't dismiss their emotions by saying, "You'll be fine."
• Remain firm, but compromise on small details that help them cope.
• Validate their feelings, then help your child come up with solutions.
• Remember that your child is doing the best he can.

Keeping all of this in mind in the heat of the moment can be more difficult than it seems. Here's a typical interaction between a frustrated, well-meaning parent and an avoidant teen:

> *Mom: It's time to sign up for summer camps. I found some great ones!*
>
> *Finn: I don't want to go to camp. I just want to stay home.*
>
> *Mom: That's what you said last summer. Remember, we said we aren't doing that again.*
>
> *Finn: Why can't you just let me be me?*
>
> *Mom: If I let you be you, you would never do anything!*

It's easy to imagine saying something like this. Avoidant and negative behavior gets old, but this interaction is ineffective at best. The parent is right to insist that her avoidant teen do something, but the parental challenge here is to see this gentle nudging as a long-term project. Therapists often refer to the following techniques for effectively building skills and self-control: desensitization (helping the child become less sensitive to challenges with experience), scaffolding (giving them extra supports as you nudge them to greater challenges, then removing those supports), and exposure (exposing them to fear-inducing but benign events, so that they experience the rise and fall of their anxiety, without the reward of avoidance taking precedence over the reward of mastery). The general idea is that once the child safely rides the wave of anxiety up and back down again—and finds that he is safe and sound—he starts to believe that he'll be OK and maybe even enjoy the activity.

Just *telling* an anxious kid that "planes are safe," the "party will be fun," and "people like you" doesn't make it so. Perception is reality. When the amygdala perceives danger, it will always trigger an alarm, false or not. Until the physiological arousal of that hijacked emotional brain can settle down again, you are talking to someone in the middle of an emotional seizure. Let's try it again, employing some of our new wise-minded strategies:

Take Two:

> *Mom: I know you dread the camp talk, but as we told you a month ago, we want to find one that you will try.*
>
> *Finn: I already told you: No way. I'm not going.*
>
> *Mom: I understand that you have a lot of negative feelings about what it will be like.*
>
> *Finn: Why can't you just let me be me? I'm not the camp sort.*
>
> *Mom: I know you are the reluctant sort, and that you are slow to warm up to new things. I'm going send you links to videos that you can look at so that you can get to know the settings better. I'll also let you know which of your friends are going to which camps.*
>
> *Finn: Suit yourself. I'm not going. You can't make me.*
>
> *Mom: I know new stuff always seems terrible to you at first. I'll circle back and talk to you about this later.*

Here, Mom also could have said, "It's awful when the brain registers a 10 on the distress-o-meter. It's the worst. I'll tell you a story of the last time that happened to me, if that will help. Or rub your back. Or just get out of your face. But I want to help you figure out a way to deal with this when you are ready." The teen still may not engage, but at least Mom won't be making it worse with criticism.

On a scale from 1 to 10, extremely sensitive children will give you a 7–10 reading for how distressing it feels to join a team, club, or group, even though an average kid might give it a 5, and a sensation-seeking kid will give it a 1. Ideally, registering a 10 should be reserved for a life-threatening emergency, not a birthday party. But that's the thing—if you have an anxious and avoidant kid, they can't help the fact that their brain registers a 10 when a 7, 5, or even 2 is more appropriate. Naming the emotion and giving it a rating can put the child in an "observing" and analyzing mode.

In one study, brain scans showed that subjects whose amygdalae were activated by looking at photos of fearful faces began to fire neurons in their prefrontal cortices when they translated their feelings into words (Lieberman 2007). Since fear is one of the biggest obstacles to self-control and problem solving, this research has significant implications. Once a flooding person puts feelings into words, he can start checking the facts and begin to cope.

ESSENTIAL
TIP

Name That Emotion
When your child is flooding, ask him to identify his emotion (fear, anger, frustration, etc.) and rate it on a scale of 1–10. See if the two of you can figure out what triggered the emotion and what your child's negative assumptions are, and then check the facts together.

Anxiety and sadness squelch zest and motivation. But the research on what parents can do to help kids become more resilient and venturesome is heartening. Parents who encourage their shy children to be brave and arrange for them to experience incremental masteries of social challenges are likely to raise teens who can face their fears and even overcome their shyness (Zimbardo and Radl 1999). These kids can't help being triggered by their low fear and anxiety threshold; but like the hyper kid who needs to learn to control his impulsive urges, the anxious and highly sensitive child needs to develop skills for coping with apprehension while forging ahead. And parents need to be tenacious about helping these kids manage the frequent false alarms they receive while helping them cultivate self-control. If you can find ways to get the initial anxiety under control, you can introduce new experiences to these children and teens, in the hopes you'll not only hit upon situations that offer a tolerable anxiety level, but provide growth experiences that even inspire enthusiasm and passion over time.

SHY AND RELUCTANT

If you have a tween or teen on the shy and reluctant side, but not extremely anxious or avoidant, you can get them over the hump of emotional resistance by telling them choices will be made for them if they don't engage in the process of decision making themselves. Give your child a deadline for choosing a sport or extracurricular activity; tell them that they get to choose *which* activity, but not *whether* they will participate in an activity. If they refuse, then choose for them. For these reluctant kids, sign them up for the more benign option, such as an individually focused, noncompetitive sport that offers adult support (martial arts), an easy-to-learn musical instrument, such as an African drum, or a low-key volunteer job, such as helping out at a retirement home. Your child can always choose an alternative—but there needs to be one (or two!).

A sensitive child's reactive, fearful, and cautious tendencies usually continue in some form throughout childhood and adolescence. The good news is that parents who continue nudging—exposing their kids to incremental challenges—may be happily surprised at the growth spurt that can accompany the college launch. College usually provides a huge leap forward in social competence, since it provides daily exposure to a zillion new experiences.

Wise-Minded Strategies for Parenting High-Energy and Impulsive Kids

"I'm going to start a car-washing business this summer!"
"I'm writing a graphic novel that will be a science fiction version of The Odyssey*!"*
"I raised money for a girls' school in Iraq!"

Oh, yes, you say to yourself, my child is a real go-getter. Always dreaming up big ideas, even if he doesn't always follow through; a kid who thinks this big is going to go places! But are they always the best places?

"Let's get some beer and meet in the park!"
"Let's skip class so we can skateboard on the new half-pipe!"
"Everybody loves the photo of you in your underwear that I posted on my Facebook wall!"

Parents of high-energy, impulsive teens know well the darker side of this temperament. Failure to think before acting can lead to negative—even dangerous—results. Kids like this can commit to big projects without understanding the consequences and then fail to follow through. And all that nonstop, go-getter energy? It can be exhausting to find enough appropriate outlets for high-energy teens to blow off steam. But blow off steam they will, and in ways you may not always like.

A child comes by a high energy, risk prone temperament as innocently as any genetic trait, such as blue eyes or left-handedness. However, parenting plays a significant role in how the child's energy level is harnessed, regulated, and directed. High zeal kids can end up in a lot of trouble, or become quite successful. Parenting these kids is a marathon event, and it requires a lot of stamina and skill to guide that gonzo energy toward positive outcomes.

ESSENTIAL
FACT
The Nature of High-Zeal Kids
A child comes by a high-energy, risk-prone temperament as innocently as any genetic trait, such as blue eyes or left-handedness.

These kids need more limits set for them than other children. As a parent of a high-energy and impulsive tween or teen, you may feel that you are being terribly restrictive compared to other parents, but that's exactly what your child needs (though they won't tell you that). These kids are often driven to seek the next thrill. It is the parents' duty to draw clear limits and find appropriate outlets for them, so that they will one day be able to do the same for themselves. Parents of kids like this wish for and dream of more self-control every day of their child-rearing lives! Sometimes, when I'm consulting with the desperate parents of a high-voltage eleven-year-old, I reassure them that in ten or fifteen years, their son will have self-control and probably be a successful adult. I often see stricken faces at this news ("Fifteen years?"). Yes, fifteen years for the development of optimal self-control, but these kids can also provide their families with a lot of fun and positive energy along the way. In the meantime, parents can help their kids with the executive functioning skills they lack.

Here are some typical behaviors of high-energy, impulsive children and teens, and some strategies for dealing with them.

1. **Your child operates at a supercharged energy level, compared to other kids.**
   Here's a child you should not worry about overscheduling; she actually needs a lot of different activities because of her temperament and energy level. Your job is to provide lots of good ways for her to burn off that energy, so she doesn't find her own less desirable methods for getting the job done. These kids often badger their parents for more freedom, privileges, and online access; it's a smart idea to keep them busy with highly engaging activities. Typically, these tweens and teens love anything electronic, since it jacks them up to that optimal state of arousal. It's a good idea for parents of preteens to be very careful about giving these kids a lot of freedom in the Wild Wild West of the media world, given their impulse-control difficulties and craving for excitement.

2. **Your child can't sit still, finds a lot of things boring, and revs things up to have more fun.**
   Like it or not, you are just going to have to accept this truth: For this child, you need to have different expectations. Because home time can feel like solitary confinement (if he isn't online), he can get very crabby and resentful of the limits you set. Furthermore, his sensation seeking outside the home can get him into more trouble than the average kid. For all of these reasons, parents have to work hard at conveying acceptance. Remember that part of secure attachment that relates to "accepting the child just the way he is"?

Since early childhood, these kids have no doubt been getting more than the average "time-outs," notes from the teacher, loss of privileges, and yes, the results of their parents' amygdala hijacks. Thus, these kids often question their parents' love in the face of all the "trouble" they cause. A wise-minded parent must figure out ways of staying more positive in their responses to this child; they even overlook many infractions to keep that positive bias intact; and they arrange for activities that make this kid a star. You can't win this one by talking him into changing; you must start with that bedrock of acceptance and trust that he will change with maturation and your good parenting. Setting reasonable expectations is critical to avoid setting him up for failure. You will still expect this child to attend his sister's choir concert, but you may think twice before buying him a ticket to the opera.

3. **Your child is impatient and easily frustrated with linear or tedious tasks.**
Remember: This frustration is not a choice; it's his emotional response to obstacles and part of his genetic predisposition. His tolerance for frustration will evolve with the maturation of his prefrontal cortex and his many opportunities over the years to practice "effortful control." Every day at school, he is practicing effortful control when he sticks to a task, doesn't act out in class, and fights his temptations to entertain his friends with constant verbal asides. These kids should really get medals for all the trouble they *don't* cause, given their level of frustration, temptation, and boredom. Yet because they often cause so much trouble, the only attention many receive is negative.

Make it a priority to periodically commend your highly exuberant child on the self-control he does exercise. These kids need as much positive reinforcement as they can get to offset all the negative attention they attract. Remember that DBT mantra: He's doing the best he can, and he needs to do better. You can help by accepting and validating, which creates a better context for cheering him on to do so. Since homework can feel like torture for these kids, you'll want to help them figure out how to break it up and make it tolerable. When this child really needs to engage with homework or another task, allow him to take lots of breaks. Control distractions and disallow access to social media. Help him come up with a structure and make a plan for getting a task done, perhaps using a white board or other list or chart.

4. **Your child dives in without thinking about consequences.**
This happens with children in general, especially during the big teen-brain remodeling project; but for these kids, the effect is supercharged. You need to have realistic expectations that this will happen with your high-energy, impulsive teen—and there will be collateral damage. Accept that you will have to be less permissive than parents of other kids her age, but at the same time less outraged when she messes up, since it is to be expected. When other eighth-graders are allowed to spend all day at the mall, you know it's just too much freedom for your kid. Stand your ground. But figure out more structured (more supervised?) ways that she can still have a lot of fun. As with a

thoroughbred horse, you'll want to give your child freedom to run, making adjustments to the corral as needed.

Parents sometimes get frustrated when these kids lie about their whereabouts, receive a consequence, such as being grounded, and then repeat the offense. When they get aroused and excited out there on the range, they are not thinking about consequences. Some parents believe they need to pile on harsh punishments or keep them grounded, but sitting at home is not where they learn self-control. They learn by being in a some-what open range with rules and limits (spot checks, check-ins, and pullbacks), and practicing the self-control of complying with those rules over and over again. These children need much more monitoring than others, to keep them safe and provide fewer opportunities for damaging decisions. With this type of child, you need to pay special attention to peers; sensation-seeking kids seek like-minded friends to double the fun, which can also double the trouble.

It's tough to parent a child who falls at either end of the temperament spectrum. Just as parents who deal with anxious and avoidant kids often feel embarrassed by their kids' awkwardness or timidity; parents of high-energy and impulsive kids meet with their fair share of parental embarrassment, and sometimes many more trips to the principal's office. Impulsive kids are especially good at drawing harsh judgments from other parents because their behavior is often blamed on lax or absent parental discipline. But not only are these behaviors a natural result of his temperament and not necessarily of insufficient discipline, *they become worse with harsh punishment.* Remember, these behavioral tendencies are inborn, and no matter what other parents might think, you are no doubt working very hard to manage them the best way you can. Keeping your child safe is the number-one goal. And the second goal is to stay as positive as possible as you balance the setting of limits with encouraging independence on the long road toward self-control.

ESSENTIAL
TIP

Wise-Minded Strategies for High-Energy and Impulsive Kids
• Redirect the energy and seek settings for positive engagement.
• Set reasonable expectations based on your child's temperament.
• Remember that frustration is not a choice; it's a natural part of your child's temperament.
• Control distractions and help collaborate with your child to set and meet goals.
• Vigilantly monitor your high-energy child.
• Remember that your child's inborn behavioral tendencies are not reflections of your parenting skills.

You might see yourself in this typical scenario in which a parent sets unpopular limits for his high-energy, impulsive teen:

Darrell: *Dad, I'm going skateboarding at the park.*

Dad: *Not right now. It's too close to dinner time.*

Darrell: *You never let me do anything!*

Dad: *You're right, because the last time I let you go with your friends, you ended up with stitches, and I got complaints from the other parents. I just don't trust you anymore.*

Darrell: *You will never be happy unless I grow up in a jail.*

Dad: *I'd rather have you safe in jail than free and in trouble.*

This is a classic power struggle, with both sides making valid points and both sides escalating. A better, more wise-minded approach for the parent might be:

Take Two:

Darrell: *Dad, I'm going skateboarding at the park.*

Dad: *Not now. It's too close to dinner time.*

Darrell: *You never let me do anything!*

Dad: *I know it's frustrating when you are all ready to have fun and I put the kibosh on it.*

Darrell: *Yeah, well, do something about it and let me go to the park.*

Dad: *Nothing doin'. You can relax some more in your room, or if you're restless for action, I'd love it if you'd set the table.*

ESSENTIAL
TIP

Structuring for Sensation-Seeking Teens

Parents of high-energy, impulsive kids should set expectations and consequences for noncompliance, and then follow through with as little emotion as possible.

Kids with extreme temperaments benefit from especially skilled parents. However, all kids need their parents to praise good behaviors, ignore a lot of low-level violations, and impose consequences for breaking rules. Since energetic, impulsive kids create so much havoc, parenting efforts need to be multiplied to stay positive, manage conflicts, and keep the lid on risk taking while creating outlets for high-energy fun.

A parent's first challenge with a high-energy, risk-taking kid is to accept that trying to tame his sensation seeking is akin to riding a bucking bronco. Parents of children with "spirited" or "difficult" temperaments need to control and structure the environment to compensate for the child's lack of self-control.

Parents will want to anticipate situations that are likely to trigger zest gone amok. Any activity that jacks up energy to a frenzied level is likely to be risky. Thus, parents of these kids are advised to increase supervision and safety plans for big events (school field trips), fun outings (birthday parties, sleepovers), and special social occasions (prom and graduation). As a group, teens benefit from parental monitoring. High-energy teenagers who enjoy thrill seeking need even more supervision than the average teen, for obvious reasons: Sensation-seeking teens are at higher risk for teenage pregnancy, substance use, truancy, smoking, and juvenile crime.

Of course, there are also plenty of straight-arrow, high-energy kids who are uncomfortable painting outside the lines and who direct their laser-like attention toward loftier goals, such as competing in a prestigious chess competition or winning the state swimming championship. But most kids with high levels of zest are like garden hoses. They flail around, moving their energy and focus from one new interest to another— learning juggling from YouTube one day, rereading *Calvin and Hobbes* for the umpteenth time the next day, daring to write a poem to a new love interest the next, and on the fourth day, blowing off class to go to the mall. Since parental monitoring and necessary restrictions on freedom can be such a huge bummer for risk-attracted kids, parents need to work twice as hard to maintain good relationships and positive feelings in the home during the rambunctious adolescent years.

What's Your Temperament?

Take a moment to reflect upon your own temperament. You can use the scale on page 46 as a starting point and then answer the following questions as honestly as you can:

True False

1. ☐ ☐ I usually don't like a new idea at first.
2. ☐ ☐ I really prefer a quiet night at home to going out most of the time.
3. ☐ ☐ I haven't taken a new class or tried a new hobby in years.
4. ☐ ☐ I am reluctant to initiate social invitations.
5. ☐ ☐ When I plan a vacation, I like to try places we've never visited.
6. ☐ ☐ At parties, I am pretty good at mixing and mingling.
7. ☐ ☐ I hate doing things that are boring.
8. ☐ ☐ Long meetings make me want to jump out of my skin.
9. ☐ ☐ I love a busy, challenging day.

If the majority of your "true" checkmarks are at the top of the list, you probably tend toward the anxious/avoidant end of the spectrum. This may come as no surprise to you, and you may find your tween or teen on the same end of the scale. The opposite holds true for the bottom of the list, where high-energy and impatient temperaments are described. This simple exercise in self-observation is just a start to get you thinking about how your own temperament might be interacting with your child's to affect your parenting style.

Your Temperament—And Your Teen's

Now that you've thought about your own temperament and your teen's, consider how the two might interact. If you co-parent, have your partner answer these questions as well, then compare your responses.

1. What traits do you share with your tween/teen?

_____

_____

_____

_____

2. What traits are different?

_____

_____

_____

_____

3. What traits in your teen cause you the most distress?

_____

_____

_____

_____

4. In your own judgment, do you overreact to or over-control any of these shared traits you see in your teen?

_____

_____

_____

_____

5. Do you underreact or pass up a chance to work on any of these shared traits?

_____

_____

_____

_____

6. Which of your teen's temperament traits would you like to learn to accept?

_____

_____

_____

_____

7. What strategies would you like to try to help your teen develop better self-control?

_____

_____

_____

_____

8. What self-control practices would you like to model more for your tween or teen?

_____

_____

_____

_____

Your answers to these questions can provide launching points for acceptance and ultimately, change.

High-energy kids are hard to nail down with chores and reasonable expectations. Wise-minded parents know that verbalizing a lot of "shoulds" causes shame, disregards the temperament issue, and doesn't get the job done. With as little emotion as possible, they set realistic expectations and consequences for noncompliance, and then follow through.

As you work to understand your teen's temperament, remember that your view will be colored by your own temperament. Unless your kid is adopted, he's destined to share certain personality traits with you, his grandma, your spouse, or anyone in the family. If you're aggressive, bossy, and "out there," you shouldn't be surprised to find that your teen is, too. Often, it's the traits we share with our children that we'd most like to "fix." Good luck with that!

Authoritative Parenting

It can seem a daunting task to correctly analyze your child's personality and then tailor your parenting accordingly. But in spite of the fact that children possess a whole host of individual differences in their budding personalities, research has documented that one particular parenting style is most predictive of adolescent competence and psychological health: authoritative parenting. By adopting this style of parenting, you will be doing your best to cultivate strong self-control in your child.

Authoritative parenting has stood the test of time, through decades of research, examination, and practice. Authoritative parents are emotionally warm with their children while setting firm limits and providing solid structure. They are also respectful of their adolescents' feelings and need to explore independent opinions and beliefs, and in doing so, give their children what is called "psychological autonomy." Authoritative parents stand in stark contrast to other parenting styles that are linked to poorer results, such as *authoritarian* parents, who issue edicts, lack warmth, and disregard their children's emotional needs; *permissive/indulgent* parents, who don't provide structure and lack authority; and *neglectful* parents, who pay little, if any, attention to their children or their psychological or emotional needs.

Compared to children reared by authoritarian, permissive, or neglectful parents, children of authoritative parents do better in school, are emotionally healthier, and are less likely to have behavior problems, including drug and alcohol abuse. They have a warmer connection with their parents, respond better to external discipline, and develop stronger and more effective self-control. By any measure, children of authoritative parents thrive and succeed beyond their peers. To understand how to work on your own authoritative parenting skills, it's helpful to understand the science behind why this style of parenting is so effective.

ESSENTIAL
FACT

Authoritative Parenting

Authoritative parents are emotionally warm with their children while setting firm limits and providing solid structure. They are also respectful of their adolescents' feelings and need to explore independent opinions and beliefs, and in doing so, give their children "psychological autonomy."

AUTHORITATIVE PARENTING AND TEEN DEVELOPMENT

The sheer volume of research that associates authoritative parenting with positive outcomes in late adolescence is remarkable (Larzalere et al. 2012). More than forty years ago, developmental psychologist Diana Baumrind conducted longitudinal research with parents and children at the University of California, Berkeley, in order to establish which parenting style resulted in the best adjustment of children and adolescents (Baumrind 1971). Among the three styles she studied—authoritative, authoritarian, and permissive—authoritative parenting was the hands-down winner.

Adolescents from authoritative homes achieve higher grades in school, possess greater self-control, and are less likely to have conduct and behavioral problems. They also report less depression and anxiety, and score higher on measures of self-esteem (Steinberg et al. 1994). And in the four decades since Baumrind's study was first published, these findings have been replicated time and again in research conducted all over the world using a variety of methods.

Developmental psychologist Laurence Steinberg and his colleagues have researched authoritative parenting and examined the literature from many perspectives (Steinberg 2001). His conclusions suggest something quite fascinating: Authoritative parenting practiced by just one parent is more important than consistency between parents and the so-called "united front." Steinberg has also examined the long-term impact of authoritative parenting, and figured out that for every year of high school, teens from homes in which parents are lacking in authority and warmth—parents they call "indifferent"—lose ground to their authoritatively reared counterparts in measures of competence and psychological health. He surmises that the prolonged advantages in this parental nurturing and disciplinary style helps to explain why authoritative parenting has been shown to have such robust power in determining positive outcomes for teens throughout the child-rearing literature.

Like his predecessor Diana Baumrind, Steinberg emphasizes the three emotional strengths that underlie authoritative parenting: warmth, structure, and psychological autonomy. Warmth—expressed in nurturance and parental engagement—makes the child more receptive to parental influence, which allows for more effective implementation of rules and guidance. It seems obvious: Nurturing and engaged parents are more effective at discipline and creating structure, because their family exists in the context of relative emotional harmony. A warm and strong support system, together with limits, consistent discipline, and structure in the home, promotes the development of self-control in the child. And finally, allowing a teen to develop psychological autonomy—giving her the freedom to express independent thoughts and feelings—enhances trust, self-expression, and analytic thinking.

It takes effort, but this parenting style helps the teen become a successful and happy individual over time. Get your pen and journal ready for a series of exercises in the coming pages that can help you focus on these truly essential parenting strengths.

ESSENTIAL QUIZ

Are You an Authoritative Parent?

Take a moment to appraise your authoritativeness by completing this quiz.

True False

1. ☐ ☐ I want my kids to do chores, but it's too much of a hassle to enforce these tasks.
2. ☐ ☐ Our family doesn't focus that much on a consistent bedtime for our kids.
3. ☐ ☐ I have daily goals and meet most of them every day.
4. ☐ ☐ We prefer letting days naturally unfold to keeping an organized household.
5. ☐ ☐ Keeping my children happy with me is more important than making sure rules are followed.
6. ☐ ☐ When my children express an opinion that contradicts my values, I set them straight immediately.
7. ☐ ☐ My children are never snippy with me because they know I won't stand for it.

If you answered true to all of the above—except for number 3—you, like the majority of parents, have work to do on your authoritative parenting.

AUTHORITATIVE PARENTING IN ACTION

Scene: *When fifteen-year-old Henry gets home, he goes straight to his room to post a music review on his Facebook page and check ESPN for sports scores. Ever since his last dismal report card, a family rule was established: There is to be no "play" or social time on the computer until homework is done. Still, he thinks, maybe he can slip in a little fun while he downloads his history homework and readies himself for the wireless blackout.*

Mom's blood starts boiling the minute she hears Henry crooning along with his favorite hip-hop artist. To calm herself, she repeats her favorite mantra for meltdown moments: "You might be right, but are you effective?" She knows that to maintain her authoritative credibility, she needs to keep calm, firm, and level-headed. Instead of barging into Henry's room and yelling at him about the rule violation, she tries a different approach. Her conversation with her son is in the left column below; the underlying dynamics are on the right.

Mom: Henry, I see that you're online. What's up with your breaking the homework rule?	*Mom is trying to be direct but not too accusatory, in an effort to avoid a power struggle.*
Henry: Mom, I'm downloading my history chapter, so I can do my homework offline, the way you make me. God, you're on me like a vulture.	*Henry feels like he can't get away with anything under his mother's vigilant watch. He finds her supervision infuriating.*
Mom: Henry, I appreciate that, but the rule is that you don't go online until 8:30 p.m.	*Mom ignores his snarky remark to stay on the issue of the rule. She wants to remind him of his bad grades before they had the homework policy, but she knows that it would just make things worse.*
Henry: I know the rule, Mom. It's not like you don't nag me about it a million times a day. It's like you are just waiting to catch me. I bet this is the most exciting moment of your day. You love the big "gotcha!" don't you?	*Henry's voice drips with disgust. He knows that his grades made the "wireless" homework policy necessary, but nonetheless, he feels controlled and treated like a baby. He enjoys making his mother feel as miserable as he is, as he anticipates the drudgery of homework without the distraction of social networking.*
Mom: I actually hate the monitoring of the homework rule as much as you do. But that's mother love for you. Mothers will do anything to help their kids become successful.	*Again, Mom fights the temptation to respond to his nasty remarks. She knows that if she gets as negative as Henry in her communication, the chance of his getting down to business with his homework is nil.*
Henry: Yeah, right.	*He hates it when his mother stays upbeat when he's trying to pull her into the mud pit. It always makes him speechless.*

Mom: I know it's a drag to come home after school and baseball and then face the homework pile, Henry. It takes a ton of self-control to turn off the wireless and tackle it.

It takes self-control for Mom to turn on her heel and leave the room without making sure he complies, too. But she knows that she is more likely to get Henry's cooperation with a pleasant exit than by belaboring the issue.

In this scene, Henry's mom is demonstrating wise-minded parenting by controlling her emotions and not indulging in self-righteousness (i.e., dwelling on "reason mind" facts and how justified she is for instating the policy to begin with), taking his disrespect to heart, or fixating on how much his violating the rules angers her. She is demonstrating authoritative parenting by keeping a warm rapport, providing structure around his home-work time in a way that will helps him learn self-control, and giving him wiggle room for his negative feelings.

If Henry's mom were authoritarian, she would have punished him for breaking the homework rule and cared not one whit if Henry thought her a tyrant for not hearing his defense. Also, without a history of her commitment to warmth and relationship building, he wouldn't be motivated to cooperate and would probably just rebel.

If Henry's mom were permissive (and indulgent), she might have tried to interact with Henry positively, and may have reminded him of the rule. But she would have avoided putting her foot down when he charged her with "vulture-like" behavior and been ineffectual in making sure he complied, either by leaving in a huff or by engaging in a nonproductive power struggle. She might have talked about her hurt feelings (after all, her emotion mind is no doubt flooding over his remarks), and then gone on and on about why she is concerned about his grades, his online activity, and his disrespectful attitude (her reason mind supplying copious facts). Because TMI ("too much informa-tion") and the guilt trip would trigger his hostility and defensiveness, Henry would likely counter with retorts and verbal missiles for every one that she lobs.

Sometimes, parent-child power struggles look a lot like marital bickering or sibling conflicts. When this is the case, there is usually a parent-child boundary missing that is a major part of the authoritative parent's personal strength (the power to stay out of power struggles!). Without boundaries and self-control on the parent's part, the teen often learns very little about self-control, but instead gets a lesson in how to pick fights with the permissive parent, or to con them into caving in on rules and consequences.

If Henry's mom were permissive (and neglectful), she would not have a rule about homework in the first place, nor would she monitor his computer use or the completion of his homework. Henry would be one of those kids who lives online and does pretty much whatever he wants. And his grades likely would not improve.

Authoritative parenting is a lot harder than it sounds. It requires picking your battles, monitoring without hovering, and being realistic about the fact that teenagers will never be perfectly compliant. Although flexibility is required so that life with a teen doesn't become a war zone, consistency with policies and routines is paramount. Charting a constant course toward competence and responsibility is the goal.

ESSENTIAL
ACTIVITY

Build Your Authoritative Parenting Skills

Here's an exercise to help you determine which, if any, of the three main traits of an authoritative parent you need to work on.

More warmth?

Think about the overall tone of your interactions with your child. How much of it is warm and loving? Imagine someone is videotaping and then evaluating your interactions with your child, rating them as neutral, positive, or negative. What's your ratio? If you see room for improvement, try for a 5:1 ratio of positive to negative interactions. Kids don't like gushing praise, but they appreciate subtle and specific acknowledgments. Your bids for connection count as warmth, whether your kid blows you off or not. ("Want to play a game of pingpong?" "I couldn't wait to show you this comic!" "Thanks for getting your stuff out of the hall," "I know you are facing a tough deadline with that paper—do you want to talk about it?") And remember that when you're talking to your teen, nagging—even just reminding them to do their homework!—counts as a negative interaction.

On an average school day, try estimating the ratio of positive to negative interactions:

	Positive	Negative
Before school		
After school		
After dinner		

More structure?

You can't overhaul the whole system at once, but if your household is lacking structure, now is a good time to tighten things up, one step at a time. Introducing structure by increments will get you there in a more stable, less painful way.

Here are some ideas for increasing the structure in your home. Try checking off a few that you would like to introduce into your family's routine.

☐ Set regular hours for homework. (If your child claims she has no homework, she can read.)

☐ Establish clear rules around recreational use of the Internet, video games, and social media.

☐ Set a family bedtime, collect the cell phones, and turn off the wireless router.

☐ Insist on a regular family dinner at least five nights a week. (If you are at zero, start by adding one or two.)

☐ Expect your children to sit down with you for breakfast.

☐ Assign—and then regularly enforce—chores.

☐ Keep a family calendar posted in a common area so kids can see that there is a plan for their week.

☐ Post "to do" lists for weekend projects.

☐ Have a regular "library day," on which the entire family goes to the public library (or bookstore) together.

☐ Establish a family game night, movie night, breakfast-for-dinner night, or other fun ritual.

☐ Give your child a regular allowance; have an expectation of savings and charitable giving as part of that allowance.

More psychological autonomy?

Allow your child to be an independent thinker—even if their thinking is outrageous! Yes, the goal is self-control, but clamping down on your child's crazy ideas and strongly held opinions will backfire. Remember: You can control actions to a large degree, but not thoughts and feelings. Draw the line at things that are truly unacceptable, such as profanity or unkind and humiliating statements to siblings. Try to let a little backtalk slide ("You don't know anything!" "You're the meanest mom!") and ask open-ended questions about some of their new ideas ("I think anarchists are cool," "College is a waste of time"). We'll walk you through this process—called the Socratic method—in chapter 4. It's a worthwhile exercise; why chock up more negativity on your relationship ledger if you don't have to?

Think about a few recent times you allowed more "psychological autonomy" for your child by avoiding criticism of his/her feelings or thoughts. Record here or in your journal any offensive, off-putting things your child said that you let slide instead of responding negatively to them. (If you validated their feelings or said, "Tell me more about that," give yourself extra credit!)

_____

_____

_____

_____

_____

The wise-minded parent stays out of power struggles because she understands that the core principle—"Do not criticize thoughts and feelings"—makes room for the crucial task of teen autonomy in thought and belief. Avoiding power struggles by not arguing about your teen's views or exaggerated pronouncements—or even about the truth!—is extremely important. Remember, the truth has many sides.

TOOL

The Anti-Nagging Intervention

No one likes to nag (or be nagged) and besides, it knocks points off the warmth ratio. So how do you get your kids to do as you ask without nagging?

1. **Set clear expectations and consequences.**
   "I'm sorry I've been nagging so much lately. I have an idea for a win-win solution. I'll give you one reminder after I make a request. That way you always have a choice whether to comply or not. If you don't, I will assume you are ready to take a twenty-four-hour break from your cell phone. Chores are like work; cell phones are like a paycheck. First you work, then you earn your paycheck!"
2. **Give only one reminder. Do not threaten.**
   "Here's your one reminder. I need the garbage bin out by 6 p.m. I hope you get it done."
3. **Follow through.**
   "I noticed that you didn't take the bin out by 6 p.m., so I did it. You know the deal. Your cell will be out of service for twenty-four hours."

THE ROLE OF EMOTION COACHING

Cultivating self-control in your child involves helping them regulate their emotions, and a powerful tool for doing that is the practice of emotion coaching. We'll explore this practice more deeply in chapter 5, but because self-control is ultimately about learning how to cope with emotions—and emotion coaching is key to building that control—we'll touch on it here first.

University of Washington psychologists Lynn Katz and John Gottman conducted a groundbreaking study that followed families over time with comprehensive assessments. They coined the term "emotion coaching" to refer to the set of parenting qualities that are associated with children's greater concentration skills, fewer behavior problems and instances of negative play, and less physical illness. This set of qualities also resulted in higher academic achievement (Gottman et al. 1997). Katz has gone on to associate one emotion-coaching skill in particular—parents' emotional awareness—with fewer depressive symptoms in adolescents, fewer behavior problems, and closer mother-daughter relationships (Katz and Hunter 2007).

Parents who practice emotion coaching treat negative behaviors and emotions as opportunities for teaching children how to label and solve problems, and in doing so, eliminate some of the negative feelings (especially rejection) that are very likely to occur at these times. These parents are keenly aware of their emotions and those of their children, recognize that all feelings are valid (even the unpleasant ones), and utilize some basic skills for helping children deal with their emotions. Parents' emotional awareness is an essential ingredient in emotion coaching; it helps them more intuitively respect their kids' feelings. That intuition and empathy makes emotion coaching an important part of wise-minded parenting.

Here's an example of emotion coaching in action:

Adeela: *I only shoved Joe because he used my iPod without asking and wouldn't give it back.*

Dad: *I'd hate to have my stuff taken or used without permission. I know your little brother drives you crazy. There will be consequences for both of you, but let's talk about you and your brother first.*

Adeela: *You spoil him rotten. Just because he's eight and I'm twelve, you let him get away with murder. You treat him like a baby.*

Dad: *So the way I handle Joe infuriates you because you think I should punish him more for his actions.*

Adeela: *Yes! I think you just pat him on the head and take some little privileges away, but really you treat him like he's this cute little baby. And you always say I'm supposed to take the high road. I'm sick of it. I hate it.*

Dad: *You think I'm way tougher on you than I am on him. I'm sure that's true. I have much higher expectations for you as a twelve-year-old. I also give you a lot more privileges, but that's beside the point. Being older is a drag when it means your little brother takes stuff, irritates the heck out of you, and gets more room for being the child that he is. Right?*

Adeela: *Right!*

Just because parents respect the importance of emotions doesn't mean they don't also believe in the importance of discipline. This emotion-coaching dad disciplines his kids for their infractions and takes the time to process negative emotions.

And he does it while remaining calm. A parent's ability to develop and deploy self-control plays a big role in their children's abilities to do the same. Parents who can't regulate their own emotions when kids are yelling or defiant can't help their kids identify which emotion they are having and why, and can't model what a calm and reasoned response to strong emotions looks like. Comparing thirty pairs of mothers and daughters, Katz and Hunter (2007) found that maternal acceptance of negative feelings was associated with fewer externalizing symptoms (conduct problems) in the teens. One of their conclusions was that parents who model emotional competence, accepting their own and their daughters' negative feelings, serve as approachable supports for teens who might otherwise maintain their distance during adolescence. This important body of research on emotion-coaching suggests that parental emotional awareness is another parenting pillar that builds self-discipline, competence, and psychological health in teens.

As an author, university faculty member, and practicing psychologist, I have given hundreds of lectures on child and teen development, family life, and parenting. On the following pages are some good questions that I am frequently asked. I think the answers help flesh out some important concepts related to parenting adolescents and influencing the development of self-control.

Q: Authoritative parenting sounds good in principle, but giving teens autonomy for feelings and thoughts that are disrespectful sounds wrong to me. I don't think I should tolerate rudeness.

A: When families are run like boot camps, children don't develop warm relationships with their parents. Furthermore, parents who don't listen to their teens' feelings and perspectives may lack moral credibility from their kids' point of view. They think, "All you care about is perfect behavior, grades, and looking good. You don't care about me!" As a parent, you may think strict discipline is a form of caring, but teens are focused on their perspectives and don't agree. Authoritarian parents do not rear the most well-adjusted or even well-behaved children, even though they may feel self-satisfied that they don't give in to feelings or soft-pedal on the discipline.

Q: I understand that feelings are important, but why can't you just say "Because I said so!" sometimes?

A: Authoritarian parents suffer from an overdose of "reason mind," believing that kids should learn self-control through the setting of rules and the doling out of punishments when they meet with resistance. They have the notion that telling kids what they should do will get them to do it. These parents may handle meltdowns and protests with stale responses like "Because I said so," "Get over it," or "I'll punish you if you don't." All of these responses are understandable, but they don't work. With resistance and moodiness so common among teens, parents who pick their battles and keep things mostly positive will finesse chores, screen limits, and bedtimes more deftly than those who just lay down the law. Tyrants don't inspire good behavior; they just alienate.

Respecting and understanding the complexity of emotions takes time and patience, but it communicates acceptance, thus helping the child tolerate firm boundaries and consequences. When parental authority is seen as fair, kids internalize rules and adopt self-governance more effectively. The evidence is on the side of authoritative parenting.

Q: I know I should be prioritizing chores, bedtimes, and screen limits, but the fights I get into with my teen just don't seem worth the trouble.

A: Permissive parents who lack rules and structure may worry that limits will destroy the parent-child bond, intensify the teen's anger, or generally cause more problems than they are worth. Whatever the source of this avoidance or neglect, permissiveness usually causes as many problems as authoritarianism does.

Permissive parents may want their children's love and delight so much that they can't tolerate their children's vitriol when they are enforcing rules. These parents cave or become inconsistent, and fail in their attempts to hold the line. Some of these parents are very invested in their children, but their busy lifestyles make them seem neglectful, because they are not engaged enough with the heavy demands of responsible child-rearing.

Developing a habit of authoritative parenting, while demanding, pays off because it results in a more harmonious household down the line. It also results in a secure bond between parent and child, because the children become more well-adjusted (and happy!) teens and adults than children reared in permissive, neglectful, or authoritarian homes. Competence is a good setup for happiness; it feels good to learn self-control and accrue the rewards our society offers to high-functioning individuals.

Q: Accepting negative emotions is one thing, but the torrents of negativity I get from my teen are over the top!

A: Socialization, and the development of self-control, is a major project, involving seemingly endless tasks, such as enforcing manners, good behavior, homework, chores, and rules, and monitoring the teen's whereabouts, to name a few. All kids, no matter what their temperament, are going to buck the system once in a while and engage in some negative behavior. Tolerating negative emotions is part of the "acceptance" principle of parenting, which also includes the expectation that child-rearing will require enormous time, sacrifice, and patience. Too many parents have the erroneous impression that if they are good and wholesome parents, they will have pleasant family dinners, obedient children, and kindly sibling interactions. When conflicts and teen grumpiness prevail, demoralized and disappointed parents may stop trying. Don't.

Parents who give up because of the enormous negativity and conflict unleashed by adolescent emotions are missing one key aspect of socialization: To a kid, life can feel like a series of nonstop demands. This road to self-control, especially if parents lack realistic expectations and impose too many expectations, taxes a child's ability to practice self-control. It doesn't mean that we just abandon our routines, expectations, and rules; it means we need to understand that we risk emotional backlash if we continue to press on without taking into account the teen's perspective. Remember: Teens often tell researchers that they have "mostly good" relationships with their parents, even while sending constant torrents of negativity their parents' way. We take it all personally, but really, they are just reacting to all those rules and expectations. Having empathy for children's feelings about this forced march through socialization can help. It doesn't mean parents should ease up on behavioral expectations; it just means that policy implementation needs to be mixed with heavy doses of tolerance, acceptance, and perseverance. Kindness and humor help, too.

Q: I want to accept my teen's negative moods and practice wise-minded, authoritative parenting, but I'm incredibly busy and stressed, and I don't see how it relates directly to my teen learning self-control.

A: If we are good CEOs of our own lives and our family lives, there's a greater chance that our children will learn these skills from us. All parental goals, including managing family dinners, chores, screen controls, bedtimes, homework monitoring, emotion coaching, and special time with individual kids, require parental executive functioning. But as explained in chapter 1, parents can only tap into those important executive functioning skills when they are calm enough to access their thinking brain—the prefrontal cortex—which controls brain functions such as reflection, evaluation, and decision making.

Neuroscience is helping us understand crimes of passion—and parental tirades. Any of us can end up yelling at our kids about their homework, sloppy rooms, and nasty attitudes, instead of engaging our CEO brain, utilizing our wise-minded parenting strategies, and collaborating with our spouses and children about routines and policies. Remember: Perfection is not the goal; "good enough" is the goal. Raising a teen is ambitious business!

Q: I see that all these limits and structures help my teen internalize self-control, but it's all too much for me to do on my own.

A: It's never truer that it takes a village to raise a child than in the tween and teen years. You can have a huge, positive impact on your child's development of self-control by enlisting that village. Choose neighborhoods, schools, activities, camps, and other social contexts that positively influence your child.

This is an enormously powerful tool for parents. Putting children into settings that build character, provide adult role models, and offer challenging activities does some of the heavy lifting of socialization for you. These settings may include religious group activities, athletics, boys and girls clubs, scouts, music lessons, and all manner of volunteering.

THE MYTH OF THE OVERSCHEDULED KID

All organized activities and social settings have expectations that implicitly build the self-control muscle. Lately, it's very much in vogue to criticize parents for overscheduling their kids. But the "overscheduled child" epidemic has been declared a myth, because only a small fraction of children participate in more than twenty hours of extracurricular activity (Mahoney et al. 2006).

Some children are "overscheduled" relative to their appetites for organized activities, but in truth, the average participation level is about five to seven hours a week. Compare that to the average time spent using various screens for social media or entertainment—more than seven hours per day!—and you can see that overscheduling is hardly the risk it's often made out to be. The real issue, aside from the amount of screen time kids engage in these days, is that 40 percent of children partake in *no* extracurricular activities, and this disadvantaged group is of much greater concern than those teens who participate in excess.

Participation in after-school activities correlates strongly with income. Generally speaking, parents with resources and more flexible jobs and lives are more likely to get their children into scouts, youth groups, schools with high-achieving students, summer camps, athletic opportunities, and music lessons. These days, with most parents working outside the home, parents who can afford to arrange for extracurricular activities often do so, and impoverished families are burdened with concern over unsupervised afternoons and early evenings. Given the relationship between problem risk-taking behavior and unsupervised time, it is a common plea among developmental psychologists that after-school activities be made more widely available—not less (Larson 2000).

Developing Willpower

One of the crucial skills possessed by all self-controlled kids is willpower. You know willpower: It's what keeps your hands out of the office doughnut box. What you lean on to make it to those 6 a.m. workouts. And how you stay focused on a project at the end of an exhausting, harried day. How is it different from self-control? It isn't, in practical terms (at least for our purposes—if researchers want to slice and dice the differences, they can). Essentially, child psychologists use the term "self-control" because it is one of the main features of executive functioning, and adult-psychology researchers use the word "willpower." They are both great words because we want *control* over *ourselves* (and our temptations), and we need to exercise *will* and *power* to withstand the desire to nab that doughnut. Your child needs willpower (or self-discipline, or self-control) to meet most of her daily goals—but her immaturity means she needs you to help her hone it and provide guard rails until she can do it all on her own. And that's one of the keys to willpower: It gets easier to tap into with more practice. But there's a catch: Research has found that willpower can be used up. Expend too much of it on something trivial, such as resisting that doughnut, and it will flag when you need it the most (Gailliot and Baumeister 2007).

Roy Baumeister and John Tierney have summarized a mountain of research on willpower in their recently published book, *Willpower: Rediscovering the Greatest Human Strength* (Baumeister and Tierney 2011). It is common sense that self-control makes the practice of any virtue and compliance with any parenting policy possible. But what is less well known is that self-control can be enhanced by developing willpower. Lab studies have demonstrated that willpower is like a muscle that needs to be strengthened, maintained, nourished, and rested. Other studies (and plain old logic) have shown that the lack of willpower and poor self-control are associated with just about every negative outcome in life—violent behavior, a poor work history, financial ruin, drug use, academic underachievement, criminal activities, and unstable relationships with friends and family.

In the late 1960s, Stanford psychology professor Walter Mischel conducted his now-famous "marshmallow study," which gave us some indication of how important willpower can be in predicting life outcomes, even when measured in young children (Mischel et al. 1988). In the original study, a group of four-year-olds were each left alone with a marshmallow and told they could either eat it immediately or wait a few minutes, after which they would be allowed to eat two marshmallows. The results were predictive of the children's future success in school, work, and relationships. Compared to the children who instantly ate their marshmallows, the children who were able to wait fifteen minutes demonstrated their ability to delay gratification, and went on to achieve better grades, higher SAT scores, stronger friendships, higher salaries, better weight control, and fewer substance abuse problems later in life (Mischel and Ayduk 2004).

Analyses by Baumeister and his colleagues over the years found that willpower was more powerful than nearly three dozen other personality traits in predicting a college student's grade-point average, as well as a student's IQ and SAT scores. An exhaustive study in New Zealand (Moffitt et al. 2011) tracked one thousand children over thirty years and also demonstrated positive outcomes: Self-control predicted health, wealth, and safety (less traffic accidents, violence, and criminal behavior).

Baumeister also found that willpower is a limited commodity. It can be exhausted for a time, until we rest and ready ourselves to use it again. Therefore, willpower should be called upon selectively for reaching our most important goals, such as homework, making big decisions, and sticking to our routines. In one study (replicated in several ways), students who were told to fight the urge to eat cookies before engaging in difficult cognitive tasks did worse on those tasks than students who were allowed to eat the cookies (Baumeister et al. 1998). In other studies, researchers found that immediately after making decisions, people had less self-control. After a long day at school or work, people have a harder time sticking to a diet, refraining from bad-tempered outbursts with family members, or persisting at difficult tasks; no doubt because they're tired and have probably used up their willpower for the time being (Vohs et al. 2008). We truly do "run out of gas" (willpower) at certain points and have a harder time summoning it for important tasks until we've rested it for a while.

A physical basis for the depletion of willpower has been found in experiments conducted on glucose metabolism. Glucose is the chemical in the bloodstream that carries energy to the brain, muscles, and other parts of the body. Acts of self-control reduce blood glucose levels, and those reduced levels predict poor performance in future tasks requiring self-control. Replenishing glucose—just by drinking a glass of orange juice, for instance—improves self-control.

The good news about willpower is that it's essentially transferable: People who build this "muscle" will be able to use it in other parts of their lives. Stick with your regimen to study Spanish or meditate every morning, and you may be able to control your impulses to eat junk food and watch too much television at night. In a series of studies conducted by Australian psychologists Megan Oaten and Ken Cheng, people were recruited who wanted to work on one area of self-control, such as exercise, homework, or money management. Not only were they successful in increasing their self-control in their chosen area of self-improvement, but they also got better at exercising self-discipline in other areas. The students who studied more also reported doing more physical workouts, and cutting down on impulsive spending (Oaten and Cheng 2006). While these studies were conducted with young adults, this kind of experiment would make any parent's mouth water, but remember: These participants were motivated adult volunteers, and children are not just little adults.

That said, kids who practice willpower learn to do things that are difficult, even if they don't want to do them. If they are used to a challenging daily workout with the team, they may be able to tap into that same well of willpower to accomplish a fiercely difficult homework project. The key is pacing. The willpower muscle gets tired and needs rest. It develops best with the use of rewards, accountability, and "default settings" that remove potent distractions. The essence of this willpower training is to exert deliberate control over your actions. Over time, this practice may improve self-control in other behavioral areas.

One of the most important implications of this research on willpower is that we need structures in place (those "default settings") to protect us from wasting precious willpower fighting temptations. Resisting temptations depletes the energy we need for accomplishing difficult tasks. For instance, if parents and children do not have access to electronic distractions, they are more likely to do their homework or other onerous tasks. Another implication is that we need to eat and take breaks regularly, restore and refresh ourselves, and spare ourselves from unrealistic expectations.

PARENTS AS HABIT BUILDERS FOR WILLPOWER AND SELF-CONTROL

This research on willpower provides a strong case for parents taking an active role in creating routines for their children that promote its development. Practicing morning and evening rituals—such as brushing teeth and taking care of family pets—are all tasks that parents impose on young children, knowing that these routines are important ways to establish good habits of self-care and other responsibilities. Other behavioral expectations, such as practicing manners and overriding impulses to use profanity and aggression, are more than just "the right thing to do"; they are important "muscle-strengthening" exercises for your child's development of willpower.

Research on habits has demonstrated that once people learn a new skill, they don't expend as much mental effort doing it as they did at the beginning, because the learning is stored in the basal ganglia in the limbic system of the brain (Graybiel 2008). This phenomenon is apparent in everything from learning to drive to learning a new language, dance, sport, or math skill. At first, we use our prefrontal cortices to learn a new skill, but once that skill becomes a habit, it's relegated to our "lower" brains, preserving our thinking brains for more complex tasks, such as doing difficult homework, making tough decisions, and finding creative solutions to problems.

Teens need to preserve thinking-brain activity for the willpower and reflection required for managing friendships, planning Saturday night (with or without risk taking), and settling on a topic for their research paper that's due next Tuesday. Especially with young teenagers, parents should spare them the thinking tasks of whether or not to eat a bunch of junk food, turn off the media, and do their homework. Older teens obviously need more autonomy on these issues, but having "default settings" (curfew, entertainment limits, requirements to engage in extracurricular activities, etc.) can establish guard rails. Rules, limits, and structure allow tweens and teens to direct their energies toward the practice of important behaviors such as social skills, emotional regulation, chores, hobbies, and homework.

Evolution embedded in humans a strong drive to pursue rewards (sex, warmth, sleep, and food) for survival purposes. Modern life has created an abundance of other rewards, such as gaming, social media, and materialism, to name a few. Research shows that most adults spend about one-quarter of their waking hours actively engaged in fighting the urges to eat, sleep, pursue sex, and seek pleasurable outlets online (Hofmann et al. 2012). There are more temptations at our fingertips than ever before, thanks to the many distractions available on our smartphones and other electronic gadgets.

Teenagers, who are especially sensitive to reward-seeking stimuli, thanks to those enormous brain-structure changes that begin in adolescence, may have tremendous difficulty with self-control and task completion. Their brains are just not equipped to fight all the dopamine-rich, cyber temptations available in their bedrooms, not to mention the sex, drugs, and other risky choices available in their social lives. No wonder decades of research show that parental monitoring plays a vital role in promoting teen psychological health, achievement, and competency building (Dishion and Patterson 2006). There are undeniable biological reasons for parents to set limits, ones that far exceed the "It's the right thing to do" argument. Your child's very safety and success—and the critically important development of their self-control—depends on it.

ESSENTIAL
ACTIVITY

Willpower

Here are some ways you can support your child in developing willpower. Take a moment to note a few things that might work for your family.

1. Limit access to entertainment media while your middle-school or under-achieving high school student does homework (except for music). Otherwise, they'll quickly use up their willpower trying to fight their temptation to keep from checking Facebook (often an unwinnable battle for teens). Multitasking is a myth. Tweens and teens can't focus on complex cognitive tasks while interacting with media.

   Changes I can make:

   _____

   _____

   _____

   _____

2. Bring a teen a snack while they're studying. Their brain needs to be fed with glucose, so that their thinking brain receives its necessary brain fuel. Like so many other external boundaries in child-rearing, parents initially need to provide the structure that allows children to take care of the needs of their bodies and brains. Four hours of homework without a break or food and drink is not ideal. Your kid may interpret willpower fatigue as a cognitive

weakness on her part, when she actually just needs a break and a glass of orange juice or handful of nuts.
Things I will try:

_____

_____

_____

_____

3. Impose a clear structure for homework, chores, and more. If your child doesn't have successful routines for these expectations already established (which is common), help him out. Remove distractions, set clear guidelines, and provide a bit of reward for compliance, if needed. Once kids are successful in establishing new healthful habits, the habits become intrinsically gratifying, and parents can remove the rewards and monitoring.
New routines to implement:

_____

_____

_____

_____

4. What kind of willpower exercise do you want to instigate in your own life? Turning off the television more often, nagging less, and walking for twenty minutes a day all provide good role modeling. Then you can talk with your teen about the strategies you both use to make success more likely (such as a piece of paper taped to the TV screen reading, "Think twice," a rubber band on your wrist signifying a reminder to avoid nagging, or running shoes at your bedside). When teens feel like you are in the trenches with them, they feel your support more genuinely.
Strategies I use and will share with my teen:

_____

_____

_____

_____

Choosing to do difficult things is incredibly hard for adults, and even harder for kids who are experiencing the intense emotions of adolescence. They need our help. One of the gifts (or curses, depending upon your perspective) of child-rearing is that there is a certain pressure to clean up our own acts. After all, it's a lot harder to require a teen to practice healthy new habits if we aren't doing the same.

The Rewards of Self-Control

Self-control can seem like a fuzzy virtue to develop in your adolescent child, but it is one of the most important predictors of a child's success. Our self-control systems are under a huge strain every day to fend off temptations, do the right thing, get work done, and withstand exhaustion. The research outlined in this chapter demonstrates the importance of self-control, the role of the brain's executive functioning, and your child's unique temperament.

Parents make decisions about how their children spend hundreds of thousands of hours during childhood and adolescence. Given the power of routines and structured activities in forming healthy habits—and given the power of our teen's urges to pursue pleasures—parents will want to avoid overtaxing those teen brains by expecting them to consistently make good choices. Putting those healthy habits on "auto-pilot" frees up teen brains for the more challenging willpower tests of adolescence.

Tweens and teens need a lot of practice at self-control, especially since sensation seeking increases during adolescence. The authoritative parent uses his influence to set up "guard rails" (structure, rules, and expectations for behavior), which are removed when the teen can steer straight—well, fairly straight, anyway—on their own.

Wise-minded parents practice the three basic tenets of authoritative parenting—warmth, setting firm limits, and allowing psychological autonomy—and become adept at emotion coaching. This style of parenting requires enormous energy and determination. And it requires something else, too—a huge amount of self-control on the part of parents. It's a lot of work, but the rewards are many: first and foremost, a successful, thriving, and happy teen.

CHAPTER 3

Academic Success

Scene: *It's Thursday evening, and this dad has some tough business to attend to with his teen. Dad got a call today from his son's physics teacher, and he's horrified to learn that his teen's grades in that class have been slipping for some time; his son currently has a D and is in real danger of failing. The dad had no idea his teen was struggling in physics.*

> **Dad:** *Your physics teacher—what's his name?—called today and said you're failing the class. What is going on?*
>
> **Marcus:** *He called you? What a jerk. I told him I would get it under control. I'm on it, Dad. You don't need to be involved.*
>
> **Dad:** *What do you mean, you're on it? You're failing! Failing at physics! How are you going to become a doctor without passing physics?*
>
> **Marcus:** *Geez, Dad, calm down. I'll fix it. I just need to turn in a bunch of assignments. That teacher is an idiot. No one understands what's going on in that class.*
>
> **Dad:** *This is the first I've heard of it! Why didn't you tell me your grades were in the toilet? You're grounded! And you'd better fix this or you'll ruin your chances of getting into medical school.*
>
> **Marcus:** *God, Dad, you're so dramatic.*

For teens and parents, academic failure of any kind is a frightening proposition, because of its potential long-term consequences. With so much on the line, it's hard for both sides to stay calm and keep things in perspective.

Parents consistently rank academic performance as the biggest factor in determining their child's future happiness and success. It's safe to assume that if you could figure out a way to bottle academic success, you'd have a lot of customers. But since that magic elixir is not coming to a store near you anytime soon, your family will have to strive for success the hard way, by carefully choosing and then strictly following a course that you set for yourselves. Deciding how to set that course in a wise-minded fashion—taking into account a variety of values, attitudes, and strengths—is the focus of this chapter.

Why Academics Matter

No one disputes the importance of education in modern life. It's the rare parent these days who falls back on the "I never went to college, and look what a success I am" story. What was once considered a luxury for the lucky few (and lucky rich), a college education is now all but required for anyone who wants to be competitive in the majority of well-paying careers. Sure, there will always be high school dropouts who hit the jackpot, and stoners who strike it big, but those anecdotal stories are statistically rare. The simple fact is, for the majority of teens, a college degree is a major advantage in today's workplace. Most parents place high values on a college education and a strong work ethic, but few know how best to go about promoting academic success. Parental involvement in a child's education can range from absolutely nil to full-time hovering, with a lot of variation in between.

Parents must strike a critical balance when deciding how involved to get in their children's academic lives. They should place emphasis on academic achievement without exerting too much pressure, which can result in negative consequences, such as underachievement, stress disorders, or a disconnection between parent and child. Beginning as early as pre-school, the number-one factor that generates the energy for long-term and genuine academic motivation is *love of learning*. But cultivating that love also involves tending to other factors that enhance academic performance, such as discovering and coping with any learning challenges, supporting a strong work ethic, and placing an appropriate—but not obsessive—emphasis on grades. As with all of parenting, striking this balance can be tricky.

Some kids need a lot of parent involvement, and some need very little. Some love school and are born strivers, and some have been bruised along the way and already see themselves as underachievers. All children arrive at middle school and high school with internal school "histories" and academic identities. Some thrive while others wither, and it all depends on a host of factors. Yet there is remarkable consensus among educational experts about what gives parents the best shot at tipping the balance toward high achievement for their kids. Here's a clue: High IQ is not the be-all and end-all that you might think.

The Science of Academic Success

When you're thinking about your child's school success, don't get hung up on IQ (i.e., intelligence quotient, which is a measure of general intelligence). It's important, sure, and predictive of success, yes—but it's just a starting point. Just as most men would rather be six-foot-four than five-foot-two, most people would like to have as high an IQ as possible. But it's not what you were born with that matters as much as what you do with it. IQ is just one factor among many in the academic success equation.

One of the most exciting discoveries in cognitive science is the debunking of the IQ myth—the idea that a person's overall brainpower is unchangeable (this is often referred to as the "fixed-brain myth"). In fact, our brains change daily in response to experiences. This remarkable ability to adapt to environmental influences is called *neuroplasticity*. Researchers have discovered that neuroplasticity can be triggered by both negative experiences, such as adversity and deprivation, and by positive ones, such as effective, authoritative parenting (Bryck and Fisher 2012).

Children's brains are especially pliable and trainable. And when it comes to academic success, the challenge lies in figuring out the most nurturing educational environments. From a neuroscience perspective, achievement depends on three things:

- sustained attention
- engaging curriculum offered at the optimal level
- practice

The attentional networks in the brain are of fundamental importance because they allow the student to be alert, stay attuned to relevant events in the classroom, control emotions, and make discerning choices related to goals (Posner and Rothbart 2007). Social and emotional factors are important in learning and memory, as well (more on this in chapter 4).

Furthermore, the sweet spot for learning seems to lie in challenging students just enough so that they stay engaged and stimulated, and rewarding them at key junctures so that they feel a sense of mastery. What results is a student who's excited by the premise of reaching for new, achievable goals. The reward may be intrinsic or extrinsic to the experience of learning. For instance, a music student might feel the reward of a well-played piece internally ("It felt really good to play that piece so beautifully"). Or, for the frustrated student who has all but given up, an extrinsic (external) reward may do the trick, perhaps in the form of a thoughtful comment from the teacher ("You played those stanzas so well that time, with just the right precision").

And finally, practice is powerful. By practicing newly learned concepts, we create neural pathways and memory for the material. An expression in the neurology field, "Neurons that fire together wire together," refers to the connections that are formed in the brain with repetition (or practice).

ESSENTIAL
FACT

A Formula for Successful Learning

Just enough challenge to stay engaged and stimulated + rewards at key intervals = a student who is excited about reaching for new goals

Every child has his own individual "academic operating system," which is a combination of the skills important for learning and achievement (such as IQ), grade-level achievement in various academic areas, attention skills, processing skills, memory capacity, sequencing skills, and self-regulation. This operating system is pliable and undergoes changes based on certain influences, many of which a parent can control. By adolescence, the system will reflect all sorts of influences, including inborn abilities, family environment, parenting practices, and school experience. A child testing in the superior range of intelligence at age six can end up flunking out of high school, and the slow reader at the same age can morph into an academic superstar. What makes the difference?

Biological, social, emotional, and cultural factors all interact over time to determine academic achievement. These factors include the IQs and personalities of child and parents, peer dynamics, school quality, parenting practices, and even neighborhood safety, as well as many random circumstances that affect a child along their path to adulthood. If the brain is a garden and cognitive abilities are the plants, then optimal nurturing, wise-minded parenting, positive social experiences, and excellent teaching and curricula are akin to miraculous fertilizers. Extreme stress and trauma are like poison.

The Essential Role of Parent Involvement

Decades of research have demonstrated that parent involvement in children's academic lives is associated with elevated grades and test scores, higher graduation and college admission rates, increased motivation and more ambitious educational goals, and better classroom conduct, as well as decreased use of drugs and alcohol, and fewer instances of violent behavior (Epstein et al. 2002; Fan and Chen 2001). There's no doubt that parents can have a positive impact on their children's school performance in ways both direct and indirect, and a review of thousands of studies over the last half-century gives us insight into the powerful role they play (Epstein 2005).

As described in chapter 2, a child's executive functioning—his ability to plan ahead, prioritize, organize behavior to meet goals, reason, manage distractions, and self-regulate—is correlated with his parents' executive functioning abilities. These qualities—so necessary for academic success—are not just passed through the genes; they are transmitted from parent to child through role modeling.

ESSENTIAL
QUIZ

How Well Is Your Family Set Up for Academic Success?

Here's a quiz to give you a baseline reading of how well your family is set up for academic success.

True False

1. ☐ ☐ I know my child is completing his homework every night.
2. ☐ ☐ I rarely get into fights with my child about grades.
3. ☐ ☐ I understand what my child is capable of and expect him to do his best.
4. ☐ ☐ My child understands that learning is a top priority in our family.
5. ☐ ☐ My family has real connections and/or substantive discussions at the dinner table.
6. ☐ ☐ I know the first and last names of my child's English teacher.
7. ☐ ☐ I'm comfortable with a hands-off attitude toward school.

If you answered "true" to all of these—except for number 7—congratulations! Your family probably has some critical structures in place that provide the underpinnings of potential academic success. If you answered "false" to any of the first six, the information provided in this chapter will help you understand how your personal history, attitudes, and habits may be having an impact on your child's performance at—and attitudes towards—school, and what wise-minded changes you can make to create an environment that optimizes your child's academic potential.

SUPPORTING SCHOOL SUCCESS AT HOME

Meta-analyses of thousands of studies have shown that an academically stimulating home environment is one of the chief determinants of school achievement (Hill and Craft 2003). The researchers concluded that the intellectual richness of the home is twice as powerful as socioeconomic status in predicting academic success. When you talk to your child about the events of the day, exhibit an active interest in their academic and personal growth, or even just discuss the books that you're both reading, you're creating a rich environment for intellectual growth. And when you put long-range goals ahead of immediate gratification (by flipping off the television to finish a report for work, say, or shunning a great shoe sale to save for a big vacation), you're modeling self-control, which underpins academic success. School choice is important, too, but getting your child into a fancy school is less important than many other steps parents can take at home.

There is also a significant relationship between a parent's involvement in a student's academic life and the child's academic performance (Topor et al. 2010). Research suggests that when parents show *sincere* interest in and dedication to their child's achievement (e.g., by making sure homework is completed, showing interest in academic progress, and conveying faith in their child's ability to master school material), the child internalizes a sense of "cognitive competence" (Gonzalez-DeHass et al. 2005; Kohl et al. 2000).

When wise-minded parents believe in their children's abilities, expect them to achieve, and follow up with routines in the home that help them meet academic goals, children tend to believe in themselves, too, and do the expected work at higher levels than students whose parents are less involved.

As children get older—and especially when they're in high school—parents tend to be less involved in their academic lives. In one study, researchers found that high schools were perceived as not as welcoming to parents as elementary and middle schools (Eccles and Harold 1996). Parents reported that their child's high school contacts them less often about problems, and that they were rarely, if ever, encouraged to volunteer at the school. The researchers conclude that sometimes it is the disadvantaged families that can benefit the most from involvement, but they are also least likely to receive information about promoting achievement, overcoming barriers, and partnering with the schools on problems. Additionally, I often see in my practice parents of teens who believe that they are fostering independence by taking a hands-off attitude toward school. Combine these factors with a teen's general preference for autonomy, and it's not surprising that parental involvement drops during these years.

While this transition to independent academic functioning is fine for high achievers, it can be a disaster for teens headed into a tailspin, as depicted in the opening vignette. Here, the father has lost touch with what is going on in his son's academic life, and both are paying a painful price. The dad is not sure of the physics teacher's name, which probably means he hasn't met or touched base with him, an all-too-common scenario for parents of high schoolers. Further, he has probably stopped checking in with his teen about school, or has been previously shut out for asking too many questions.

The vignette that began this chapter might not have happened if wise-minded parenting practices had been firmly in place. Still, even the most attuned parent can be sideswiped by a teen's defensive shutdown or outright dishonesty. Let's run the same scene again with a more wise-minded approach to handling the challenge.

Take Two:

Dad: *Mr. Lincoln called today and said you're failing physics and that you have eight outstanding assignments.*

Marcus: *He called you? What a jerk. I told him I would get it under control. I'm on it, Dad. You don't need to be involved.*

Dad: *Oh, actually, I do need to be involved, and I'm sorry I didn't see this problem sooner. Mr. Lincoln said he'd be glad to help you figure out a way to get partial credit if you set up an appointment to talk about it with him.*

Marcus: *Yeah, fine, whatever. I can't believe he called you. What an A-hole. I'll handle it. I'm going to turn the assignments in.*

Dad: *It was clear from our conversation that you need to discuss this situation with him so that you get partial credit. You must feel kind of overwhelmed and in the pits. Can I help you figure out ways to dig out?*

Marcus: *What I need is for you to stop breathing down my frickin' neck! As if physics isn't enough!*

Dad: *Look, I can see that this is a big, horrible mess for you right now. You've probably been dreading my finding out and where all this was headed. I know you're upset by the whole thing, but with your great track record in school, I know you'll be able to turn this around. Everyone needs a little course correction now and again. I've been slacking off myself. I should be more in tune with your school. We'll work together on getting you out of this jam.*

Marcus: *God, Dad. Please…just let me handle it.*

Advice for this dad: You can only get so much done in one exchange with a flooded and defensive kid. Instead, plan to circle back the next morning and see if he's ready to talk. If so, focus on conveying your expectation that by the day's end he will have met with Mr. Lincoln and formulated a schedule for improving his performance. You know that you are going to monitor his homework completion and consider getting a tutor, but you can address these agenda items later. Your son is overwhelmed right now, so comfort and empathy come first, and then partnership and structure. Marcus learned four important things in this exchange: that you know about the disaster, haven't freaked out, will help him create a plan of action, and are going to stick by his side to make sure he's successful.

When parents institute certain habits and home-enrichment practices that support academic success, their children are likely to internalize those habits and values relating to education and intellectual achievement. Obviously many factors can interfere with even the best-laid plans, including trauma or family strife, but parents can still have a positive influence on their children's academic life by enacting a few of the "best practices" listed opposite.

ESSENTIAL
ACTIVITY

Home Enrichment Practices that Support Academic Success

Check off the practices you feel you have in hand (keeping in mind that it's a rare parent who gets a perfect score on this ambitious list).

- ☐ Establish daily routines (set times and places for doing homework)
- ☐ Monitor out-of-school activities
- ☐ Make sure homework is completed daily
- ☐ Make sure screen time is limited
- ☐ Model a value of learning, self-discipline, and effortful work
- ☐ Express high but realistic expectations for achievement by setting goals and standards that are appropriate for your child's age, ability level, and maturity
- ☐ Engage in an authoritative parenting style, characterized by warmth, interest, and concern, and instill a value on independence, clear rules, and plenty of structure
- ☐ Encourage your child's progress in school, as well as her special talents
- ☐ Inform friends and family members of your child's successes
- ☐ Encourage reading, writing, and discussions among family members
- ☐ Value verbal articulation through sharing stories, discussing current events, sharing problems, and thinking dilemmas through
- ☐ Volunteer at school, maintain communication with faculty and administration, and participate in school and/or district-wide activities
- ☐ Procure extra academic help for your child when needed
- ☐ Avoid negative interactions about schoolwork and instead take a collaborative approach to solving problems
- ☐ Prioritize the parent-child relationship over school performance so that your child does not feel extreme pressure

Now, go back over the list and circle one or two to work on in the coming months. The goal is not perfection; it's to continue to grow and improve as a source of support for your child's academic success.

THE ROLE OF PRAISE

Self-esteem was a parenting buzzword in the 1980s. Back then, parents were led to believe that academic success depended on their child possessing a great deal of self-esteem, and a cornerstone of fostering self-esteem was praise. Understandably, parents got the idea that if they showered their kids with compliments, warranted or not, their kids would feel self-assured, and would achieve as a result. But what the '80s got wrong—or what the '90s and early 2000s misunderstood—is that children can see right through false praise. Worse, if they believe all their own good press, it can actually undermine success.

Keep it Real
Children can see right through false praise.

In survey after survey, a huge majority of parents today still believe that it is important to tell their kids that they are smart. According to conventional wisdom, praise encourages children, and without it, they may underperform. In fact, it seems to have the opposite effect in many cases. A comprehensive review of the research shows that self-esteem enhancement programs are ineffective at best and actually backfire at worst (Baumeister et al. 2005). Instead of enhancing performance, heaps of praise can hinder motivation and effort.

Stanford psychologist Carol Dweck studied the effect of praise on students over the course of her career and has concluded that commending effort is far more constructive than focusing on pure smarts (Dweck 2006). In a groundbreaking series of six studies, she and her colleague Claudia Mueller found that just a single line of praise, depending on how it was given, made a huge difference in cognitive performance (Mueller and Dweck 1998). In the initial study, a group of fifth-graders each were given a fairly easy puzzle to solve and then were told, "You must be smart!" The researchers gave a second group the same puzzle, but when the students had completed the challenge, the researchers altered the wording of their praise, saying, "You must have worked hard!" Afterward, each group was given a chance to choose between two tasks, one difficult and one easy. Ninety percent of the group praised for their efforts chose the task labeled "hard," while the majority of the group praised for their smarts chose the easier task.

In the next part of the study, the test was rigged to ensure that all of the students failed. The kids were then retested a third time. Kids in the group praised for their effort rebounded impressively, achieving scores 30 percent higher on average than their results on the original test. Students who had been praised for their intelligence earned scores 20 percent lower than they did on their first test. Since the original study, this pattern in the test findings has been found to be consistent for kids from every socioeconomic class and racial group, and among both girls and boys (Dweck 2006).

What does this study tell us? The findings seem to suggest that children who are praised a lot for their intelligence have more to lose when approaching cognitive tasks. If they make mistakes or fail, they are sacrificing their valued identity as a smart kid, so they may avoid challenges. Students deemed gifted and innately talented may not try as hard when their perceived competence is on the line. Conversely, when children are praised for their efforts and instructed in what is called a "growth mindset"—told that the brain is a muscle and that it gets stronger with exercise—they become more motivated. A study of low-achieving seventh-graders showed that when students are given a "growth mindset" workshop, they improved markedly on motivation and math scores when compared to a group that focused on the importance of memory. One of the conclusions Dweck and her colleagues reached is that study skills should be powered by a belief in *effort*.

In both animal and human studies, intermittent praise (also called "reinforcement") is the most powerful motivator. From a behavioral perspective, these findings make sense: When children are told that they are wonderful *all* the time, the compliment loses power, just as eating ice cream all the time, every day, loses its appeal (if you don't believe it, ask someone who has worked in an ice-cream shop). In other words, if everyone gets a trophy for simply showing up, the trophy is meaningless, and the kids know it.

Neuroscience research also sheds some light on this phenomenon of intermittent praise. The orbital prefrontal cortex—the part of the brain that monitors the availability of rewards—is like an air traffic controller. It intervenes when there is no immediate reward on the horizon and switches our motivational systems off. When it perceives that a reward could be coming in for landing, it keeps us attentive, motivated, and ready to pursue that reward. It is gratifying to finish tasks successfully, and persistence helps us stay focused on that pursuit. However, if we are flooded with reinforcement (e.g., praise, ice cream, trophies) along the way for small or negligible efforts, we stop trying so hard because the reward is devalued.

Does this research imply that parents should never praise their children? No! Praise is good, and it is a vital part of the warmth and acknowledgement that parents bestow on their children as encouragement. However, just as too little praise deprives, too much praise can overwhelm and ultimately become meaningless. Parents who overpraise can't be trusted, because even small children know that they can't be the smartest and most wonderful at everything. Teens, with their tuned-in and newly abstracting minds, wither in the face of excessive hyperbole, because they understand their vulnerable standing in the universe of extraordinary brains, bodies, and talent.

Praise is best when it is specific, genuine, and trustworthy. Wise-minded parents offer thoughtful and appropriate praise that integrates an instinctive understanding of their child's abilities and emotionality with reasonable expectations for their child. A kid would rather be praised for a "good pass," an "engaging first paragraph," and a "kind gesture" than for being a spectacular basketball player, brilliant writer, and perfect friend. Irish poet William Butler Yeats said wisely, "Education is not the filling of a pail, but the lighting of a fire." A positive self-concept is not built by filling a pail with copious praise, but by lighting the fire of belief in oneself.

ESSENTIAL
FACT

The Power of Praise
Intermittent praise (also called "reinforcement") is a more powerful motivator than constant praise.

QUIZ

Are You a Praise Junkie?

Take a moment to consider your own approach to praise, and the effect it might be having on your child's academic motivation and success.

1. Your kid comes home from school crying and saying that he's dumb after getting a B-minus on a test. You say:
   a. "Don't worry, you're really smart. I'm sure you'll do better next time."
   b. "How did you prepare for this test? Do you see any difference between this time and a time when it went well?"
   c. "You should talk to your teacher about how to bring that grade up."

2. Your kid just got the highest grade in the class on a history test. You say:
   a. "It's great being on top, isn't it?"
   b. "What did Susie get?"
   c. "That's great! You really worked hard."

3. Your child's report card went from mostly A's to mostly C's. You say:
   a. "I know you can do better. You have tremendous potential."
   b. "Next term, we'll give you $100 for every A and $50 for every B."
   c. "Let's look at what happened and come up with a plan to turn this around together."

4. Your child is very frustrated and underperforming in math class. She says, "Math is just not my thing." You say:
   a. "You know what, I'm terrible at math, too. Math is hard! You are great at a lot of other things."
   b. "You clearly need more practice so you can develop a math brain. Let's make a plan."
   c. "You just need to try harder."

The optimal answers for each of the above are: B, C, C, and B. Note that each of these options emphasizes problem solving and the child's own ability to work toward her success, rather than the suggestion to fall back on basic gray matter or work the system through teachers.

THE MYTH OF LAZINESS

The praise-junkie quiz includes one word that struggling teenagers hate above all else. Can you spot it?

The word is "potential." Parents think it is reassuring to tell a teen he has a lot of potential, because it implies that they believe in the child's IQ—his natural abilities—and that he could do better if only he tried. But that is not what the child hears. To the child, this seemingly innocuous phrase comes loaded with all kinds of criticism. It's a slam: "You are lazy. You're not doing what you should."

In fact, when it comes to most teenagers, laziness is a myth. It just doesn't exist. Every child has a natural burning curiosity about the world, until we stamp it out or make learning a joyless chore. Instead of fixating on how lazy your child is, figure out how to relight that fire. All kids want to do well, feel good about learning, and satisfy their acute curiosity and particular interests; some of them just lose steam along the way. A child who is underachieving may look lazy to the parent, but chances are it was the adults (parents, teachers, school administrators) in his life who unwittingly made him that way!

So, as part of your mission to reignite your tween's or teen's passion for learning, eliminate the phrase "You have tremendous potential" from your repertoire. Skip the judgmental (yes, it sounds judgmental to your child) phase and move straight into problem solving. So what do you say if your child brings home a stinker of a report card? Try this instead: "We're stumped. We need to figure out what to do about this. You might never like math, it's true, but it's important; so let's figure out how you're going to do well enough to pass this class." Then move through a list of possibilities to address the achievement issue at hand.

ESSENTIAL
FACT

The Laziness Myth

Teenage laziness is largely a myth. Every child has a natural burning curiosity about the world, until we stamp it out or make learning a joyless chore.

Authoritative Parenting for Academic Success

By far, the most effective academic problem-solving teams are composed of a kid and an authoritative parent. In chapter 2, you were introduced to authoritative parenting. So why bring it up again? Because authoritative parenting is key to helping your child master all seven essentials, including academic success.

You'll recall that authoritative parenting is marked by three major qualities: warmth, structure, and psychological autonomy. To a child who is neck-deep in challenging homework and overwhelmed by hormonally fueled emotions and social chaos, parental warmth is like a balm on an aching wound. Your ability to stay warmly connected—avoiding criticism, derision, and sarcasm at the tender end of the day—can make all the difference in her mood when she sits down to study. You'll read more on this in the "Strategies for Homework Success" section (page 95).

Structure in the home and specifically around homework expectations is one of the most basic and important ways parents can promote academic success. Homework charts, regular homework hours, clearly articulated rules about studying—all create a foundation that helps kids succeed. There are also the tangential but crucial family expectations that help support this foundation, things such as regular family dinners, the expectation that kids participate in at least one sport a season, and an overall sense that "this is what we do in this family, and we're a family with a plan." All of these structures contribute to an overall sense of order that mitigates some of the chaos of modern life and soothes raw nerves.

And since you're always encouraging your child's budding intellectual autonomy, you keep your lip zipped when they spout off at the dinner table about why Shakespeare can't hold a candle to their favorite rapper when it comes to poetry.

Authoritative parents convey warmth, impose structure, foster individuality, and encourage self-regulation, and this parenting style has been directly attributed to academic success in longitudinal studies (Dornbusch et al. 1987; Spera 2005). Authoritative parents are effective because they engage in setting limits—tracking academic performance, monitoring homework, and other success-oriented practices. By contrast, the authoritarian parent—whose style emphasizes control and punishment, and lacks warmth and responsiveness—might punish their teens for poor academic performance, which rarely results in improvement. At the other end of the spectrum, permissive and indulgent parents lack authority in setting up the structures and boundaries that help their kids achieve.

Research also shows that authoritative parents are better at controlling one of today's biggest distractions from studying: online social media and entertainment (Rosen et al. 2008). A 2010 study by the Kaiser Family Foundation found that there was a remarkable increase in media use by eight- to eighteen-year-olds over the previous five years. The study found that the average kid uses media for approximately seven and a half hours a day (often on more than one gadget at a time). This puts school performance problems in perspective: With so much highly rewarding entertainment available, how can it *not* take a toll on schoolwork?

Rosen found that the parents who limit online access in an authoritative way succeed in preventing excess. He examined the relationship between parenting, online activity, and academic performance, surveying one thousand parents about how much time their kids spent online, and their mental, physical, and academic health (Rosen 2012). Even when controlling for the effects of family income and parental-education levels, Rosen found that high media use was associated with poorer school performance. Moreover, students who switch back and forth between devices and homework had worse grades than those who worked undistracted on their homework until completion.

ESSENTIAL
FACT

Bad Grades?
Punishing kids for poor academic performance rarely results in improvement.

Rosen also found that, in addition to poor school achievement, kids who engaged in high media use were less well-adjusted across the board, took more sick days, suffered more depression, and had more behavioral problems at school. Previously, the term "digital divide" referred to the gap between those who had access to computers and those who did not. With the ubiquity of laptops and smartphones among teens these days, the new digital divide is the chasm between kids who have parents who put limits on digital media use and kids who do not.

A New Definition

The new digital divide (*noun*): the chasm between kids who have parents who put limits on digital media use and kids who do not.

PARENTAL FACTORS THAT AFFECT SUCCESS

Virtually all parents, regardless of income or ethnicity, want their children to achieve in school and go on to college. But a child's academic success is linked to his parents' own educational history. A recent study found that when a large sampling of parents of Caucasian, African-American, Asian, and Hispanic ethnicities were separated into groups according to income and parent education, the kids from homes with parents who had received a four-year college degree or higher achieved greater academic success than their peers whose parents had not (Spera et al. 2009). On the whole, most parents believe in the value of education, but those who have achieved higher educational goals themselves find it easier to shoot for the stars with their teens.

Income is another factor that has an enduring effect on academic achievement. Although parents from different ethnic and socioeconomic groups (or social classes) have similar goals for their children, their financial position affects their ability to influence those goals. One study, which examined the role poverty plays in creating stress among students, compared the stress levels of kids from different social classes (Felner et al. 1995). Students from the most economically disadvantaged circumstances were among the most stressed; poverty can be emotionally devastating, and brings with it the associated tolls of crowded schools, dangerous neighborhoods, lack of support systems, and unemployment. When stress levels were factored in, the differences in grades and on math achievement tests among students from higher and lower social classes disappeared. Still, poverty does not doom a child; if parents are able to shield their children from the stressful effects of financial instability, then children have a good shot at performing well at school.

Stress is not limited to financially disadvantaged families. In many affluent homes, overinvestment in grades can create stress for students, impacting their academic performance and contributing to depression, anxiety, and substance use (Luthar 2003). Suniya Luthar's research has made a strong case for the association between affluence, overpressure regarding academic performance, and disconnected parent-teen relationships. The teens who experience these difficulties often feel isolated from their parents or feel that acceptance by their parents is contingent upon school performance.

Whether caused by academic pressure in an affluent home or poverty-related hardships in a lower-income home, stress undoubtedly impedes learning and achievement, and it can be spurred by the broader social environment or by a parent-child problem. Either way, the amount of stress a child is under and their ability to manage it is a powerful variable in determining success.

Social stressors and economic strife take a huge toll on parents, as well (Hoff et al. 2002). Stressed parents often produce stressed kids. But regardless of external pressures, financial and social stressors can be mitigated if parents foster a positive relationship with their kids, and create clear and consistent structures around homework, free time, media use, and family time.

GRADE FIGHTS

Grades are one of the biggest sources of conflict I hear about in my practice. And in surveys, teens consistently report that academic pressure is among the top stressors in their lives. Parents know that if grade-point averages drop too low, college admissions and merit scholarships go out the window. So how are you supposed to keep a lid on your stress about school performance?

When one person's red-hot emotions collide with those of another, you have the makings of a fiery explosion. Let's take the example of a mom who just found out that her sophomore daughter received another report card covered in C's. Here are some "right," reason-minded comments the mom might be tempted to make to her daughter, and ones I hear in my office on a regular basis:

- *You won't make it into the state university with these grades.*
- *You will be miserable in community college when you are left at home and all your friends have gone off to the university.*
- *You are cavalier about your low grades now, but you are shooting yourself in the foot in terms of future prospects.*
- *You will be happier if you can make it into a college with lots of opportunities and ambitious classmates.*
- *I can structure homework time and pull the media distractions, but I can't force you to buckle down.*
- *I provide you with such a good life, and you are not doing your most important job, which is doing well at school!*

By applying a wise-mind filter, you can screen out the lectures that naturally spring from these thoughts. (Remember the mantra: "I may be right, but am I effective?") In reality, parents with "underachieving" teens have already made these points (a lot), but still, they repeat the admonishments, with the fantasy that kids will suddenly be enlightened by the "facts" and raise their grades. However, to paraphrase Albert Einstein: "Insanity is doing the same thing over and over and expecting a different result."

What's a parent to do? The wise-minded parent knows she needs to validate herself for caring deeply, and her daughter for being a complicated teen juggling many pressures. She needs to keep these twin factors in mind as she quells her anxiety and digs deep to find empathy. While looking at those panic-inducing grades, she knows to focus on being mindful—remaining present in the moment, suspending judgment, and taking a deep breath before responding. Then, when she is ready to face her daughter, she knows she should emphasize acceptance—that her child's behavior makes sense and is understandable given the situation—before focusing on any change.

> ESSENTIAL
> **TIP**
>
> **Validation**
> Validation refers to the act of letting someone know that you understand, empathize with, and accept their thoughts, feelings, and behaviors in the context of their life experience (Linehan 1993). It can take the form of:
> • sitting quietly and listening;
> • telling someone you are listening carefully;
> • acknowledging someone's feelings, or paraphrasing them;
> • trying to understand what someone is feeling or telling you.

Whatever form of validation you choose, make sure it works for your child. If one approach bugs her ("Stop repeating everything I say!"), try another. If it feels too robotic, shrinky, or fake, it will not work. Teens are laser sharp in their abilities to detect baloney. And remember, validating someone's feelings does not mean agreement or approval. It means you are listening and trying to appreciate her point of view.

Here's an interaction recently relayed to me by a mom who has really done her homework on repairing old patterns of nagging, pleading, and threatening her daughter, Brooke, about her grades. You might be surprised at Brooke's openness, but this mom has spent about six months abstaining from criticism, making only supportive and empathic remarks, and acknowledging that it really is up to her daughter to figure out how to use her homework time, as well as her teacher's support.

Mom: It's been a couple of days since we received your report card.

Brooke: Oh, God, I knew this was coming.

Mom: We made a deal that if I gave you two days, you'd tell me how you were feeling about school right now. I feel like there is an "elephant in the room" if we don't talk a little about what you refer to as the worst stressor in your life. And I am sorry that you suffer so much with the pressure you feel to make better grades.

Brooke: You don't know what it's like, Mom. All we hear about is the bad economy, college competition, and how important grades are. With my 2.8 as a sophomore, it feels hopeless, OK? So that's why even the mention of grades makes me crazy. Every time I even think about school, my stomach aches.

> *Mom:* It's awfully hard to fix something if it feels hopeless and it gives you stomachaches. No wonder going into your room to do homework feels like entering a snake pit.

> *Brooke:* Exactly, entering a torture chamber with snakes, bats, and spiders. That's why I hate your stupid homework rules. If you didn't let me do some of my homework at Starbucks with Janie, I would probably have a nervous breakdown.

> *Mom:* Having a friend around makes it less torturous, huh? Sorry it took me a while to trust that homework was really happening there. Do you think that has helped?

> *Brooke:* Yeah! I would have made a D in Spanish without Janie. I can get more done when I'm not jumping out of my skin.

> *Mom:* That makes sense. It sounds like we need to figure out more ways for you to get stuff done and mix in positive things so homework isn't so torturous. Not Facebook, but maybe other study buddies? Or breaks, or something?

> *Brooke:* Maybe some nights I could Skype with Preston on math. Or with Lisbeth on English.

> *Mom:* Yeah, they could help you wrangle those snakes. That sounds like a great idea.

> *Brooke:* God, Mom, you are so cheesy.

You may be thinking, "But it sounds like Brooke is still struggling with her grades this semester despite the new measures!" or "What if she plays around with her friends on Skype?" or "What can be done to ensure that she raises her grades?" All these concerns are understandable. However, since Brooke's mom knew going into this conversation that she could only control herself, her goals were clear:

- to remove herself from the power struggle over grades so that she didn't make things worse with a coercive parenting style—the same one she had employed during the previous three semesters of high school;
- to attempt to seek some more solutions with Brooke about supportive measures (like meeting Janie at Starbucks);
- to validate Brooke so that she felt like her mother was truly a support, not another burden in her life.

Did you notice that Brooke's mom stuck with validation instead of reacting or correcting the perception that improving grades was "hopeless" or making her daughter "crazy"?

Instead of a lecture on effort and the importance of grades, Mom kept her focus on empathy and support. Brooke got to experience her mom as trustworthy, and thus confided in her about how stressed the homework was making her and how that stress actually felt (like "a torture chamber"). Mom had done the hard work of nailing down the homework structure and removing distractions earlier, so this time she got to prioritize parent-child connectedness. Mom was also working on not overreacting and on intrinsically accepting what her daughter was telling her, repeating to herself, "The most important thing for Brooke to feel is that I care and that I love her, accepting her just the way she is. Whatever happens with her grades and college prospects is in the future. I need to be present, focusing on the balanced approach I'm taking now—structure and support; that is all I can do, and I'm doing a good job."

Sometimes we can't make things better, but we can certainly make them worse.

This mom has learned one of the hardest parenting lessons: Sometimes we just have to accept that we can't make things better. But we can certainly make them worse—by conveying judgment, panicking, and trying to change things to the detriment of acceptance. And maybe, with the bedrock of acceptance, and with some skillful engineering in study habits, Brooke will stop feeling that her school efforts are hopeless and start making some real progress with her grades. At the very least, knowing her mom is there to support her—without criticizing or shaming her—might stave off the "nervous breakdown" and halt a downward spiral.

STRATEGIES FOR HOMEWORK SUCCESS

In many families, homework is a source of numerous tense discussions and negotiations. Many parents have fought valiantly to draw lines in the sand around social media use during homework hours; or employed such elegant tactics as nagging, threatening, and promising "serious consequences" to get teens to fall into line. If you've gone down this road, you are in good company, but it's a bumpy road that will most likely lead to nowhere. To get where you want to go, you need to devise a homework strategy—with your child's input—that sets your student up for success and takes you (and your nagging) out of the equation.

Let's debunk some common homework myths:

• *For a student to get the most out of any given subject, they should focus on one skill for an extended period of time and not jump around.*

In actuality, focusing on several related topics within one discipline—such as studying the vocabulary, reading, and oral skills of a new language—seems to deepen learning (Rohrer and Pashler 2010). It's just like an athletic workout: Switching between several drills keeps you attentive, deepens muscle memory, and enhances skill training.

• *Memory and retention are improved by intense immersion (i.e., cramming).*

Recent research indicates that studying in regular sessions spread out over time is best, with the expectation that relearning will increase memory and long-term retention (Carpenter et al. 2012). Cramming for a test can work for the short term, but it isn't effective for long-term retention.

• *All children require a quiet corner with a well-lit desk to study most effectively.*

For some students, this is certainly true, but for others, studying in a kitchen is just as effective as buckling down in a quiet, well-lit corner. We all have different preferences and tolerance for distraction, and some of us are really good at tuning it all out, while others are not. And, as was illustrated in Brooke's vignette, for some of us, a homework spot with people around actually reduces stress and opens the mind to learning.

- *Regardless of the venue, students should do their homework in the same place every night.* In fact, it's actually better for the student to mix up their study locations for optimal retention of the material! The theory is that varying the study locale enriches memory skills and forces more neural associations with the material (Rohrer and Pashler 2010).

These are interesting research findings, but there is no reason to assume that these ideas alone will work to improve your kid's homework habits. Good study habits depend on accurate monitoring of ongoing learning and appropriate use of study strategies (Kornell and Bjork 2007). Parents and kids should work together to figure out what study environment is optimal. Although students' preferences for a work space are important, they should not dictate it; many teens would prefer a homework space littered with electronic devices, even though concentration and quality of work would probably suffer. Students who are struggling with their homework especially need their parents to step in and restrict distractions.

Remember that while sitting in silence at a desk by a window might be ideal for you or me, our teenagers live in a different world, and have different brains, personalities, and preferences. Also, keep in mind that old adage: "If it ain't broke, don't fix it!" If homework is going just fine in your home, be thankful and stand down.

ESSENTIAL ACTIVITY

Homework Factors

In what environment does your child do his best work? Begin by checking off the factors that you think your child needs for optimized homework success. Then ask your child what he thinks and add those to the list, too (applying your wise-mind filter to such suggestions as loud music and unfettered access to social media).

- ☐ Bedroom, at a desk
- ☐ Bedroom, sprawled on floor
- ☐ Kitchen table
- ☐ At a café
- ☐ Social media access
- ☐ Adult supervision
- ☐ Music
- ☐ Total silence
- ☐ Regular snacks

- ☐ Regular breaks
- ☐ Clearly articulated homework plan
- ☐ Whiteboard schedule for bigger projects
- ☐ Tutoring
- ☐ Really cool, fancy school supplies
- ☐ Study groups with classmates
- ☐ Other:_____
- ☐ Other:_____

While neither you nor your teen may have checked the box marked "adult supervision," here's a bid for you to reconsider. Especially with tweens who struggle with focusing on homework, supervision has a lovely hidden benefit. Try sitting next to your child, reading a magazine in companionable silence while he works. By this simple act, you are holding him accountable for doing his homework, sending a signal about your commitment to his education, and altering his brain chemistry by sending him messages of empathy, support, and warmth. (If you are in bad mood, skip it. This job is for the parent who can deliver those positive messages.) In fact, it is this companionship—this warm, willing body nearby—that is the real reason some tutors are so effective.

Many kids can't get their homework done, not because of learning disabilities or a poor work ethic, but because they are swimming in anxiety hormones, sexual hormones, or the twilight zone of hijacked amygdalae. It's not the academic support, per se, that they may need from you, it's the message that "I am here as cheerleader, consultant, commiserator, or calming agent." Resist coaching or nagging, or you'll just end up compounding the parent-as-tyrant rap.

It may seem logical to you that you should try to tutor a tween or teen who is having problems with homework and school performance, but that rarely works out well. The reason parent-led tutoring devolves into conflict so frequently is that for many kids, homework involves frustration, anxiety, and other negative emotions. When the parent is involved in these moments, they frequently get dumped on. But when the tutor is a resource teacher at school (or a cute upperclassman), the dumping is less likely to happen. In addition, with a non-parent tutor, the teen might be more inclined to dig deep to find some untapped motivation, out of sheer pride, if not an honest desire to show his stuff. Although some parents can tutor their own kids successfully, it's usually more than a parent-child relationship can tolerate, given the strong feelings associated with the individuation process during these years.

Don't underestimate the power of frequent snack breaks either. Most kids live at a breakneck pace—school, sports, clubs, workouts, friends, elaborate social media routines—and that, combined with the massive biological changes they undergo during the late tween and early teen years, means that they are just plain out of gas by 8 p.m. Offering a break and something delicious to eat sends messages of support and empathy, provides a crucial blood-sugar recharge, and helps shore up dwindling reserves of willpower, which help teens stay on task.

If your child doesn't usually snack, suggest a break anyway. You can watch your favorite YouTube videos or take the dog for a walk together. When it comes to homework, you can choose to be a jail warden or a cheerleader. Ask your child to show you their favorite music video (they'll have many!) or ask to hear one of their recently created playlists. Another study session, another break—maybe a quick backrub this time (physical touch can be a big stress reliever). Parents who have to work late into the night or are exhausted by piled-up laundry, dishes, and other responsibilities will benefit from these quiet interludes of connection and support, too.

The benefits of an effective homework strategy extend well beyond learning. A study of the relationship between homework and self-regulation (self-control) among students, from elementary school to college, revealed that self-management practices are more important than the amount of time spent doing homework (Ramdass and Zimmerman 2011).

Kids with good study skills ignore distractions, feel a responsibility for their learning, set goals, self-reflect, manage time, and create an effective environment. For kids who struggle with homework, parents, teachers, or tutors need to help them target these skills and help them structure an effective environment. Obviously, the quality of homework given is a factor, too, and ranges as widely as the quality of schools does. But the parent's job is to make sure homework is completed and satisfactory; homework grades that are slipping are a red flag that parents need to take action.

But here's a major caveat: Before you attempt to "improve" things in touchy areas such as academics, social life, or physical fitness, consider whether new policies could make things worse. For instance, if you have a child who gets A's and B's (and maybe an occasional C), you might think that severing the media cord will help them make all A's. After all, your reason mind tells you that even though your sixteen-year-old son is in his room for four hours every night supposedly doing homework, you know he is spending more than half of that time surfing around the Web and iChatting with friends. Subtract social media, and you'll add more homework time, and *voila*! Straight A's! Right?

Not so fast. Consult the wise mind. What is your son thinking, feeling, and experiencing? Deeper reflection might bring an appreciation for everything your son has told you about homework: that he works very hard (from his perspective) on his school responsibilities, tolerates the homework load by toggling back and forth from homework to online study breaks, and would be furious if you tried to control his study habits. Is it worth the risk of pulling media to investigate the possibility that he will be more motivated to produce improved grades? Is there a collaborative approach that may work? It may be that he really feels that he is working at *his* top speed, and any suggestion to the contrary just makes him less motivated to up his game. As with all "new improvements" in parenting, remember this: First, do no harm.

PARENT INVOLVEMENT AT SCHOOL

Study after study concludes that kids whose parents are actively involved at their children's schools are more successful academically, and more and more, schools recognize the importance of parents in the equation; the parent-school partnership is a cutting-edge issue for elementary school reform (Epstein 2011). Involved parents demonstrate an investment in this important part of their children's lives and are more likely to take action when needed. Although frequent contact with a child's school drops significantly after the elementary years, parents should still attend curriculum nights, volunteer at school functions, and connect with teachers when problems arise. Given how hard it can be to turn problems around after they've become entrenched, if you are not already doing *something* at the school, now is the time to start.

When your child was little, it probably wasn't hard to find ways to feel connected to her during that huge chunk of her day spent at school. Even parents who work full-time can often find a few hours every few months to chaperone a field trip, assist with a library book sale, or frost cookies with the kindergartners at the class Valentine's Day party. But fast-forward to high school and it's a different story: Teachers and staff don't reach out as much, the opportunities for engagement are less obvious, and your kid doesn't want you hanging around, anyway. And aren't you supposed to let your tween or teen have more space, independence, and privacy?

The truth is it matters very much that you stay involved, even at the risk of objections and eye rolling. This doesn't mean you have to be on the PTA board or chaperone the dance (heaven forbid!). Opportunities to connect actually abound in high school; you just have to search them out. You can be involved in ways that don't mortify your child, but rather reassure them that their world at school is extremely important, to both of you.

ESSENTIAL
FACT

School Involvement
Kids whose parents are actively involved at their schools are more successful academically.

Start by making a copy of your child's school schedule and familiarizing yourself with his teachers. Often there are very brief bios on school websites that will give you a basic understanding of teachers' backgrounds and philosophies. Keep this knowledge in quiet reserve, as something you can draw on to contextualize child complaints or class conflicts in the future. Never miss a parent curriculum night—it's your big chance to meet teachers and get a taste of what your child's daily life at school will be like.

Reach out to teachers via e-mail to ask questions or offer support (or praise). If you have concerns, ask for a one-on-one meeting right away. Read all PTA bulletins and school and team newsletters, and sign up for something—*anything*. Bake cookies for a track meet. Hand out yearbooks at the end of the year. Help the librarian with inventory. Even small tasks like these will help you stay connected with the school, other parents, and the larger learning community.

To the extent that you can, attend your child's practices and games. Parents with full-time jobs often see a sports season slip away without ever making it to the sidelines. If your work allows some flexibility, schedule an hour on the sidelines every once in a while, or leave a little early to make it to a school volunteer opportunity. And make these efforts really count by staying off your cell phone and in the moment. Consider e-mailing your child's coach or teacher afterward with a word of appreciation or to ask any questions.

Knowing your teen's teachers and showing your face around school—even in quiet ways—send the message to your child that his school life is important to you. It's a key way of connecting with one of the biggest parts of your child's life. It's also a mainstay of authoritative parenting and puts you in a much better position to understand your child's myriad academic challenges and successes.

When addressing problems at school, the biggest bugaboo for parents is handling their own emotions. Parents get emotional about their child's underachievement, whether perceived or real. (And remember that, short of failure, "underachievement" is a very subjective concept.) Kids get emotional about being judged and pressured, and even teachers get emotional when it's suggested that they should adjust their teaching for one particular child among their scores of students. As a parent, your best approach is to stay wise-minded as you collect information, consider everyone's perspectives, and create an effective plan to address the problem.

Factors for Learning

LEARNING STYLES

As a parent of a tween or teen, you may have already heard a bit about "learning styles"—the specific way in which each child learns best. "Visual-verbal," "kinetic," and "audio-verbal" are some of the terms used for these various styles. You may have decided which style best describes your child and wondered if his teachers should be tailoring instruction accordingly. Perhaps you've even noticed that your child's learning gets a boost when the teacher writes things down, or lets your son or daughter walk in circles while trying to articulate complicated thoughts.

Differences in learning definitely exist among children, but the concept that classroom teaching is improved by focusing on these styles has become controversial in recent years. Although categorizing and teaching children according to their learning styles was in vogue a couple of decades ago, the trend has faded, as research has raised questions about its efficacy (Mayer 2011). The central question is: Does tailoring a teaching approach to a student's learning style truly help them learn more effectively? Although children express personal preferences, and academic testing may reveal strengths and weaknesses in processing information, there is a lack of evidence that either identifying a student's learning style or tailoring educational approaches to this style produces better academic outcomes (Pashler et al. 2008).

The most likely reason for this dearth of evidence is that the learning process is very complex. It's affected by overall IQ, motivation, socioeconomic background, racial and cultural issues, time, effort, health, class environment, psychosocial issues, and myriad other factors. Even if research identified some advantages to matching style with teaching approach, the findings would have to be quite significant to justify the costs associated with overhauling general educational practices to accommodate individual learning styles.

You may especially like the idea of individualized educational programs if you've noticed your child struggling with certain teaching approaches. That's understandable, and there are still those who advocate teaching to the individual learning style of students. Since we know that learning is enhanced by a student's emotional well-being, it makes sense that teachers incorporate whatever methods they can to connect with students, present the material in ways that reach the most students effectively, and maintain the rigor and relevance of their academic goals. With or without a specific goal of teaching to learning differences, the master teacher will intuitively use many mediums for galvanizing learning in a classroom of diverse students.

GENDER

For years, many researchers have posited that kids have varying levels of success in certain school subjects depending on their gender. These theories have received widespread media coverage and left parents (and psychologists) confused about what's really happening on the gender front. Take a moment to assess your assumptions about gender and learning by taking the following quiz.

ESSENTIAL
QUIZ

How Does Gender Affect Learning?
Test your basic knowledge of learning differences between boys and girls with this simple quiz.

True False

1. ☐ ☐ Research has shown that boys are naturally more talented in math and science.

2. ☐ ☐ Girls do better in school these days because of their superior verbal abilities.

3. ☐ ☐ It's important to understand the differences between boys' and girls' brains if you're going to teach them effectively.

4. ☐ ☐ It's important to talk to your child about the natural differences between girls' and boys' brains.

5. ☐ ☐ Considering all the variables, girls have a natural advantage in school.

6. ☐ ☐ Considering all the variables, boys have a natural advantage in school.

The correct answer to all of these is false. That may come as a surprise; after all, many of these concepts are the very ones that have been bandied about the most in recent years. But increasingly, research is debunking these recent notions about learning, especially when it comes to boys and girls.

Twenty years ago, "gender equity" and the claim that the educational system was set up to favor boys was all the rage. The assumption was that boys had an advantage because they tend to be assertive, vocal, and intrinsically inclined to excel in math and science. The concern led to an outcry for single-sex schools with the assumption that girls could learn and thrive better without boys in the classroom.

As with many education-reform ideas, research has finally caught up with theory. A highly credible review referred to the studies on which this reform was based as "pseudo-science" and claimed that single-sex education is misguided; justified by weak, cherry-picked, and misconstrued scientific claims (Halpern et al. 2011). In fact, the authors point out that there is evidence that sex segregation is actually harmful, because it magnifies gender stereotyping. They consider gender segregation as analogous to racial segregation, and point out that segregation sends a message that there are actual reasons to separate boys and girls. Since kids (and all humans) are ferocious pattern analyzers, they go looking for those reasons, trying to figure out why the institutional separation is relevant, important, or potentially unfair. This can exaggerate differences that may or may not exist; for instance, the ideas that all boys need more recess and physical expression, and that all girls need to be away from boys to be assertive. Even the degree to which boys and girls hang out exclusively within coed contexts can accentuate sex-typed behavior—for instance, boys becoming more aggressive or girls becoming more catty. Ask any teen, and they'll tell you that getting a person of the opposite sex into a group can tone down the girl drama or the boy goofball quotient. Gender differences do exist, and there is some truth to stereotypes, but the experts maintain that these differences are socially constructed—and probably best socially deconstructed.

Another debunking appears to be afoot, involving the more recent claim that the educational system favors *girls* and discriminates against boys. Indeed, boys are more frequently diagnosed with a range of behavioral/learning/attentional problems, and they're hard hit when recess and athletic programs are eliminated due to funding cuts. Therefore, some are saying that girls have the advantage, because they are often better behaved, more verbally skilled, more organized, and naturally better suited for collaborative learning.

In 2006, psychologist Janet Shibley Hyde synthesized data from 165 studies examining the gender differences in verbal ability—the characteristic most often cited as giving girls an advantage in school (Hyde 2005). She found that female superiority in this ability was so slight as to be meaningless. And an analysis of data available from the National Center for Educational Statistics, called the National Assessment of Educational Progress (widely known as the "The Nation's Report Card"), has also revealed findings that call for a much more complex interpretation of the data on gender advantage (Perie et al. 2005).

Some groups of boys, especially those from low-income Hispanic and African-American homes, are at high risk for low educational achievement. But the most significant problems are those of race and class, not of gender. Boys are said to be "falling behind," but in fact, overall academic achievement and attainment is higher for boys in general than it has been in the past. Girls are catching up, however; overall, they have improved their performance even faster than boys, thereby "narrowing the gap" that previously favored males (Mead 2006). The number of young men attending college after high school is rising, but the number of young women is rising more quickly. Girls now make up a higher percentage of the student population at most colleges across the country. In the first decade of life, boys still achieve at higher levels than girls do in many subjects, but they tend to fall behind their female peers by high school. Combing through the national data is interesting reading, but the "take-away" is that girls simply have opportunities they've never had before to achieve, and boys need much more academic support during the transition to high school.

And let's dispel the math and science myth once and for all. We hear time and again that "girls just aren't as good at math and science as boys." Research on the cognitive abilities of girls and boys, from birth to maturity, does not support any claim that males have greater aptitude for these disciplines (Spelke 2005). Although there are differences between males and females regarding many psychological and cognitive characteristics, there are far more differences *within* gender groups than *between* gender groups (Halpern 2012). Also, when cognitive profiles are compared, the differences are subtle and complex. Boys are not necessarily naturally spatial, and girls are not always more verbally inclined. And while boys do have higher SAT math scores, high school and college males and females are *equally* proficient in math classes.

ESSENTIAL
FACT

The Real Gender Difference
Although there are gender differences regarding many psychological and cognitive characteristics, there are far more differences *within* male and female groups than *between* males and females.

A fundamental issue with teaching to differences—aside from the lack of evidence that it's in any way effective and may even be harmful—is logistical. It places a tremendous burden and expense on already stretched schools and teachers. And, one could ask, where do you begin and end with teaching to differences? Why stop at gender differences? Why not emphasize teaching kids differently based on their sexual orientation, family income, religion, or race?

One of the reasons that stereotypes still exist is that attention is not often drawn to the research meta-analyses. It's the splashy headlines on gender inequality (or "oversched-uling" or "learning styles") that get attention, not the densely written, thoroughly researched findings. The media has played up the gender war in a way that distracts from school-reform efforts that could offer teens a better chance of getting the support they need for academic success, especially among disadvantaged populations. Furthermore, gender differences remain in academic-course choices, social attitudes about gender, and underrepresentation of women on math and science faculties. If you look closely in the areas where you still see disparity, you're likely to find persistent stereotypes at play that perpetuate the problem far more than any difference in brain structure or capacity.

If brain-based research on gender differences doesn't hold up, then why do we see so many girls who hate math and love fashion, and so many boys who hate romantic poetry and love war games? The answer most likely lies in the fact that our brains are moldable and socially sensitive to all influences beginning at birth, and parents are just more instinctively action-oriented with boys and use more emotional vocabulary with girls. Instead of a "hardwired" assumption about differences, experts are increasingly documenting the strong influences of social and cultural forces to explain gender differences (Fine 2011).

Given the diversity among American students in regard to many characteristics—cognitive abilities, grade-level preparation, personalities, race, culture, religion, income level, and parental support and style—assuming that significant gender differences exist and should command priority in educational reforms is ill informed at best, and probably a costly mistake at worst.

Risk Factors for Poor Academic Achievement

School failure is a significant turning point for some adolescents, and greatly influences their life-course trajectory (Bersani and Chapple 2007). Depending on the school and socioeconomic setting, the percentage of students who are at risk for school problems or failure can be as much as 50 percent.

When children fail to thrive in school, it sets them up for many other negative social and emotional consequences, such as behavioral problems, parent-child conflict, and illegal activities (especially with substance abuse), all of which compound and escalate problems in school.

A History of Difficulty

The most powerful predictor of school failure among teens is difficulty in elementary school. School problems during the elementary years and in early adolescence are also linked with later substance abuse and delinquency, as well as ongoing behavioral problems, unaddressed learning disabilities, and deficits in parenting practices.

Times of Transition

It has long been known that tween and teens are particularly vulnerable during times of transition—both to middle school and high school (Eccles and Midgley 1990). With all the heightened emotions of puberty, changes in peer systems, and the academic challenges associated with attending new schools, adolescents encounter a number of stressors all at once. If a kid struggled in elementary school, it should be assumed that school transitions—with all their intrinsic demands of new academic, social, and emotional pressures—will be especially difficult, and may be too much to handle without significant adult support.

Peer Acceptance

Classmates play a role, too. Seminal research on peer rejection shows that it's a significant risk factor for academic problems during both childhood and adolescence (Asher and Coie

1990). Children who are aggressive and disruptive are particularly disliked by peers, and that rejection plays an incremental role in making school an all-around bad experience. Rejected kids are more likely to bully and be the victims of bullying, which serves to make school an even more negative environment for learning. Rejected children have more academic problems, are absent more often, have more discipline problems, and drop out of school more often than kids who are accepted and liked by their peers.

Poverty

The most dramatic risk factor for children trying to learn—in and out of school—is poverty. Students who live in impoverished communities face significant disadvantages, ranging from ineffective or overwhelmed teachers and low-quality schools to low parental and administrative support. While a review of the problems in school settings is beyond the scope of this chapter, it suffices to say that schools that lack resources deprive children of the chance to learn in a fertile environment. It's like throwing ripe seeds on barren ground.

READING THE WARNING SIGNS

Academic performance is a measure of adolescent thriving, so many parents pay particular attention to achievement tests. Compared to many other important developmental issues—emotional and social skills, peer-status concerns, ego development, body image—academic performance is clearly measurable. Additionally, these tests are familiar; most parents took them at one time or another themselves. In addition, achievement tests operate like objective measures of future promise, along with grades, teacher comments, and even what teens say about their school experience (e.g., loving, hating, or just tolerating some classes). These measures are not absolute in any sense, but they should be considered extremely important barometers of teen adjustment—and not just academically speaking. Because of the importance of school performance to future success, when kids fail academically, it signals that they might fail in life as well, whether financially, occupationally, or in their interpersonal relationships.

There is help available. If your child isn't thriving at school, consult with teachers and school psychologists, and find out what special programs exist at the school to help struggling students. If the school is unresponsive, you can move up the chain of command to the district level, or elsewhere, to seek the services your child needs and deserves. Although paying for tutoring or academic services outside of the school system can be a financial burden, it's important to intervene in school problems before they intensify. Like any problem, the longer an academic difficulty goes unaddressed, the more "expensive" (financially, emotionally, and socially) it becomes for the child and family alike. The ultimate cost to the child can be a loss of self-efficacy, pride, and hope. There is simply too much at stake to ignore the warning signs.

When a child fails at school, the consequences reverberate outward, like ripples in a pond. From the initial plunge and sinking of academic failure come the spreading rings of behavioral problems, conflict in the home, substance abuse, poor peer relationships— all of which can result in a flood of escalating problems at school.

ESSENTIAL
ACTIVITY

Academic Risk Factors

What risk factors could be barriers to your child's academic success? Gaining a clear understanding of what your child is up against can help you better support him.

Check any and all that apply to your child today:

- ☐ body-image issues
- ☐ poor physical health
- ☐ lack of neighborhood safety
- ☐ low acceptance from peers
- ☐ friendship problems
- ☐ marital discord, divorce
- ☐ illness, mental disorders
- ☐ family conflict
- ☐ financial stress
- ☐ emotional issues (anxiety, depression, etc.)
- ☐ preoccupation with social issues
- ☐ distractibility
- ☐ learning problems
- ☐ extreme sensitivity to frustration
- ☐ overuse of video games/social media
- ☐ risk-taking behavior
- ☐ belief that "I'm not a good student"
- ☐ negative attitude about school
- ☐ unhappy or unmotivated teachers
- ☐ racism in school
- ☐ school violence
- ☐ high dropout rate in school
- ☐ sleep deprivation
- ☐ problematic adjustment to a new school
- ☐ other _____

If you checked even a couple of boxes, your thoughts about how to help your child should focus on much more than just academic performance. Life issues like the ones presented above filter down to have a profound effect on your child's education. Addressing them is key to helping your child do his best; solving any of these problems will take him much further than paying him to get A's or even hiring a tutor will.

The Social-Emotional Component of Optimal Learning Environments

Schools should provide an environment in which children can master reading, writing, math, and science—and that environment should take into account far more than academic proficiency. In the chapters ahead, we'll tackle social and emotional well-being—two of life's essentials that should be supported and nurtured at school as well as at home.

Social and emotional parental support, positive student-teacher relationships, peer groups that value learning, a school culture that helps kids feel like they belong, and a supportive classroom atmosphere are all critical factors—along with an engaging academic curriculum and homework, and solid study skills—in a child's academic success. This attention to the "whole child" may be what Margaret Mead had in mind when she so eloquently said, "If we are to achieve a richer culture, rich in contrasting values, we must recognize the whole gamut of human potentialities, and so weave a less arbitrary social fabric, one in which each diverse human gift will find a fitting place."

Studies demonstrate that finding that "fitting place" for every child pays off in spades. A national research consortium called the Collaborative for Academic, Social, and Emotional Learning (CASEL) took a long look at the benefits to students when curriculum emphasizes the roles of social and emotional skills, including attitudes toward self and others, positive social behavior, behavioral adjustment, and emotional stability, along with academic performance. A meta-analysis of 213 school programs that emphasize these points showed big payoffs: improvement in students' achievement test scores by 11 percentile points; improvement in students' social/emotional skills, and in positive behaviors and attitudes about peers, self, and school; and a reduction in conduct problems and emotional distress (Durlak et al. 2011). These programs benefitted students with and without behavioral and emotional problems, and were effective for racially and ethnically diverse students from urban, rural, and suburban settings across the K–12 range.

In other words, everyone benefits from school programs that emphasize the integration of social and emotional learning into academic curricula; even teachers report better job satisfaction. If children are distressed and overwhelmed, they cannot learn. If children are adequately supported, both emotionally and socially, as they learn, the entire school community thrives.

Your Mission

School performance is influenced by countless cognitive, social, and emotional factors that begin at birth. When adolescence happens—and those hormonal and brain-remodeling changes occur—the number of factors multiply. It is not simply a matter of "good parenting + good brain = good grades." And anxiety about the high stakes of school achievement just makes parenting that much more challenging. With an appreciation for all these facts and emotions, we really do need a wise-minded approach to promoting academic success.

When we set up an effective homework schedule and volunteer in the school library, we create a sense of importance and commitment that sets the tone for achievement. But true parental involvement runs deeper—deep enough to tap into the well of the authoritative parenting traits of warmth, structure, and the encouragement of autonomy. This type of parenting creates the underpinning of an academically supportive environment. Add to that encouragement and genuine praise, the understanding that a child's brain power is not static, and an appreciation that you can only do so much to help your teen pull those high grades, given the hurly-burly of adolescent development.

Not every school year can be outstanding, but parents need to insist that school failure is not an option. Parents can't control whether their kids make top grades, but they can step up their involvement in a variety of ways to prevent a grade slump from becoming a nose dive. Don't be thrown if your child gives you the "Back off! I'll handle it!" message about school: Academic success really is one of those parenting battles worth waging. But don't think of it as a battle; it's more like a mission—a mission to ensure that your child gets the support they need to achieve one of life's essentials: academic success.

CHAPTER 4
Social Thriving

Scene: *This mom has just gotten home from curriculum night at the high school, where she got some disturbing information about one of her ninth-grade daughter's closest friends. She is terribly worried about the influence this girl might be having on her daughter. She finds her daughter in her room and launches right into the subject.*

> Mom: *Honey, I need to talk to you about something.*
>
> Sara: *Mom, I'm busy. We can talk tomorrow.*
>
> Mom: *Updating your playlist can wait. I need to talk to you about Molly.*
>
> Sara: *Oh, what now? You never liked Molly. Everyone knows that.*
>
> Mom: *Well, I've always said she's too promiscuous. Those super-short skirts and skimpy tops! But now I find out she's been having oral sex with boys. Multiple boys!*
>
> Sara: *How do you know that? It's none of your business anyway!*
>
> Mom: *A couple of the parents were talking about it at school tonight. Are you saying it's not true? Is it true? That girl has serious problems. I'm mortified at the thought that a friend of yours would cheapen herself like that.*
>
> Sara: *Mom, you don't even know her and you judge her! Just because of gossip! You are so the one who has serious problems! You parents are disgusting to do this to Molly!*

It's an all-too-common parental worry: Does my child have the right kind of friends? Good-enough friends? Or even just enough friends? Is what I heard about so-and-so true? Will he or she get my child into trouble? When should I draw the line with a friend of whom I just don't approve?

As your child enters her late tween years, you'll probably notice a changing of the guard: As scintillating as you used to be during her first decade of life, her peers are taking center stage now. You are still welcome to drive her places—and may still be permitted a quick hug or a peck on the cheek—but if you could please refrain from embarrassing her with slobbery shows of parental affection, it would be greatly appreciated. Failure to comply may be met with a roll of the eyes, but don't be fooled: Research indicates that most parents are still the main attachments in their teens' lives (Cassidy and Shaver 2010). It's just that the relationship is so secure—such an utter mainstay—that the teens feel safe to relegate their parents to the wings.

If this seems familiar, pat yourself on the back. Your child probably has a normal, thriving social life, complete with all the thrilling aspects of newfound independence, the exploration of new ideas and social mores, and peer influences—for better or for worse.

And that "better or worse" is what this chapter is all about. Because your child, whether you like it or not, is in the process of developing an intricate, critically important web of peer relationships that will alternately elevate him, challenge him, thrill him, and devastate him. Learning to keep his head while on this social roller-coaster ride is one of the seven essentials for your budding, blooming, exasperating teen. And for parents, learning to stay wise-minded while watching the ride from the safety of the midway is one of the most challenging—and messiest—essentials to navigate. But if you can get this one right and encourage your child to thrive socially, then you'll be helping him gain all kinds of important skills that will serve him well in practically every aspect of his life, now and in the future.

Why Social Skills Are So Important

As tweens become teens, friends become increasingly important, until they reach a stage in which making and keeping friends becomes positively central to their overall sense of happiness. Those vital friendships enhance well-being, social skills, and peer acceptance. Friends can also serve as a buffer during stressful times. Most adults know this to be true: A high-quality friendship provides intimacy, fun, and validation.

But the benefits of friendship go deeper than that. Numerous research studies have shown that teens are psychologically better adjusted when they have friends. Isolation and peer rejection have been associated with all manner of negative outcomes, ranging from depression, bullying, victimization, school problems, and conduct disorders. In fact, in one study, teen respondents who just *believed* that they were thought poorly of by their peers—even when this was not the case—experienced a host of psychological problems as a result (Sandstrom et al. 2003). Social exclusion can be damaging, and it's another chicken-and-egg problem: For a long time, it wasn't known whether shy kids were more likely to be rejected, or that rejection caused kids to be shier. But a longitudinal study, following a sample of five- to eleven-year-olds, revealed that exclusion increases shyness and social withdrawal. It also has a negative effect on academic perfor-mance (Buhs et al. 2006).

You probably know how important social skills are in the workplace. Employees who are socially adept are far more apt to be well liked and successful on the job, and more likely to be promoted. One review of the literature on traits that employers look for in entry-level workers found that interpersonal effectiveness, resilience, and communication skills were always at the top (Goleman 1998). And how do people learn secrets of social success, such as empathy, assertiveness, cooperation, and the building of consensus? In the home, and in the ever-expanding social contexts of adolescents' lives. High-quality social relationships with parents, peers, and other adults are powerful predictors of adolescent thriving and success in adulthood. And teen dating is, of course, a testing ground for adult romance and family life.

We'll begin by addressing the many ins and outs of tween and teen friendships—and yes, romances, too—but first, take a moment to assess your basic assumptions about your child's social life.

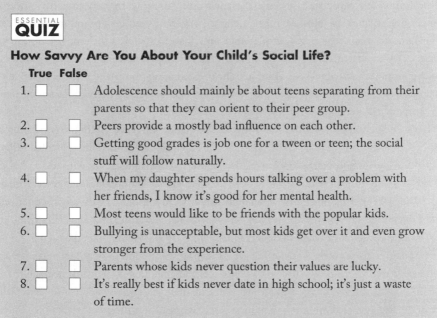

The Science of Social Development

From the moment they are born, babies are driven to explore the world with their eyes and mouths. Toddlers engage people with smiles and mimicry and investigate their social environment by crawling over and under things, seeking contact with people, and enjoying a game of peak-a-boo. Young children, depending on their temperaments, either burst or tiptoe into the socially rich environment of preschool and elementary school. Regardless of temperament, every child's innate developmental "thrust" is to seek the company of others—to find those who like what they like and play at their favored pace and level of psychological arousal.

Brain growth in adolescence is greatly influenced by social experiences. During these years, social interactions of all kinds affect the brain construction process, as the brain "fine-tunes" its neural connections, consolidating its synapses based on experience. With the pruning of unused grey matter, some mental abilities are lost, such as the ability to speak a foreign language without an accent. But new synapses are established through experience, and the ever-more-sophisticated social experiences adolescents have "wire in" some impressive capacities. These experiences help them learn how to contribute to conversations, enhance good feelings among members of their group, and regulate their emotions, especially the negative ones that may lead to social exclusion. The desire to hang out with friends has a function, one that is as important as learning algebra—maybe more so. Kids need social interactions the same way they need to engage actively in sports, extracurricular activities, and academics, because those interactions strengthen the synaptic connections in the associated brain regions.

Because the brain is wired to be sensitive to *all* outside influences, with the good comes the bad. The teen's drive to be social results in the expansion of refined interpersonal skills, but it also means adolescents are more susceptible to experimentation with alcohol and drugs as a way to experience novelty, seek arousal, and/or gain peer acceptance. What starts out as experimentation with alcohol can lead to various negative consequences including mental health problems (Kandel et al. 1997), academic problems (Hawkins et al. 1992), and use of other substances (Duncan et al. 1998). Remember, the teen brain is very sensitive to rewards and the release of dopamine, which is why teens can be so vulnerable to the effects of drugs and alcohol. Temperament, mental health, sociocultural factors, and family dynamics will all play roles in the process by which some teens will navigate drug and alcohol experimentation safely while others progress (sometimes quite rapidly) to abuse and addiction. The social implications of this brain construction phase are fraught with opportunity and risk.

This expansion of social and emotional competence is complicated by the tween's or teen's quest for independence, and often a desire for peer-related risk taking of all sorts. By this point, parents have usually developed a heightened awareness of the potential dangers of their child's social life. Parents—and the entire community—naturally worry about the welfare of kids and the health-related concerns that can accompany these years, including traffic accidents, bullying, substance use, pregnancy, and mental health problems. But putting too heavy an emphasis on the potential problems is shortsighted and can actually blind us to the wonderfully adaptive aspects of tweens and teens pushing for independence, learning from peers, exploring values, and acquiring self-regulation skills through experiences with risk. In other words, research about and emphasis on the *positive* ways that teens influence one another is sorely lacking in our common perceptions of peer relations.

Until recently, it was assumed (possibly by you!) that teens must "separate" from their parents and "break away" to join a detached peer culture, but this notion has evolved into a more nuanced understanding of social development. Ideally, teens will have constant exposure to varied social experiences with caring and principled peers and adults within social networks, both informal and formal. Additionally, the arrival of social media as a key player on the teen scene can both hinder and advance this agenda, depending on the nature of the activity and amount of time spent online. Although teens will send a strong message to parents to back off, the wise-minded parent will artfully balance independence with a nurturing connection. You'll see how this works in the coming pages.

As teens progress through adolescence, their social development is influenced by evolving friendships, socialization in larger and more diverse groups, and the exploration of ideological questions. It's a journey best traveled with the support of wise-minded parents who understand (and have empathy for) the complexity of social forces at work during this dynamic period of growth.

Friendship 101

In the second decade of life, it's normal—and actually desirable—for children to spend more time with their peers and less time with their families. In early adolescence, the choice of friends is often determined by common interests, hobbies, and affiliations (e.g., religious institutions, sports teams, or clubs). Over time, teens are also drawn to peers who have traits and talents that may be different from their own, although common interests continue to have a strong influence on friendship choices.

Teens conduct their increasingly complex social lives on multiple levels at once: one-on-one friendships, romantic relationships, small cliques, larger crowds, and extended and wide-ranging networks, thanks to social media, which has altered the teen social scene significantly. But here again, it's often the negative aspects—especially online bullying and inappropriate information sharing—that draw the most focus from parents and the public at large. Supportive texts sent late at night to reassure and encourage one another often fly beneath the radar of parents and researchers. The bottom line is that teen friendships, no matter what form they take, can be volatile, changeable, supportive, and destructive, and sometimes all these things at any given time.

It appears that it's quality, not quantity, that counts. A seminal study on friendships found that having a friend, the quality of the friendship, and overall group acceptance greatly affect whether or not a tween feels lonely (Parker and Asher 1993). Over the last twenty years, studies have documented that friendship depth (quality and mutuality) as opposed to breadth (sheer number) has been associated with psychological adjustment even into early adulthood (Pettit et al. 2011). Although this research may seem like common sense, I can't count the number of consultations I have done with distressed parents who worry about their teen's lack of socializing. But teens who prefer to stay close to home, avoid school dances, and rarely seek opportunities to socialize may not actually have a problem, especially if they deny loneliness, feel accepted at school, have a few mutually enjoyable friendships, and feel satisfied with their social life. Parents of such teens might do well to ponder that wise maxim: Accept the kid you have.

Also, as your teen learns to navigate her emerging social world, she may be taking a page from your book. One study found that both the quality of teens' friendships and the level of their emotional expression with best friends were associated with their mothers' positive relationships with husbands and friends (Markiewicz et al. 2001). Teen perceptions of the quality of their mothers' relationships were also related to positive teen behaviors, such as school achievement and participation in extracurricular activities. Not surprisingly, teens who have the opportunity to observe positive social skills are at an advantage. Furthermore, teenagers who have experienced the security of a strong bond with an attachment figure (usually a parent) are better able to trust and enjoy—and perhaps tolerate the inevitable ups and downs of—intimate relationships.

You may have just a couple of close friends, or many; most people have tiers of friends, some close, others who are seen only socially or in a work context, and still others who fall somewhere in between. Parents who have tumultuous social lives or problems making and keeping friends can be particularly sensitive to the goings-on of their kids' social lives. Like any "hot button" issue, those parents will need to be especially careful about not over-reacting to the social ups and downs so common in adolescence. When parents bring intrusive, judgmental, or coercive reactions to friendship issues, they lose trust and credibility with their teen, as well the chance to support their child in a time of need.

GIRL FRIENDSHIPS VS. BOY FRIENDSHIPS

It may come as no surprise that girls tend to expect more from their same-sex friendships than boys do. In studies, girls report greater intimacy and more self-disclosure in their friendships with same-sex peers than boys. On the flip side, girls also seem to experience more stress in their friendships. An analysis of preteen and teen brain scans (fMRIs) found that girls respond differently than boys when they think they are being judged by their peers; the scans of girls' brains showed reactivity to social stress that does not occur in boys' brains (Guyer et al. 2009). The study was constructed to measure responses among participants to peer evaluations during an online chat session. The specific brain regions associated with emotions lit up during these peer evaluations for the girls, but not for the boys. Teenage girls have always reported a significant concern for what others think of them; now there are brain scans to prove it!

Another gender difference researchers found was that girls "co-ruminate" with their friends more than boys. Co-rumination refers to a process in which teens confide about problems, talk about them repeatedly, encourage and support one another, and dwell on negative feelings (Rose 2002). This is primarily a girl thing, especially in middle school, but boys catch up a bit over time. Researchers discovered that the levels of co-rumination varied less widely between genders within college-age groups. Boys seem to learn to self-disclose and confide more as they get older.

Co-rumination has trade-offs. It contributes to relationship quality and social support—but it also increases depression and anxiety (Tompkins et al. 2011). Findings like these lend some insight into how female friendships can both enhance and hinder coping. Dwelling on problems is harmful to girls' well-being, yet they benefit greatly from the depth of their close relationships. Even with the downsides of co-rumination, boys would do well to seek more social support and confide in one another. They could discover that they share similar worries and vulnerabilities.

A WISE-MINDED APPROACH TO FRIENDSHIPS

Every parent wants their child to have strong friendships of the "right" kind, but overt manipulation of the friendship process—even for the best reasons!—can backfire terribly. Though you will naturally nudge and sometimes overtly steer your middle schooler away from negative peer groups and toward more positive ones, as your child gets older, this kind of influence becomes increasingly difficult.

Most of us make the mama- or papa-bear mistake of only wanting our children to associate with nice, wholesome, motivated, high-achieving—let's face it, perfect!—kids. Really, doesn't that make our lives easier? Assuage our fears? While that seems reasonable on the surface, a reality check is in order: Our child's choice of friends is not about us, and should not be about making us comfortable. Your child is choosing friends as part of that crucial process of individuation (forming a unique identity). She will choose according to her own tastes, personality, and developmental needs.

Whenever our kids pick friends we consider less than desirable, we need to ponder an essential question: What does our child see in this kid? A rigid, slightly obsessive girl will sometimes choose a wilder girlfriend, because she is exploring the terrain of adventure from a safe distance. And the converse can also be true: A boy who operates on the margin of self-control might be drawn to a stable, down-to-earth friend who serves as a touchstone or an anchor. In both cases, the friendships, which might appear harmful or just mismatched to parents, may actually fulfill a particular need in a child's social development.

WISE-MINDED
MANTRA
My child's choice of friends is about _his_ needs, not mine.

There is no single set of rules for parents who want to support their child's quest for healthy friendships and curb (or at least monitor) their child's attraction to unhealthy ones. But wise-minded parenting can help you point your parental compass to the intersection of what you objectively know to be "good" for your child and what your child actually needs and is actively seeking.

Let's revisit the scene from the beginning of this chapter. The mom is afraid of Molly's negative influence on her daughter. This time, as she drives home from the parent meeting, she thinks deeply about how to best open channels of communication and handle the situation with a wise mind. Here's a look at the result.

Take Two:

> Mom: *Honey, I need to talk to you about something.*
>
> Sara: *Mom, I'm busy. We can talk tomorrow.*
>
> Mom: *I'd like to talk to you tonight about some disturbing information that was going around school this evening.*
>
> Sara: *What?*
>
> Mom: *I struggled with whether to share something that amounts to gossip, but you'll find out through the rumor mill anyway, so I decided that I owe it to you to confide in you.*

Sara: Oh, no. Just tell me.

Mom: The story is that Molly has been engaging in oral sex with several boys.

Sara: I can't believe that this is what the stupid moms are talking about at curriculum night! Parents are so two-faced. You tell us not to gossip, and then look at you guys.

Mom: You are absolutely right. And I'm feeling really bad for Molly—and that this is happening at all. I'm concerned about Molly, not just that this might be going on, but how she is going to feel when she finds out that people are talking about it.

Sara: Me, too. She must be dying right now!

Mom: I'd like to talk to you about oral sex, values, and all that. But would you rather talk right now about how you want to support Molly?

Sara: God, yes, Mom, would you let me text her right now? Obviously, she is in big trouble. I've been really worried about her lately. She's been kind of going off the deep end, and now this....

Mom: Sure, let's talk about what might be the best way for her to feel safe, supported, and hopeful. This is a terrible situation for her. And we have a lot to talk about, too. Let's do both.

This wise-minded mom proved herself to be trustworthy and nonjudgmental in a situation that would make many parents quite reactive and critical. She took some time while driving home to put herself in Molly's shoes, the same way she knew her daughter would, thereby cultivating empathy for her daughter's friend and creating a common departure point for this tough conversation with her daughter.

As parents, our instinct is to distance ourselves and our children from negative influences. But if we can quell our fear and tap into empathy instead, we're bound to be far more effective conveying important information to our kids and modeling supportive, nonjudgmental behavior.

If you've ever made a negative comment about one of your child's friends, you may have experienced the powerful backlash it can provoke. Tweens and teens have a jumble of feelings, both good and bad, about their friendships. When a well-meaning parent calls out a negative feature of a friend—putting a thumb on the seesaw, so to speak—the only way the kid can restabilize the fragile balance is by climbing up on the friend's side. Your child will also call you out for having the *nerve* to even *think* that you might be right about even one tiny piece of the complicated friend puzzle.

This mom still plans to discuss Molly's behavior and underlying motivations with her daughter—the consequences of engaging in this kind of sexual behavior and the long-term implications for self-esteem, social adjustment, and reputation—but she wants that discussion to happen in the best possible way. The daughter's appreciation now for her mom's empathy and understanding about Molly's situation makes it much more likely that those future discussions will be productive.

ESSENTIAL
TIP

Wise-Minded Tips for Supporting Teen Friendships

1. Make an effort to know the families of your child's friends. You can share notes and agree on rules (and hear about how wonderful your kid is at their homes, when you aren't around to see it!).

2. Adjust your support based on your child's temperament. Nudge your shy child forward (even though he won't like it). Maneuver your sensation-seeking child away from the wild crowd (even though he won't like it).

3. If you have concerns about your child's choices, try encouraging friendships with high-functioning friends. Offer to chaperone a trip to the movies or a baseball game, or host a simple pizza and movie night.

4. Be aware of your own baggage. If you have issues with your own childhood experiences with friends, you might be "overcorrecting" when it comes to your kids'. Given the importance of social thriving, now's a good time to talk to friends, your spouse, or a professional counselor to help you work through your own issues on the subject.

5. Remember that you are your child's first love relationship. If they had a good experience with you, chances are they will ultimately apply their positive expectations, relationship skills, and emotional sensibilities to their friendships.

6. As your child matures, you may earn the privilege of being their confidante about complicated social matters if you haven't blown it by bad-mouthing their friends. Keep reciting the wise-minded mantra "I may be right, but am I effective?"

7. Although restraint should be exercised when considering direct action regarding peer relations, sometimes rescue maneuvers are appropriate and mandatory—in situations involving suspected abuse, bullying, illegal activities, social threats, and the like.

8. Keep up with what's going on in your child's social networking world. Insist upon access to phones and computers as you see fit, according to your assessment of their healthy social development IRL (in real life).

9. Should you find your child's attraction to a peer mysterious, consider that she may be exploring a part of her identity by proxy. ("My friend is brave and a nonconformist. I know I lack those traits myself, so I'm fascinated by her and enjoy the vicarious experiences she offers.")

10. Believe the good things that you hear about your children from others. Children save their "best selves" for their social relationships outside the home. Since parents are the secure base, kids usually feel safe about really letting their hair down at home. Aren't we lucky?

Popularity

Research into peer relations has generally been conducted on two fronts. In "sociometric" surveys, children and teens are asked whom they like or don't like among an identified group of peers (usually classmates), to determine a person's likeability. In other research, children and teens are asked about the "perceived popularity" of their peers. Recent research has shown that likeability and popularity can be two different things (Cillessen and Mayeux 2004). These two concepts can be associated with one another (e.g., "She is popular" and "I want to be friends with her") or not (e.g., "She is popular" and "I do not want to be friends with her").

For younger children, especially girls, perceived popularity and likeability go hand in hand. But as kids grow, they seem to learn to discern the difference between a good friend and a popular peer. While both types of friend ratings can be associated with positive behaviors in teens, perceived popularity can also carry the nasty baggage of dominant and aggressive tendencies, including both indirect and direct cruelty.

Popular kids can be both naughty and nice. Research has identified two distinct subtypes of popular boys in a sample of fourth through sixth graders (Rodkin et al. 2000). "Model" popular boys were seen as expressing positive traits (e.g., cool, cooperative, athletic, studious, take-charge—sure to earn the parental seal of approval!). "Tough" popular boys were perceived as exhibiting a combination of athleticism and aggressive behaviors. Recent research has confirmed what most of us know experientially: Popularity can have a dark side.

Indeed, research that tracked teens through high school found that boys and girls who were perceived as popular engaged in greater alcohol consumption and sexual activity by twelfth grade than their less popular peers (Mayeux et al. 2008). This research also seems to indicate that there is a "cycle of popularity," in which popularity leads to risk taking, and increased risk taking leads to increased popularity. In another study of affluent teens, the ones with high popularity rankings and low grade-point averages were found to use more nicotine, alcohol, and marijuana (Luthar and Becker 2002). The popularity/affluence/risk-taking axis can be a recipe for trouble, since kids from well-heeled families are more likely to have cars, money for illegal substances, and sometimes disconnected relationships with their parents.

Popularity can be a risky proposition, not only for the popular kids, but also those who become the victims of their sometimes mean and aggressive behavior. Tweens and teens who are perceived as popular by their peers can be some of the most aggressive members of a social group (Rose et al. 2004). Though overt aggression can make an adolescent less desirable as a friend (less likable), especially among girls, perceived popularity stays stable despite undesirable behavior (Cillessen and Borch 2006). The link between relational aggression and perceived popularity is the strongest during the transition from middle school to high school, peaking in ninth grade and then beginning to decline around tenth grade.

In others words, as kids mature and become more confident themselves, the mean, popular kids begin to lose their appeal. So if your daughter struggles with the "mean girl" dynamics of middle school, take heart: What goes around comes around. Speaking ill of others to become popular may have a high pay-off early on, but it extracts hidden costs later in likeability and friendship.

The Dynamics of Peer Influence
BIRDS OF A FEATHER

Kids influence each other, it's clear, but the processes by which they do so are complicated. While peer pressure gets a lot of bad press, peer relationships are probably fueled more by peer *conformity*—children *wanting* to be like each other—than by being *pressured* to be like each other. Researchers call this reciprocal process "bidirectional"—meaning that children choose friends because they are similar to themselves, and then, once they are friends, the friends influence each other. Birds of a feather flock together, and then orchestrate their flight patterns during formative years.

Certain activities are often the outcome of friendship choice and subsequent influence, activities such as substance use (Dishion and Owen 2002) and eating behaviors (Story et al. 2002). One child might have an interest in the French horn or ballet and another in skateboarding or computer gaming, and those preferences will have a significant impact on whom he chooses to hang out with and be influenced by—and on whom he is having an influence. Certain behaviors, such as nicotine use or dieting, may be associated with those interest patterns as well. Skateboarders are more likely to smoke together than diet together, and the opposite is true of ballerinas.

While most of the research on peer influence relates to "externalizing" behaviors—those problematic, risk-taking behaviors such as antisocial (criminal or illegal) behavior and substance use—recent research has documented that peer influence may also play a role in "internalizing" behaviors, such as depression, negative body image, prejudicial attitudes, and low academic motivation (Brechwald and Prinstein 2011). The more we learn about peer influence, the greater that influence appears to be.

The mere physical presence of a peer can change teen behavior. In one study, adolescent boys taking part in a computer risk-taking exercise had increased arousal and willingness to take chances when a friend was in the room (Gardner and Steinberg 2005). The fact that peer contact increases risk taking is probably no surprise to you. However, brain-scan studies such as this one help expand theories on peer influence and suggest that the mere presence of a friend can trigger the brain to release dopamine, the neurotransmitter associated with pleasure.

I often get a laugh during lectures when I posit the theory that for every peer you add to a group of teens, you lower the collective IQ by ten points, but I'm only partly joking. When teens are in the presence of peers, they are far more likely to be aroused and do stupid things. They don't "process" the possible consequences of their risk taking because of their immature prefrontal cortices (discussed in chapter 2), and they don't want to, anyway; that dopamine spike is a lot of fun.

THE POSITIVE SIDE OF PEER INFLUENCE

Although the research emphasis is on *negative* peer influence (understandable, given the potential impact of these behaviors on the health of the teens and others), it should be noted that peer influence is also associated with the development of healthy behaviors (Barry and Wentzel 2006; Prinstein et al. 2001). Teens who feel satisfied with the quality, interaction, and stability of their friendships can motivate each other toward positive goals, which may include school achievement, participating in healthy extracurricular activities, and staying away from drugs and alcohol.

As children mature through the second decade of life, the interlaced processes of peer pressure, social conformity, and mutual influence can be difficult to tease apart. Children learn about social codes from their peers. And adults worry about the negative peer influences that are all too easy to focus on: profane language, sexual behavior, and substance use. Less obvious to parents are the tremendous pressures on teens to be kind, generous, thoughtful, fair, and honest. In fact, teens do some of the heavy lifting of the socializing agenda by teaching their peers how to be good citizens, friends, workers, and even students. Haven't we all heard stories of a teen confronting a peer who didn't pull his weight on the group project, show up on time, or share the ball? It's important for parents to remember that peer pressure can come in different forms, both desirable and undesirable.

ESSENTIAL
FACT

The Upside of Peer Pressure
Teens exert tremendous pressure on each other—to be kind, generous, thoughtful, fair, and honest.

HOW PEER PRESSURE WORKS

Peer pressure occurs during the tween and teen years as kids chide, deride, and ridicule each other into engaging in "be like me" behaviors. Kids at this age rely on peer feedback to figure out their status; it's a source of information about how well they are liked, which, in turn, becomes a form of self-regard. We all want to be accepted by our peers, and this is certainly true for children and teens who learn new social behaviors by observation, especially that of high-status peers in their network. By engaging in these behaviors, which may include new ways of talking or dancing—or the less savory social behaviors of bullying or alcohol use—teens mimic peers in order to attain the ultimate goals of acceptance and validation.

It's easy to spot the visible trappings of peer pressure, such as when kids encourage each other to wear different clothes, try their first cigarette, or blow off a check-in phone call. One of the most obvious signs that your child is becoming a member of a new "tribe" is the adoption of a new (and potentially baffling) language. Teens develop their own vernacular in order to mark their territory in this new, second tribe, and exclude those first-tribe members (their parents and siblings). Every generation does this; your parents' "groovy" became your "awesome," which these days is translated as "cray cray," and who knows what else by press time. Look no further than teen texting codes ("TTYL," "POS") to see how kids use language to keep parents from understanding what goes on in their digital worlds.

But what lies beneath the surface of teen language is far more profound than what you can hear in teen speech. They are learning to interpret one another's feelings, change their ways of speaking to accommodate the person they are with, make conversation, share the floor, understand humor, make requests, assert their wishes, match the mood of the group, praise others, and persuade peers with logic and sentiment. A heady, nuanced dance is learned through repeated, attuned interaction. Thinking about this process alone might be enough to inspire a little wise-minded empathy for the Herculean task your teen undertakes every time she sets foot into her social world.

THE DEVELOPMENTAL IMPORTANCE OF SOCIAL CONFORMITY

Your child will choose his peer group based on a whole host of factors: your family's socioeconomic status and cultural background; his school, neighborhood, interests and personality; and plain old chance. Let's imagine a boy named John. By joining the high school jazz band, he gains friends. Those friends expose him to hip-hop music, which he loves, so he starts a DJ business for local dances. John feels proud of his "musically talented" identity and considers a future in the music industry. His friends, who are also interested in music, may model kind and loyal support and encouragement, alcohol and nicotine use, academic ambitions, none of the above, or all of the above.

John may in turn accept those peer influences, depending on his own temperament. He may be an introvert or a thrill seeker. He may be predisposed to depression or optimism. His parents may be authoritative or permissive. He may be from a low-income household with a single parent, or from a middle-income household with highly educated parents, one of whom is chronically ill. He may be of European-American descent and trying to be accepted in an African-American peer group, or vice versa. And what if the school eliminates the jazz band? While peer influence is still a salient process affecting John's development, this dizzying array of social contexts in which peer influence is nested emphasizes the importance of interacting social forces.

Without the drive to try new things and join peers on the march toward adulthood, our kids would stay in the family "first tribe" forever. It's necessary to put social conformity into this context to fully appreciate its importance, despite parents' chagrin as they watch the transformation of a child (whose playdates could often be controlled) into a teen (who insists on making his own social choices). Peer conformity is part of an essential process that drives social (and species') success.

ESSENTIAL
QUIZ

How Wise-Minded Are You About Social Conformity?

Now that you know a bit about the complex and essential role of peers and social conformity, take a look at a few common but tricky parenting scenarios to see how you might react.

1. **Your tween boy has a new friend about whom you've heard terrible things. He plays violent video games all day long and is often in trouble at school. You tell your son:**
   a. "Listen, I don't want you hanging around Brian. That kid is no good!"
   b. "Tell me what you like about Brian. I like hearing about what draws you to your friends."
   c. "I can see why you like Brian. But I'm sorry, he's just not a good influence on you. You can't socialize with him anymore."

2. **Your child's very close friend has just gotten into trouble for cheating on a test. You tell your child:**
   a. "Cheating is never acceptable. That is bad behavior. You'd better stay away from Sharon. What if she cheats off of you next time and you both get busted?"
   b. "What do you think about what Sharon did? Why did she do it? Does it change how you feel about her?"
   c. "Boy, Sharon blew it this time. She must be feeling all kinds of pressure to succeed, but that is going to cost her big time. Her teacher won't trust her anymore, and her parents must be furious."

3. **You have just been told by a teacher that your tween boy was part of a group that stood by and watched Tommy verbally abuse Sam. You say:**
   a. "Geez, that Tommy is nasty. Best to keep your mouth shut or he'll turn on you."
   b. "Tell me what happened so I can support you in learning from this. Did you consider intervening, or at least going for help? What were you feeling? What do you think the impact of this is on Sam? How do the other kids feel about Tommy?"
   c. "I'm ashamed of you. Watching and doing nothing is just as bad as bullying."

4. You've just heard from a hurt and outraged mother that your fifteen-year-old daughter has been repeating rumors about her daughter, Jennifer; specifically, that Jennifer is having sex with her boyfriend. You say:

a. "Is Jennifer having sex with her boyfriend? Are all of your friends having sex? *Are you having sex?*"

b. "I know you are in hot water right now with the word out that you repeated a rumor about Jennifer having sex. What do you think you should do about it? How do you think Jennifer is feeling?"

c. "Listen, gossiping is terrible. You shouldn't do it ever, whether you think something's true or not. How would you like it if people were talking about you?"

5. Your child, who has always had a cute, very personal sense of style, just came home wanting to dress exactly like her friends. She said she'd "do anything" for a pair of $200 boots. You say:

a. "Why would you want to look just like everyone else? That is just dumb. You should dress like the special individual that you are."

b. "Wow, good thing you have been saving your baby-sitting money. I would be happy to scrounge up some extra jobs around here so you can earn the difference. I like seeing you work hard for things you want."

c. "Geez, that's expensive. Even I don't own $200 boots. Kids these days are so spoiled!"

The most wise-minded answer to each of the above is B. The wise-minded parent resists the urge to lecture, to be "right" about the difficult friends and overpriced clothes, and instead focuses on cultivating empathy for the daunting process of social development and conformity that their kids are facing. Though it's natural for parents to react to some of these issues by sharing their views, criticism and shaming almost always diminish a parent's ability to influence their teen's social decisions. Wise-minded parents remind themselves that a teen's accumulation of social smarts, while messy and imperfect, is critical for future happiness and success.

THE SOCRATIC METHOD

One way that parents can help their teens explore values and develop critical thinking is through the time-honored technique known as the Socratic method. Named for the classical Greek philosopher Socrates, it's a process of debate that's based on asking and answering questions to stimulate critical thinking.

Here's how it works: Let's say there is a dad who wants to talk about the provocative clothes that his daughter and her friends are wearing. He wants to explore his daughter's attitudes in a respectful, nonthreatening way. With the Socratic method, the goal is not to win an argument, persuade, or teach; inquiry is the only objective. Here are some questions he might ask:

I've noticed that girls in your class like to dress provocatively. I know it bugs you when I comment on it. I wonder what you think motivates them to wear such revealing tops?

Why do you think girls like to dress like that?

What kind of power do you think it gives them?

How do people perceive a girl who is exposing so much with that kind of top?

Do you think offending us parental types is part of the allure of dressing that way?

To do this correctly, your tone should be neutral and respectful. Socrates called himself a man of ignorance. To reap the benefits of this method, you, too, must think of yourself as ignorant, looking for insights into your teen's psychological and intellectual world. This is how a wise-minded parent gains the understanding and empathy needed to make an effective plan of action.

In this case, the daughter's replies might reveal her naiveté when it comes to provocative dress—certainly, that's what the father expects. But it might also give the father insight into the social pressures his daughter feels, her quest for acceptance and social power, and even her preferences around clothing styles. The father's calm, respectful listening could even inspire a compromise of sorts: Perhaps low-cut is off the table, but he would allow a shortening of hems. Maybe one outfit is off-limits at school, but OK at dances. Whatever compromise is reached, the point is that this dad is working *with* his daughter, seeking common ground, rather than laying down an authoritarian edict.

Notice that this wise-minded dad avoids calling out his daughter's friends for "slutty" dress, or accusing them of putting out negative messages about their values or self-esteem. He is intuitive enough to know that dissing his daughter's friends is not the best way to maintain influence and relevance in her life. His focus is on *her*—her opinions, her feelings.

ESSENTIAL
TOOL

The Socratic Method
Use a neutral, interested, and respectful tone to draw your tween or teen out by guiding them through a series of questions, such as those on page 125.

To practice the Socratic method, think about a subject you want to tackle with your teen related to something meaty, such as the legalization of marijuana, cheating, being a bystander to bullying, social exclusion, or some specific hypothetical moral dilemma. Consider questions like the ones below. (If you suspect your teen will think this is hokey, invite an older teen or college kid to join in; they will likely enjoy the conversation, and that might be enough to encourage your teen to engage.)

Here are ten go-to Socratic questions:
1. Can you give an example of what you mean?
2. How did you reach your conclusion?
3. What do you think motivates people to do that?
4. Is it possible that it may not work out the way you predict?
5. What is the counterargument for what you just said? If you were in a debate, how would you argue the other side?
6. What else could we assume beyond what you just said?
7. What is the evidence that supports your claim?
8. What evidence might refute your claim?
9. What are the upsides and the downsides of your position on the subject?
10. Do you have examples of other situations like this one, in which your argument might apply?ß

Social Aggression

As tweens and teens experiment with social power, social cruelty inevitably comes into play. Kids test their limits by including and excluding others, directly and indirectly, via methods that involve both aggression and withdrawal. One way of gaining status, especially over those with superior abilities or talents, is to disparage them; after all, gossip, rumors, and exclusion are essentially forms of social power. It can be a gratifying way of dealing with the inevitable vulnerability of joining the peer tribe: By making others smaller, you'll seem bigger by comparison. This may work in the short term, but in the long run, it can create persistent problems in interpersonal relationships. Although we know that kids learn from social experience rather than those cautionary tales and pearls of wisdom conferred by parents, once "mean" behavior comes into play, intervention from the adult world is necessary to ensure lessons are learned and harm is prevented.

Peers can be cruel in both direct and indirect ways. "Indirect" social aggression refers to doing damage to relationships or social status through circuitous or emotionally damaging means, such as spreading rumors and outright social rejection. It can include gestures like eye rolling, aggressive humor or teasing, and overt hostility. This type of cruelty is more common among girls; direct, physical aggression is much more common among boys. Because crime and violence are such significant problems among teen boys, their indirect social aggression has probably been underemphasized; likewise, a focus on physical aggression in girls has probably lagged far behind reality. Recent awareness about bullying among both girls and boys may turn the tide of research and begin amending for some of these oversights.

There is much more to social aggression than plain meanness and grasping for power. In any one awful incident, there are often a multitude of factors to consider, ranging from the intensity of the incident; the perpetrator's intent to harm; the victim's perception of harm; the type of harm inflicted (e.g., to friendships, social standing, self-esteem, as well as physical harm or property damage) and whether it took a direct or indirect form; if the aggression was reactive versus proactive; and whether the act was perpetrated under the influence of "hot" emotion or "cold" calculation (Underwood 2003).

It might surprise you to learn that when children gossip, it is rarely with the intent of hurting a peer (McDonald et al. 2007). Kids vent. They establish solidarity. They analyze what they like and dislike in others. Gossip helps kids navigate social norms. It may be mean to talk about a girl's ugly haircut or babyish voice, but it can be helpful to know that it is unattractive to speak with your mouth full, to pick your nose, or to always talk about oneself. Kids' whispers can be weapons, but they can also be morality tales, not unlike the stories in tabloids.

BULLYING

Bullying gets a lot of press these days—with good reason—but it is important to understand that not all mean interactions between kids constitute bullying. Specifically, bullying refers to a pattern of physical or psychological torment enacted on a person of unequal physical strength, personal power, or age. Bullying can apply to verbal, physical, and social forms of aggression, and it can be as harmful in the online world as the real one. Yet the distinction between bullying and other forms of aggression bears repeating: Bullying is a *pattern* of behavior, and bullying always occurs between people of unequal power.

In large samples, up to 30 percent of respondents report feeling bullied at some point during their childhood or adolescence (Nansel et al. 2001). Bullying usually peaks between sixth and eighth grade, and involves more than schoolyard beatings; the most common forms of bullying are delivered verbally or via exclusionary behaviors.

Studies have shown that social aggression can be just as harmful as physical aggression, and even disrupt neurobiological functioning. Researchers studying twelve-year-olds who had been bullied discovered disruptions in the levels of cortisol, a hormone that is released during stressful events (Vaillancourt et al. 2010). Brain scans also revealed that young adults who were bullied during adolescence display abnormalities in an area of the brain associated with learning, visual processing, and memory (the *corpus callosum*, part of the midbrain, which connects the right and left hemispheres).

Researchers speculate that there could be a link between the intense stress experienced from bullying and a negative impact on the immune system, academic abilities, and neural growth in the memory centers in the brain (Vaillancourt et al. 2010). The long-range impact of bullying is inarguable. These researchers speculated that emotional abuse from peers during adolescence could turn out to be as damaging to a child's mental health as emotional abuse by parents.

ESSENTIAL
FACT

Impacts of Bullying
Victims of bullying may experience a negative impact on their immune systems, their academic abilities, and the neural growth in the memory centers of their brains.

Essentially, psychological bullying can hurt as much as sticks and stones, and given the choice, many would choose latter any day. The fact that many kids never report bullying, enduring it with little or no support for so long, isn't surprising given the developmental importance of peers, the hours spent with peers, the privacy among teens about their social lives, and the shame around bullying that prevents teens from confiding in adults.

Recent research on the subject, and a number of tragic teen suicides caused by intense bullying, has resulted in tremendous pressure on schools to take an active role in prevention efforts. Since a negative school climate has been identified as a risk factor for bullying (Orpinas and Horne 2005), school-based prevention programs are essential to build a culture of trust and fairness. And schools that already have programs in place that emphasize social and emotional learning have a leg up, since they prioritize the importance of feelings, interpersonal relationships, and pro-social behaviors.

Schools can't do it all, though. One hopes that with increased community-wide awareness of the bullying issue, parents and other adults can partner with teachers to encourage teens to take an active role in confronting bullies, supporting targeted peers, and getting help for each when needed. Teens, with the support of adults in their lives, need to promote kind behavior, inclusion, assertiveness, and positive forms of conflict resolution. Since virtually all children and adolescents acknowledge that they have witnessed social aggression, emphasizing the responsibility of the "bystander" to help the victim has been a particularly promising approach to curtailing bullying. Ideally, all students should be active defenders of victims and take the initiative to help loners who are targeted.

ESSENTIAL
ACTIVITY

Knowing When to Intervene

Knowing when let your child fight some of her own battles (with the help of your wise-minded coaching) is a learned art, and most parents can readily call to mind at least a few times when they haven't gotten it right. The scenarios below give you a chance to flex your wise-minded muscles.

1. Your daughter tells you another kid is always giving her mean looks in math class because she won't share her homework. You should:

   a. call the teacher tonight.

   b. tell her to just ignore it.

   c. suggest your child use humor as a way to deflect the aggressive behavior: "I know I'm good looking, but your eyes are boring a hole in my head," or, "Take a picture! It will last longer."

The wise-minded answer is C. In this scenario, a dose of humor is called for as a frontline defense to low-level meanness. Going straight to the teacher is an overreaction, but being dismissive of your child's discomfort by suggesting she ignore the staring isn't respectful of her emotional state, nor will it discourage the behavior.

2. **Your daughter is part of a tight group whose history goes back to elementary school. Recently, a member of this group had a slumber party, didn't invite your daughter, and then lied to cover it up. You:**

   a. ask your daughter how she would like to handle this. Discuss whether she wants to talk to the girls about it, and, if so, how she might want to go about that.

   b. call the parents. Your child deserves better treatment from these girls. Doesn't anyone remember the Golden Rule?

   c. tell your daughter not to overreact. This happens—it happened to you, too, when you were a kid. She needs to broaden her pool of friends and learn to roll with the punches of group inclusion.

   Wise parent, did you select A? If so, you are following your instinct to support your child's wishes in navigating this painful exclusion. This is a good moment for a little Socratic listening as you seek insight into what this really means to her. Is she afraid of losing her connection to the group? Or merely miffed at the social slight? What does she have riding on this group's acceptance? Again, you are hitting the sweet spot between overreaction (calling the mom) and dismissiveness ("these things happen").

3. **You just checked your high-school-age son's Facebook page and found that three of his friends had posted photos of themselves making hideous faces and giving the finger. Your kid says it's just a joke, but you think he's actually hurt. You:**

   a. call the boys' parents immediately. That's cyberbullying, after all.

   b. tell your son to "unfriend" those kids until they clean up their behavior.

   c. suggest your son call the friends on their behavior by posting something witty but direct on his Facebook wall ("I wonder if your future employer will see this someday"). Help him brainstorm.

   Here, the wise-minded parent chooses C. By choosing the middle path (not overreacting and not being dismissive), and then offering guidance that will give your child a way to stick up for himself without destroying important social connections, the boy keeps both his dignity and his friends, and doesn't compound the problem by seeking pity.

4. **Your son comes home from school and tells you that some kids in PE have been calling him gay because he's not athletic. You:**

   a. e-mail the coach about your concerns. He'll put a stop to it!

   b. help your son craft a retort that feels good to him. It can take a humorous bent that is clever and not defensive, or a more assertive takedown about anti-gay insinuations ("Haven't you heard? Being anti-gay is totally ignorant these days. Get with it!").

   c. coach your kid to tell the others that they are being mean and disrespectful, and that it really hurts his feelings.

Here, the best course is B, because it allows your son to address the problem directly, without drawing more fire by snitching or direct confrontation. The best retorts are friendly and witty, and throw the taunting peers off balance. If you can get a laugh, you've essentially disarmed the aggressor. There are 101 suggestions for comeback lines on the Bullystoppers website (bullystoppers.com); not all will apply to your child's situation, but they might get the creative juices flowing.

5. **For the third day in a row, your daughter is crying and doesn't want to go to school because a guy in her math class always rubs the inside of her leg and says, "You know you love it," and everybody laughs. He has continued to do this despite her telling him not to. You:**
   a. let her skip math until you can get her transferred into another math class.
   b. tell her to tell him that if he does it again, she'll tell on him.
   c. go with her that day to school and talk to the administration.

C is the wise-minded approach in this case. This is a situation that calls for involvement. Though your daughter might beg you not to, don't cave; she needs your support and that of the school administration to deal with this harassment. If something significant isn't done to stop this boy's behavior, he will continue to do this, and not just to your daughter. What should happen next? After you talk to the school administrators, they should call the boy's parents. The boy needs to understand how serious his behavior is. Remember that, as bad as this behavior seems, if he were your son, you'd want this to be handled very sensitively, giving him the benefit of the doubt first. After all, he might just be naive to the implications of his actions.

Now take a moment to turn this entire exercise on its head, for a little parental humility training. Imagine in each scenario that your child is the wrongdoer. How does that temper your reaction? Parental outrage can change on a dime. When your child is wronged socially, it's important to remember that even the best kids will experiment with power and social status, and do stupid and hurtful things on their messy, messy journey to social competence. **Remember that a child who's accused of doing evil when he was just being naive or stupid has had real harm done to him.**

CYBERBULLYING

Like a turbo version of regular bullying, cyberbullying takes tween and teen cruelty to new heights, thanks to three unique features:
   • constant opportunity through online access
   • anonymity
   • high-volume exposure

Cyberspace is a perfect breeding ground for mean behavior, offering all kinds of outlets for young people without established brain capacity for impulse control. As in the schoolyard, the full spectrum of social cruelty plays out online, too, with nasty name calling between friends or peers at one end ("You are such a slut to steal my boyfriend like you did"), and the anonymous terrorizing by groups against a vulnerable child (in what amounts to a hate crime) at the other. Here, bullies can use texting and social media to do what they have always done much more easily, frequently, and anonymously. The children and teens who engage in cyberbullying tend also to be involved in more traditional forms of social cruelty (Perren et al. 2010).

If you think your child is safe or exempt, think again: A major 2011 survey revealed just how ubiquitous social media is. Ninety-five percent of teens ages twelve to seventeen are now online; and 80 percent of online teens are users of social-media sites. Eighty percent of these users say they have defended a victim of meanness online at some time. But 21 percent—more than one out of five—of teen social-media users say they have personally joined in the harassment of others online (Pew Research Center 2011).

Victims of cyberbullying report the same depressive symptoms as those who are being physically or psychologically bullied in person. It is as yet unclear if victims of cyberbullying suffer the same long-term negative consequences as victims of more traditional forms of harassment do. However, with the ubiquity of phones wired for Internet and social-media access, it is not hard to imagine that the growing trend of impulsive meanness perpetrated through online delivery systems will result in some of these same long-lasting negative consequences for many tweens and teens.

You may think you have a handle on your child's cyber life, but do you? Cyber education is a lot like sex education: Most parents say they do it, but they don't. And we're way past the time when a parent can get away with saying, "I'm a techie dinosaur," while letting their kids have unfettered access to the Internet, social media, and cell phones. If you do not understand the media, then ask your child to show you how Facebook, Twitter, Formspring, texting, and any other social-media arena they play in works. Then put some serious thought into—and then clearly articulate—your house rules around this issue. For middle schoolers, consider filters, or call in an expert to set up a system that works specifically for you and your values. You'll find excellent websites to help you do this in the resources section of this book.

ESSENTIAL TOOL

The TECH Method of Social-Media Safety

Here's a handy acronym that will help you remember a simple action plan for monitoring your teen's cyber life:

Take time to learn it.
Exercise control over it—make and follow rules.
Consider tracking and filtering it.
Harness the best and zap the rest!

ESSENTIAL
TIP

Staying Safe Online

To stay safe with social media, teach your kids to:
- refuse to pass along cyberbully messages;
- tell friends to stop cyberbullying;
- block communication with cyberbullies and delete messages from bullies without reading them;
- never post or share personal information online (including full name, address, telephone number, school name, parents' names, credit card, or Social Security numbers);
- never share their Internet passwords with anyone except you;
- talk to you about their life online;
- never put anything online—even in e-mail—that they wouldn't want all their classmates to see;
- never send messages when they're angry; and
- always be as polite online as they are in person.

All it takes is one incident of poor judgment to upend your child's whole life. An impulsive posting on a classmate's Facebook page, and your child could be accused of sexual harassment (e.g., "Hey, nice boobs!") or bullying (e.g., "Your picture is so ugly!"). Tweens need an adult's supervision until they get the hang of life in cyber land. And if your teen has a thrill-seeking personality, get ready to supervise their online life for a long time.

Dating and Romance

A central part of social development is the emergence of romantic relationships. Sexual attraction combines with intense feelings of love to create an emotional experience that greatly affects many aspects of a teen's life. Romantic experiences are more pervasive and begin earlier than many of us probably realize. In a review of national survey data collected on adolescent behavior, 25 percent of twelve-year-olds admitted to a romantic relationship over the past eighteen months; as did 50 percent of fifteen-year-olds, and 70 percent of eighteen-year-olds (Barber 2006). While kids younger than fourteen reported relationships that lasted just a few weeks, duration increased with age; by age eighteen, relationships lasted for a year or longer.

Most boys and girls do not veer much off the path that begins with socializing among friends and leads to romantic experiences (Connolly et al. 2004). The route is pretty well-worn: Same-sex socializing merges into mixed-sex socializing, and at some point, pairing up occurs. Friends serve as facilitators, supporters, and brokers, as younger adolescents start negotiating their way on this journey. Gender differences emerge in areas you might expect, given that girls are socially and emotionally more expressive and become pubescent earlier than boys (by about two years). Girls create social contexts so that romantic interests can flourish, and hone the intimacy skills they bring to the romantic process (e.g., self-disclosure, active support, communication of feelings). Another sex difference is that girls are much more likely to date older partners than boys are, which can result in problems with coercion and other sexual consequences, legal age of consent, and deception of parents.

The terminology tweens and teens use about love, romance, and sex can be quite confusing for parents trying to get a handle on what's going on in their tween's or teen's romantic life, however. Expressions like "going out" and "hanging out" can mean anything from middle schoolers texting about liking someone, with no face-to-face interaction whatsoever, to a sexually intimate, long-term relationship. Likewise, "hookups" are usually onetime flings, with no commitment, but can refer to anything from kissing to sexual intercourse and everything in between.

Because teens socialize in groups and emphasize friendship, parents are often thrown off guard when they learn from others that their teen is involved in a romantic relationship. Fluidity, ambiguity, and uncertainty seem to characterize the relationship patterns of teens, and parents are often in the dark about what's really happening. But if a secure attachment is intact in your family, then your emotional closeness, the value you place on independence in relationships, and your open communication are likely to be transferred to your teen's own romantic relationships. Research shows that secure attachment in childhood is predictive of mutual caring, emotional investment, trust, and intimacy with a romantic partner in young adulthood (Mayseless and Scharf 2007). The reverse is also true: Kids who have negative relationships with their parents can bring hostility, avoidance, coerciveness, and aggression to their romances.

Since romance often involves sexual activity, parents frequently give short shrift to the *meaning* of a particular romantic relationship, and instead react to fears about sexual behavior. Given the health implications of teen sexuality (more on this in chapter 7), this is understandable. However, the intense feelings of love and loss felt by a vulnerable teen in a romantic relationship deserve attention, too. In the same way that newfound security and trust in a relationship can bring happiness and comfort, the dissolution of one can be devastating.

All the scary components of teen dating may leave you hoping your child doesn't even think about it until college. Why not wait until after graduation? What's the hurry? While frequent dating is associated with greater parent-child conflict, research has also found that active monitoring by parents, when combined with a positive attachment between teen and parent, leads to high-quality experiences for teens who are romantically involved (Kan et al. 2008). Once your child is away at college or living on his own, your opportunities to monitor, guide, commiserate, bake cookies, and soothe—in short, have any influence at all—shrink to almost nil. And teens who don't date often express regret and sometimes confess to anxieties over competence and attractiveness.

But starting too young presents problems, too; young teens have fewer of the personal resources needed for dealing with the complex realm of relationships. And when young teens date older peers, a whole host of psychosocial risks can present themselves, including more sexual activity, socializing with more risk-taking peers, and delinquency (Connolly et al. 2000).

THE DRAW OF FORBIDDEN LOVE

While dating is bound by ethnic, racial, and religious mores, forbidden love is everywhere—and is dealt with by parents in many different (often ineffective) ways. Let's eavesdrop on a well-meaning mom as she confronts her fifteen-year-old daughter on a common teen-romance problem. The conversation is in the left-hand column; the underlying dymanics are on the right. See if you can spot her (understandable) mistakes in this exchange:

Mom: Are you meeting up with Seth at the mall?	*Mom is doing her monitoring duty.*
Cammy: Maybe. It's just going to be the usual hanging out.	*Cammy is doing her best to shake Mom.*
Mom: Cammy, you know the rules. You need to tell me whom you're going to be with, or you can't go, and that's it. I can tell by your dodginess that you're probably meeting up with Seth.	*Mom needs to ask herself, "Is it helpful or necessary to remind Cammy of the rule right now? Does this open up conversation and understanding, or close it down?"*
Cammy: Don't do this to me, Mom! I'm fifteen! You treat me like a baby. You know how things are. I have no idea who's going to show up!	*Cammy, like many teens at fifteen, feels like the tracking of her whereabouts is ridiculous. Also, she's right; teen plans don't often solidify until the last minute.*
Mom: Honey, it's reasonable that I'm concerned. With Seth's school problems and pot use, I just don't think you know the risks you're taking. Like right now. I bet you are meeting up with him at the mall so you can go somewhere else and be alone, like you've done before.	*Again, Mom is probably right on every point. However, she is not effective in either negotiating the evening's plans or connecting on concerns about Seth.*
Cammy: Are you going to talk about that forever? Mom, you are obsessed with stalking me. Can't you get over the fact that you can't control me? You can't stand that I have a boyfriend; especially one you think isn't good enough for me. You are a total snob.	*It is clear that Mom and Cammy have divergent "stories" in their minds: Mom's is one of care and concern, and Cammy believes her mother wants to control her and keep her away from her boyfriend.*

Mom:	I'm just doing my job. I only track your social life because I care about you. You are not mature enough to understand the risks you are taking.	*Again, Mom is sincere and probably right. But she is not accomplishing her goal of having Cammy think about her choices.*
Cammy:	You hate Seth. You would do anything to break us up. And you don't even know him.	*Strong accusations are power moves and tend to derail the sparring partner.*
Mom:	You're right, I don't really know Seth, because you refuse to let me meet him.	*One retort begets another.*

Cammy and her mother are struggling with a classic dating dilemma. Mom has every right to know the whereabouts of her daughter, especially if Cammy has violated her trust before. But Cammy is in love (and older than Juliet Capulet was, and we all know how that turned out!). Parents can't "reason" their kids out of love, even with accurate information about undesirable factors and declarations of parental good intentions.

What's a wise-minded parent to do? Instead of trying to impress upon Cammy how reasonable it is to expect that her whereabouts will be monitored, and how poor a choice Seth is as a boyfriend, Mom needs to accept that she can't control Cammy's feelings. Second, since Cammy believes that Mom "hates" Seth, it's up to Mom to admit that she doesn't really know Seth, has prejudged him, possibly unfairly, and even apologize. Apologies are disarming when they come from a parent who has been perceived as domineering. It may nudge both sides away from their adversarial positions enough to open up communication channels. Toss in some empathy, and Mom may even negotiate a deal. Let's see how this might play out if Mom takes a break—maybe takes a walk or a hot shower—and then tries a different approach.

Take Two:

Mom:	I'm sorry, Cammy. You are right on several counts. I heard a couple of things about Seth and prejudged him. I don't know him at all, and I would really like to meet him. If you have chosen him, there must be a lot of good there.	*Teens love to be told they are right. Mom didn't defend her right to judge, but instead admitted that she prejudged. It allows her to make the transition to her desire to meet him, and she sweetens the bid with a sincere compliment.*
Cammy:	Yeah, you and your gossipy moms' groups. You are complete hypocrites. You have your little lectures about tolerance and all that crap, and then you sit back and freak if guys aren't as straitlaced as you are!	*Like all people who feel wronged, Cammy needs to rant a bit before she'll be able to accept Mom's apology. Not only that, she's indignant because she's got a point!*

Mom:	I know. That "mother bear" thing can make us worried about stuff that we think might take our kids off a good path. You are absolutely right.	*Mom frames the problem as protectiveness and worry, which allows her to validate Cammy again.*
Cammy:	Why would I want you to meet Seth when you've already skewered him and made him into a loser?	*Once again, Cammy has a point. Parents need to eat a lot of crow to earn the right of redemption in a teen's view.*
Mom:	Look, honey, here's a proposal. You invite Seth over for dinner, and we talk about how, when, and where you can spend time together.	*Mom is negotiating shrewdly. Instead of demands and rules, she is offering a deal: parental access to Seth for Cammy's access to Seth.*
Cammy:	No way! Subject him to dinner here? One of your wholesome little family interviews of my friends? Sounds like torture.	*Teens often think that honest interest in their friends is an interrogation.*
Mom:	OK, how about pizza at the counter, no more than five friendly questions and twenty minutes? Then you two get two hours in the den with the door open.	*Humor and deft bargaining are big assets for Mom here. She has sidestepped the digs and moved to some horse trading.*
Cammy:	Get rid of my little brother for the night, make it three nonpersonal questions, no more than fifteen minutes, and you have a deal.	*They've struck at a win-win. Cammy gets to see Seth with parental approval (at least this time). Most teens don't really enjoy lying and deception. And Mom will have more influence by being open-minded.*

Why should Mom give up trying to ban Seth? Every parent has to make her own decision about where to draw the line with her teen's romantic partners (e.g., violence, a rap sheet, older by two years or more), but parents need to face the fact that controlling love is virtually impossible. Not to be overly dramatic, but love is dramatic—it's one of the most intense emotions known to humans. Trying to stop it is like trying to stop a bullet train. Attempts to derail it can actually intensify attraction and drive a wedge into the best of family relationships. That said, dangerous situations require immediate interventions, but that's a very personal cost/benefit/risk analysis for each parent to make.

You may have heard the phrase "The brain in love is a brain on cocaine." Research has shown that the neurochemical associated with pleasure, dopamine, floods the brain under both circumstances (Aron et al. 2005). The brain is triggered when the desired target—cocaine or the truly beloved—is thought of, within reach, or even just associated with some cue in the environment. A person in love can be triggered by a favorite song, a memory, or even a smell. As part of our survival mechanism, deep in the emotional brain, our desire centers trigger us to seek out the object of our affection. While food and sex are the essential targets, love and drugs are in the target range as well. When food, addictions, or love are denied, our navigational systems turn cravings into obsessions.

Why did Mom focus on meeting Seth as part of her deal making? Mom gets several benefits from this deal: She gets to size him up for herself, so that she can perhaps get past her prejudgment; she gives relief to her daughter, who is in love and willing to drive a huge wedge in their family life; she enhances her relationship with Cammy, because Cammy now feels respected and understood; and by pulling Seth into the picture, he might even become an ally.

Kids don't usually want to deceive parents. Cammy is not really happy about hiding her boyfriend, or lying and conniving in order to see him. Kids almost always want to make things better, because children naturally seek approval from their parents. The huge majority of kids who are having conflicts with their parents want to find a solution. Wise-minded parents seek a way out of this mutual unhappiness, and Cammy's mother did a masterful job of kick-starting this process.

Additionally, unless Seth is a real cad (and c'mon—Cammy wouldn't sink that low!), he probably wants the acceptance and respect of Cammy's parents. Frequently, that desire for respect makes your kid's romantic partners motivated to follow the rules; after all, they're not the ones individuating from you! Enlisting the trust and cooperation of the partners is a great strategy. There is a good chance that Seth wants to make things better, too.

Not only does the research show that taking a collaborative approach with teens about their romantic life is best, but it makes good sense in our wise-minded parenting framework. By staying connected, realistic, and trusted by our kids, we are in a position to negotiate effectively with them about parameters, such as rules and monitoring. Teens may not be thrilled by either, but when they see their parents flex to understand their feelings and accommodate something as important as romantic love, they will usually meet you partway.

Identity Development

In chapter 1, we touched on the crucial adolescent task of identity formation and how it relates to your child's burgeoning sense of self. It's the "Who I am?" question teens so often ask, using their newfound cognitive abilities to scrutinize their own unique talents, personalities, social groups, race, and culture. They also begin to question the values that they have been raised with—your values!—and examine alternative ideas from their peers as they begin to explore new ideological frameworks.

In the nearly fifty years since renowned American developmental psychologist Erik Erikson first claimed that identity is the central developmental task of adolescence (Erikson 1968), researchers and clinicians have been tweaking the theory, making it more culturally sensitive, evidence based, and accurate. But the bottom line remains: Teens draw upon the many physical, cognitive, and social changes and experiences they go through as part of their identity exploration. Their new abstract reasoning abilities allow them to think about the future, imagine different life courses, and experiment with various ideologies in an effort to define their unique identities.

Making Things Better
The huge majority of kids who are having conflicts with their parents want to find a solution.

THE IDENTITY FORMATION PROCESS

Although the concept of identity and the "Who am I?" process can sound mushy to parents, hundreds of studies have been done about the identity formation process. Canadian developmental psychologist James Marcia identified four stages that teens experience as they progress to the ultimate goal of identity achievement—while taking religion, politics, and sexuality into account (Marcia et al 1993).

1. Teens in the **foreclosure** stage are not questioning or exploring values yet; they are still committed to their childhood values ("I believe what my parents believe"). Young people in the foreclosure stage score the highest in levels of authoritarianism, need for social approval, dependency, and reliance on parents. They are foreclosed, which means they haven't been investing in this home of theirs—their adolescent self—so they don't really "own it" yet. They have given over the individuation process to other "authorities" and are living the unexamined life.

2. The **identity diffusion** stage involves no firm commitments and no exploration ("I don't know what I believe and I'm not exploring my values right now"). Teens in this stage are confused. They aren't comfortable with the values handed to them by their parents, but they aren't engaged in the scrutiny process either. These teens can be rudderless and disconnected.

3. Teens in the **moratorium** stage are exploring new ideas and values, but are not committed ("I don't know what I believe, but I'm investigating options and not automatically accepting my parents' values"). Not surprisingly, kids in the moratorium stage score highest on measures of anxiety and rebelliousness, because they are in the midst of throwing off the dominant paradigms of their childhoods. But a good feature of this stage is that kids in the moratorium stage are the least rigid and authoritarian.

4. The **identity achievement** stage is characterized by successful development of one's own identity after a period of exploration, crisis, and commitment ("I have a complex value system customized by me from all of my social experiences"). Why is this important? Teens who have engaged in this identity formation process and reached the "identity achievement" stage are psychologically healthier than other teens in a variety of indicators. They score the highest on measures of achievement motivation, moral reasoning, relationship skills, emotional self-awareness, and career-goal setting.

ESSENTIAL
FACT
The Questioning Question
When teens explore values related to their identity formation, they can create upheaval in their own and their parents' lives, but they are happier and healthier than teens who shut down all questioning.

This research should come as a comfort to parents, especially those whose kids seem to relish questioning everything that they hold sacred, experimenting with values they may even find offensive, and engaging in behaviors that may be risky. After all, you can't examine identity questions without doing some actual exploration, and that means experimentation, analysis, questioning, and ruling some values "out" and some "in" along the way. Just as software cannot be developed without some bugs and crashes, a teen can't emerge at age twenty (or more realistically, twenty-five) with a set of tried, true, and personally authentic values without some of the same. All parents should anticipate some upheaval and conflict, both internally and externally, during this crucial identity-formation phase.

Most people don't arrive in the identity achievement phase until their late teens and early twenties. Kids this age have a basic set of values, though they continually make adjustments as they progress through life and have experiences that shape their ideologies. Our values usually end up as some combination of those of our parents and culture, our personal exploration process, and our generational influences. Young people slide around from stage to stage, but are twice as likely to progress forward to achievement than regress backward as they explore their values and identities during adolescence (Kroger et al. 2010).

What kinds of parents are most likely to raise kids who reach the healthy status of identity achievement? If you're thinking "authoritative," you're right. These parents are warm, encourage individuality, and support independent thinking (Grotevant and Cooper 1985). They are not permissive, but respectful of their teens' right to different beliefs. They apply their wise-minded skills and empathy as guides through tough teen exploration moments. Conversely, the teens who have the most difficulty with the identity formation process are those from homes lacking warmth, connection, and support for psychological autonomy.

Kids form their ethnic and cultural identities in a similar fashion, via a process of exploration, flux, and decision making (Phinney 1990). Very early in life, kids don't question or analyze what it means to be African-American, Hispanic-American, Chinese-American, etc. But as their cognitive processes mature, they start comparing themselves to the majority culture, ponder the implications, and usually experience a "crisis" as they process these unsettling feelings. Teens may start to identify with members of their ethnic group, turning away from the majority culture as a defense against vulnerability and as an affirmation of who they are. As the pride of belonging to their group is realized, they are often able to navigate back into the dominant culture, this time with a strong identification with their ethnic or racial heritage in place. Parents can foster this "ethnic socialization" by encouraging a positive identification with their culture and an awareness of racism, with a context for how to live within the dominant culture with pride and dignity.

The process of figuring out one's feelings about gender roles, personal religious beliefs, and sexual identity are similar to ethnic socialization. As preteens enter the social world with their new abstracting abilities, females often ask, "Am I supposed to be thin? Nice? Subordinate to males?" And males may wonder, "Am I supposed to be competitive? Ambitious? Aggressive? Suppress vulnerable feelings?" And if these kids don't conform to gender stereotypes, they might ask, "Will my friends still accept me if I don't act like a boy (or girl) is supposed to?" Kids who are questioning their family's religious beliefs may wonder, "Will my parents accept me if I question their doctrines?" "Is it OK to have a different faith than my family and friends?" "What does it mean for my future if I follow my family's beliefs?"

Likewise, for a young adolescent who feels attraction to peers of the same sex, it is natural to ask, "What does it mean if I'm gay?" "Am I acceptable to the majority culture, my parents, my friends, and to myself?" "What are the implications of belonging to this group?" "What does it mean if I'm a lesbian, as well as the daughter of first-generation Cambodian immigrants, and from a conservative, religious family?" "Will I lose connection with my family if I'm gay?" "Will I succeed in the world and be able to have a family of my own?"

In groups whose membership demands strict conformity and obedience, kids often struggle more with establishing a healthy identity (especially if they don't fit the mold) than do their peers from more flexible environments. It may seem desirable to postpone exploration and the questioning of values ("foreclosure"), but what is the cost? Obviously, individual differences play a major role, but research tells us that there is a huge psychological cost in trying to act like someone you are not.

DEVELOPMENTAL ASSETS

There has been an impressive amount of research done on the "developmental pathways" of teens growing up in diverse circumstances, in an attempt to alter the course of those who are at risk (Hawkins and Catalano 1992; Masten and Coatsworth 1998). Some researchers have even defined the concept of adolescent health as an "absence of pathologies" (Boorse 1977), rather than a presence of thriving. But, according to research done by psychologist Peter Benson, the best model for optimal social development emphasizes a confluence of support systems—springing from people, places, and institutions—that come together to help a young person thrive (Benson et al. 1999).

Peter Benson's survey introduced forty "developmental assets," which are really the building blocks of social and emotional development for adolescents. This pioneering framework is one of the most widely used approaches for the assessment of positive youth development in the United States. The assets are grouped into categories, such as "empowerment" and "boundaries," and include items such as a caring school climate, family boundaries, honesty, responsibility—and even reading for pleasure!

Building Blocks of Social and Emotional Development
Take a moment to visit the survey on the Search Institute's website
(*search-institute.org/developmental-assets/lists*). Print out the survey and then
note a few of the assets that you'd like to work on developing with your teen,
one action you will take toward that end, and when you'll begin that work.

Asset	Action	When

WHY YOU SHOULD WELCOME A LITTLE STRIFE

Among those who study adolescent development, there is an oft-repeated phrase: "Problem-free is not fully prepared" (Pittman et al. 2001). While no parent wishes for problems, teens develop social competencies by undergoing challenges with friends in a range of social contexts, making decisions in complicated circumstances, having diverse relationships, and experiencing events that galvanize them to action for a purposeful life. The goal is for teens to develop with a balance of support and challenge.

Parents sometimes underestimate the anxiety felt by teens as they attempt to negotiate their social worlds without a full toolbox of skills. Social bruises are frequent and painful—and kids are going to blow it occasionally or even often. But that's necessary, because venturing forth in the social world is critical. We draw strength from others. It is the responsibility of parents and other adults to help teens attain their positive goals through social connections that provide joy and gratification. The biggest obstacle to social resilience (utilizing friends or peers to cope with stress) is not just exclusion from social groups, but also the belief that social connections are harmful, threatening, or painful. It falls to the parent to help their teen find opportunities to establish and maintain positive friendships and learn the skills necessary for riding the waves of good times and bad times, and the troughs in between.

ESSENTIAL
ACTIVITY

Your Teen's Social World

Take a moment to think about the different social groups your teen is currently a part of. What strengths do you imagine your teen draws from each group? Are there important strengths missing from the picture? If so, note three new groups you'd like to encourage your teen to join in the next year. For instance, if your child is on numerous athletic teams, but doing nothing to help the less fortunate, look for some volunteer opportunities. For a variety of reasons (which we will get into in chapter 7), all teens should be involved in at least one athletic endeavor at all times. After you've done some thinking on this subject, brainstorm with your teen on what other possibilities exist to expand her social horizons.

Current Group	Strengths

Possible New Group	Strengths

From Social Caterpillars to Social Butterflies

As children move into their tween and teen years, their peer interactions are increasingly characterized by sophisticated social skills, new social roles, and novel experiences. Being liked is an advantage for kids, as is having high-quality friendships. What is less important is having a multitude of acquaintances or Facebook "friends." While there are plenty of kind and popular teens who manage popularity with grace, research indicates that it can also lead to more risk taking and social aggression. Unfortunately, the problems that arise from interactions in the peer world create a negative lens through which parents often view teen socializing, but teens offer each other many versions of positive modeling, too. They offer valuable feedback about self-absorption, hypocrisy, the dangers of taking risks, and school underachievement, ultimately influencing the development of a unique identity.

Teens from diverse ethnic and cultural backgrounds will examine their differences from the majority teen culture and hopefully create a positive identity through that exploration. Immigrant families often work hard to instill their cultural traditions and values in their teens, while encouraging them to pursue new opportunities. But whatever their culture of origin, teens have always pushed the values envelope in their quest to claim their generational era as their own.

Take the rebelliousness with a grain of salt. One of the biggest misconceptions parents have about teenagers is that they need to be cut loose to explore their yearnings for freedom and identity. Don't believe it! Teens need to be in the social world to establish their identity and become successful in many social roles, but they do this best with ongoing parental support, monitoring, and connection. Parents also benefit from all of this hard work; they get to watch the evolution of an increasingly competent, unique young person. A butterfly will emerge. Probably not the one you saw through the starry eyes of early parenthood, but one who will really impress you, nonetheless.

CHAPTER 5

Emotional Flourishing

Scene: *It's time to break some bad news to your eighth-grader. Her grandmother's seventy-fifth birthday celebration has just been scheduled, and it's the same night as the middle school dance. Your tween has been looking forward to this dance for weeks, but the family gathering has to take precedence. You know she is going to be very disappointed; you decide to tell her one night after dinner.*

> Dad: *Honey, I need to let you know that Grandma's birthday party is going to be this Saturday night.*
>
> Lily: *What? Nooooo! That's the night of the big dance!*
>
> Dad: *I'm sorry, Lil, but you'll have to miss the dance. This is Grandma's party, and the whole family is going to be there.*
>
> Lily: *No! I can't miss the dance! All of my friends are going to be there! I'm not going to Grandma's stupid party!*
>
> Dad: *Whoa! Geez. Calm down. It's not the end of the world. There will be other dances. You'll go to the next one.*
>
> Lily: *(yelling) Why are you doing this to me? I hate you! (Stomps foot, throws backpack across the room, scattering books and papers everywhere, then runs from the room.)*
>
> Dad: *(yelling at Lily's receding back) You come back here and clean up this mess!*

Ah, the zero-to-sixty surge of adolescent emotions. Know it yet? If not, you will soon. Moderately disappointing news can suddenly provoke a disproportionate reaction in your tween or teen—a reaction that feels upsetting at best, or frightening and out of control at worst. It might happen only occasionally, or you might be one of those parents who lives life on an emotional autobahn, gripping the dashboard as your child floors the accelerator.

These emotional surges can make you wonder about your child's ability to handle future stress, life, *anything*. Is he too sensitive? Is she too angry? Have I raised a total brat? Are these high and low extremes normal? Or is my kid just an emotional wreck?

Like all of the other essentials, developing and maintaining emotional health is a dynamic process. Just how healthy and well adjusted your child is depends on multiple factors, some of which are beyond your control, and some of which are not. In this chapter, we will look at the science behind emotions and offer a set of simple, effective tools you can use to help you gain insight into your child's revving emotional engine. Then, you'll learn a few new skills to help you help your child navigate the winding road to emotional health and adjustment.

What Is Emotional Flourishing?

The advantages of good emotional health cannot be overstated. But gauging what "healthy" or "well adjusted" looks like is a challenge, given the inherent moodiness and impulsiveness of the tween and teen years. This decade usually leaves parents scratching their heads, wondering, "Is this normal?"

At its heart, emotional health (which is synonymous with "mental health") means psychological stability in the face of internal and external stress. "Flourishing" connotes living at the higher ranges of emotional health and functioning; those who are flourishing are highly productive, enjoy a good life and positive relationships with others, and cope effectively with emotional setbacks and disappointments (Keyes 2002). As psychologist Corey Keyes has emphasized, mental health is not just the absence of mental illness, but the presence of goodness, growth, purpose, meaning, and happiness. It should be noted that research on flourishing has primarily been conducted with adults; parents should recognize that for tweens and teens, this is a long-term journey. Still, helping your teen reach the upper ranges of emotional health is an important goal. By modeling flourishing for them, and by practicing wise-minded parenting, you'll go a long way to helping them meet that goal, and that's the focus of this chapter.

An individual who is flourishing likely possesses some or all of these strengths:
- emotional intelligence
- social and emotional competence
- optimism
- a sense of well-being
- happiness
- resilience

One look at this list and it's easy to see why emotional health is such an essential for future success. Emotional flourishing arises out of emotional health, creating a sense of well-being that allows a person to fully realize their abilities, cope with stress, be productive, engage with the world, make positive contributions to society, and form and maintain relationships. From the perspective of positive psychology—the field that studies the positive characteristics of mental health—optimal emotional adjustment also includes a person's ability to enjoy life, develop virtues, and find meaning and purpose in the world.

> ESSENTIAL
> ## FACT
> ### Why Emotional Health Matters
> Emotional flourishing arises out of emotional health, creating a sense of well-being that allows a person to fully realize their abilities, cope with stress, be productive, engage with the world, form and maintain relationships, make positive contributions to society, enjoy life, develop virtues, and find meaning and purpose in the world.

Most parents want emotionally healthy children as much as they want scholastic success, but they are often a little hazy about what emotional health looks like and what they can do to help their kids achieve it. Unlike an academic tutor or an SAT prep class, a program to improve mental health is not at every parent's fingertips (or advertised in every parenting or health magazine). But there is a great deal of research that sheds light on this essential quality and your potential role in fostering it in your teen. And whether you realize it or not, you're already off to a good start: The essentials we've already covered—secure attachment, self-control, academic success, and social thriving—are the building blocks of emotional health.

Emotional health comes more easily to some than others; among children nine to seventeen years of age, 21 percent have a diagnosable mental or addictive disorder that causes at least minimal impairment (The Center for Mental Health Services et al. 1999). For those kids, strengthening emotional assets such as resilience and sociability may help protect them from many conditions that could undermine their ability to thrive. Techniques for promoting character strengths such as perseverance and resilience are the focus of the next chapter; everything you do to support a child who suffers from psychological difficulties will help them cope. For every child, having a wise-minded parent who understands the nature of adolescent emotions is a big advantage. To get started on that journey, take the quiz below and assess some of your existing assumptions about emotions.

ESSENTIAL
QUIZ

What's Your Emotion IQ?

True False

1. ☐ ☐ Negative emotions can ruin a child's ability to learn.
2. ☐ ☐ You can assume that children who control their impulses from an early age have more competent parents than those who don't.
3. ☐ ☐ The best way for children to learn moral behaviors is through punishment.
4. ☐ ☐ Parents should let children know that expressions of anger, hatred, and resentment toward family members are unacceptable.
5. ☐ ☐ If they get enough willpower practice as preteens, teens can override their impulsivity during adolescence.
6. ☐ ☐ Emotional intelligence refers to the innate ability some have for "people skills."

You might be surprised to learn that "false" is the correct answer to all of the above. You'll learn more about these common misconceptions and about the science behind teen emotions in the coming pages.

The Nature of Emotions

Emotions define the quality of our human experience. They form the basis for our consciousness and our conscience, our empathy and our caring, and our awareness of and responses to our surrounding environment. Emotions motivate us to accomplish goals, love others, take action, befriend, and solve problems. They inspire us to create art and to be curious. They form the basis of temperament and personality. Emotional warmth, expressiveness, and responsiveness give us the ability to form bonds and take care of the young, the vulnerable, and each other.

Parents who understand the science of emotions will better understand how behaviors are driven by emotions that children and teens simply cannot control. Emotional regulation—the ability to control the expression of intense feelings—improves with age. But even adults have breakdowns in emotional control—just read the news, spend five minutes on YouTube, or mentally review your own worst family moments. It is hypocritical to expect children and teens to have it all together when few adults can make that claim.

The opposite of emotional regulation is *dysregulation*. When tweens and teens are in this state, they do things that many parents misinterpret as bad behavior or as a sign that their child is lagging in moral development. Was Lily, the tween in our opening scene, really being selfish and unloving? Or was she actually flooding emotionally, because she was overwhelmed by disappointment and anxiety about missing a big social occasion? As you may have guessed, it's most likely the latter. Understanding and remembering that there is more to the story than the big emotional blowout is a foundational skill of wise-minded parenting; it's the part that allows for the necessary empathy to plan and execute positive outcomes.

So, before you judge this tween (or your own in a similar situation), remember the wise-minded mantra "She's doing the best she can, given her age, stage, and emotional state." That doesn't mean she can't do better—she needs to, and that's where wise-minded skills come into play. Lily can't really avoid an amygdala hijack (detailed in chapter 2) and the ensuing emotional eruption altogether; but as her brain matures, hormone peaks subside, and she gains some practice and support for regulating her emotions from her wise-minded parents, Lily should be able to control these outbursts over time.

Since emotions trigger reactions quickly—before conscious thought kicks in—they can determine actions before deliberate decision making occurs. When Lily threw her backpack across the room, it was less a "poor choice" than an out-of-control impulse. Telling her that it's "not the end of the world" may be true, but it's dismissive, and neither mindful nor wise-minded. It invalidates her feelings and it proves to her that her dad just doesn't "get it"—doesn't understand how important this dance is to her, which gets her riled up even more. Sometimes, hair-trigger emotional reactions (those amygdala hijacks) save our lives, sometimes they risk lives; most of the time, they just make life messy.

THE PURPOSE OF EMOTIONS

Until fairly recently, emotions weren't a focus of child-development research. Pioneering psychologist Carroll Izard changed that. He organized and investigated principles for understanding the motivation and behavior behind emotions (Izard 2002). According to Izard's groundbreaking research, emotions are inherently adaptive and motivational, meaning that they help us adjust to reality and then inspire us to change it. Both positive and negative feelings serve vital purposes, and we can learn to modulate those feelings to help us prevent harm and promote positive outcomes. An important part of socialization, and a crucial early-childhood skill, is the ability to read internal and external emotional signals accurately.

Izard articulated principles that describe the purpose of both positive and negative emotions; here they are, extrapolated to include examples in teen development:

1. Positive emotions increase sociability, personal well-being, and constructive behaviors. Emotions are unique in capturing our attention, influencing our perceptions, and driving our actions. Curiosity and joy motivate learning and social bonding. Emotions also encourage us to engage in behaviors that help us handle stress in a positive way and inspire us to explore the world, which expands our competence. Emotions such as curiosity and interest drive play, one of the most integral human learning experiences. And, as our children become tweens and teens, play often evolves into exploring the social world in other ways.

2. Negative emotions serve important purposes, as well. Unpleasant feelings of arousal and stress enhance memory and learning at certain levels. This makes sense from an evolutionary perspective: Negative emotions heighten memories of undesirable and often dangerous experiences that we want to avoid repeating. Certain negative feelings also provide the basis for empathy and other positive social behaviors. For instance, when a teen feels guilty after aggressive roughhousing with a friend, he learns to reign in his impulses. When he apologizes to his friend and they both feel better, his empathy is reinforced. Wise-minded parents encourage these natural feelings to shape their teen's behavior.

3. Early in childhood, children begin to have the capacity to exercise "effortful control" over their emotions, which means that they can slow down, focus attention, express themselves appropriately, and lower their voices. Of course, children differ in their ability to exercise effortful control (one kind of self-control), depending on their temperament and genetically predisposed style of emotional expression. Wise-minded parents who "emotion coach"—that is, accept negative emotions and use them as opportunities for guiding behaviors, rather than criticizing or dismissing them—have children who learn to self-regulate more effectively.

4. Different emotions may require different methods to regulate them. Anger, as you'll recall from chapter 2, is triggered in mere milliseconds by the rapid activation of

the amygdala. This does not allow the child time to think through the consequences of her actions. In fact, modulating any extreme emotion via the prefrontal cortex takes time, but practice can help. Impulsive children can learn to control their responses through role-playing rehearsal, which allows them to identify risky situations and plan emotion-control approaches in advance. The CASEL programs discussed in chapter 2 provide such training and help children slow down, identify feelings, and consider problem-solving options.

5. Multiple emotions can occur simultaneously, causing conflicting feelings and difficulties with cognitive processing. A teen who does not express appropriate regret about a selfish behavior may be experiencing scrambled emotions. Wise-minded parents step back and try to appreciate the scramble, taking the time to explore feelings with their child. Frequently, the apology comes later.

6. Children experience emotions about social features of themselves and others through the lens of those around them. Teens naturally size themselves up against others, and may feel superior, inferior, afraid, contemptuous, or confused about mingling with someone of a different race, sexual orientation, or religion. What does "different" mean to the teen? The way adults and peers interpret, support, and guide these feelings and reflections during adolescence will go a long way toward determining how tolerant or intolerant a teen becomes of others' differences—and their own!

7. A child who is emotionally deprived at a young age may suffer a dysfunctional emotion system as a result. Emotionally disturbed parents, maltreatment, trauma, and other emotional harms in childhood disrupt a child's psychological adjustment. Research on parent-child emotional attunement, responsiveness, and attachment quality has demonstrated the importance of emotions to the healthy development of humans.

8. Teens can benefit from bridging the cognitive and emotional systems through a skill called "emotion knowledge," which is the accurate recognition of emotions in oneself and in others. Intervention research has demonstrated that enhancing emotion knowledge and fostering connections between emotions, thoughts, and actions results in better social relationships, mental health, behavioral adjustment, and even academic competence (Greenberg et al. 1995). For instance, a girl who gets caught spreading a rumor about her best friend benefits from understanding the emotions behind her action: envy, worry about her own peer status, desire to curry favor with other peers, the hope that her popularity might rise with the downfall of her friend, or even the desire to become indispensable to her best friend in her time of need. As unsavory as all these feelings, thoughts, and actions are, a process of self-analysis will teach her more about herself—and help her develop her moral compass—than blame and shame will. (Her peer group will probably blame and shame her, anyway!)

It's important to keep in mind that cognitive systems develop slowly through adolescence, and they are often overruled by emotions, which are amped up by hormonal changes. To temper this, kids need to practice putting feelings into words, which will help them interpret their own emotions and those of others. They also need help understanding the complexities of situations that arouse their emotions and figuring out options for constructive problem solving, coping, and self-direction.

How can parents help with this? Techniques for expressing feelings in productive ways are presented in the next section, but first, let's replay the scene at the beginning of this chapter and see how Dad's ability to control his own emotions and understand those of his daughter can help in the heat of the moment, and again later, when it comes time to soothe and repair hurt feelings (because nobody's perfect).

Take Two:

> *Dad: Honey, I need to let you know that Grandma's birthday party is going to be this Saturday night.*
>
> *Lily: What? Nooooo! That's the night of the big dance!*
>
> *Dad: I'm sorry, but you'll have to miss the dance. I know you're disappointed, but this is Grandma's party, and the whole family is going to be there. I understand that your friends are very important to you. You worry you'll miss something important if you're not at that dance.*
>
> *Lily: I will! Everyone is going to be there! Why are you doing this to me? You're ruining my life!*
>
> *Dad: (Voice rising) Look, I am sure that's how it feels.*
>
> *Lily: (Yelling) You don't even care! Don't try to act like you do, because you can't if you are willing to do this! I hate you! (Throws backpack and storms off.)*
>
> *Dad: (Finally losing it) You get back here right now and clean up this mess!*

(A little later…)

> *Dad: I'm sorry I yelled at you. I was feeling riled up by your yelling, and angry about the mess you made when you threw your pack. I know that we were both reacting out of anger.*
>
> *Lily: Yeah. You make me so mad sometimes I can't stand it.*
>
> *Dad: I'm sorry. I need to work on not losing my temper when you do. After all, I'm the adult.*
>
> *Lily: Yeah, you should work on that.*
>
> *Dad: And you were sure angry, too.*
>
> *Lily: Yeah, but for a good reason.*
>
> *Dad: Can you express your anger and disappointment in a different way than throwing your backpack?*
>
> *Lily: How? Screaming? The thing that gets me is how you drop this bomb on me, and then I'm the one in trouble for having a fit about it. You don't get how big this is, Dad!*

Dad: Well, sometimes if you talk about how you feel in a way that helps people under-
      stand you, they'll try to work with you on solutions. Or if there isn't one, at least
      your feelings get heard, instead of people reacting only to the extreme outburst.

Lily: So if I tell you that I love Grandma plenty, but I also feel really, really, really
      strongly about this dance, you might let me go to part of it? Maybe the last
      hour...or two?

Dad: I can't promise you anything. I need to talk to the rest of the family, but
      Grandma likes earlier dinners these days. Just don't badger me about it, and I'll
      get back to you. And look, I do understand that I triggered your blowup by just
      declaring that Grandma's dinner was the priority. In your world, the dance is
      a huge deal.

Lily: Dad, I'm sorry about losing my temper. And please don't tell Grandma I threw
      a fit. You know how much I care about her big birthday year, don't you?

Dad's disarming apology for losing his own temper softened his daughter's response.
And note that he threw in a little emotion coaching when he named Lily's emotions of
anger and disappointment, and then later, when he talked about triggering her blowup.
This exchange shows how open a child can be to resolving a conflict when a parent is
nonjudgmental, encourages an expression of feelings, and demonstrates copious amounts
of empathy. Lily was also reflective, once she had the hope of catching the tail end of
the dance. Regardless of whether the dad decides to let her go, it's perfectly acceptable,
even encouraged, to reward efforts at negotiation and emotional regulation in one way
or another.

ESSENTIAL
TIP

Negative Emotions
Think of negative emotions as opportunities for practicing acceptance, identifying
feelings, and guiding behaviors. If you can refrain from criticizing or being
dismissive, you'll have children who are able to engage with you and work on
self-regulation more effectively.

Emotional Intelligence

Why do so many of us yell at our kids when it would be better to just ignore their
low-level attention-seeking behaviors? Why do we threaten squabbling siblings with
punishment when their feelings of resentment call for emotionally sensitive conversations
and problem solving? Emotions are usually the driver when good adults (and their children)
do irrational and undesirable things. But, they're also why we love, nurture, collaborate,
achieve, create, strive, and thrive. The key is to practice being aware of and using emotions
productively; this is the art of emotional intelligence.

Emotional intelligence, social intelligence, and emotional/social competence are all first cousins (or maybe second cousins, depending on which authors or researchers you read). All of these terms relate to the recognition and management of emotions. Studies show that emotional intelligence allows children and teens to understand and interact well with others, make good decisions, and behave ethically and responsibly. Emotional smarts help children avoid bullying, resist pressures to engage in risky behaviors, and do well in school. Good behavior and even intellectual functioning depend not just on our brains, but on our hearts.

Pioneering psychologists Peter Salovey and John D. Mayer (1990) define emotional intelligence as "the ability to monitor one's own and others' feelings and emotions, discriminate among them, and use this information to guide one's thinking and actions." This concept was later popularized by Daniel Goleman (1995), who expanded the original definition to include a list of such qualities as zeal, persistence, empathy, and communication skills. There has been some controversy in the field, as different researchers come up with different models for emotional intelligence (Mayer et al. 2008), but the standard interpretation is this, based on the original one: Emotional intelligence involves the accurate perception of emotions in self and others, understanding emotions, regulating emotions, and using emotional awareness to facilitate thought and expression.

How important is emotional intelligence? It essentially gives us the ability to understand our social environments and our relationships. Traditional measures of intelligence, such as IQ, are inadequate in explaining why certain individuals are so much more successful than others, *even when they have similar IQ scores*. It's believed that emotional intelligence is a determining factor in all kinds of success.

In fact, studies show that emotional intelligence predicts many aspects of positive adjustment for children, teens, and adults (Mayer et al. 2008). The critical roots of emotional intelligence lie in parental warmth; a loving, empathic parent provides the basis upon which children feel secure in exploring interpersonal relationships with others. A child's scores on emotional intelligence measures have been associated with their ability to show empathy, expressiveness, kind behavior, and social competence (Denham et al. 2003).

In short, emotional intelligence (EQ) correlates with good social and family relations, positive behavioral adjustment, school achievement, and psychological well-being. Since IQ and personality have also been found to predict these positive outcomes for teens and

ESSENTIAL
FACT

Emotional Intelligence
Emotional intelligence involves the accurate perception of emotions in self and others, understanding emotions, regulating emotions, and using emotional awareness to facilitate thought and expression.

adults (Barchard 2003), the three concepts—IQ, EQ, and personality strengths—clearly overlap somewhat, making it hard for researchers to tease apart the impact of each, especially for any one individual. How can we know which factor is truly responsible for someone's success? Being intelligent and having five specific personality traits—being open, conscientious, extroverted, agreeable, and emotionally stable—are all advantages for children as they mature into adults. But measures of emotional intelligence predict success above and beyond measures of IQ and personality alone. This makes sense! For instance, somebody can be highly intelligent and possess winning personality traits, but if they aren't tuned in to how others feel, they will not flourish in the same way as someone who possesses all three traits.

TEACHING EMOTIONAL INTELLIGENCE: THE RULER METHOD

The abilities that make up emotional intelligence do correlate with traditional IQ: In general, the higher the IQ, the higher the emotional intelligence. Those emotional abilities also help determine how effectively a person applies their IQ to meet goals, work well with others, and respond to emotional signals in the environment. The good news is that regardless of IQ, emotional intelligence can be learned and enhanced way beyond basic "people skills" and emotional stability. A simple tool, the RULER (see box) can help. Based on Salovey's model, it makes key concepts of emotional intelligence easy to remember and use.

ESSENTIAL
TOOL

The RULER: Steps of Emotional Intelligence
1. **R**ecognize the emotion.
2. **U**nderstand the cause of the emotion.
3. **L**abel the emotion accurately.
4. **E**xpress the emotion appropriately and use feelings to facilitate thought.
5. **R**egulate the emotion successfully.

You can apply the RULER any time you're confronted with an emotionally complex situation and want to use the opportunity for building emotional intelligence. This wise-minded tool will help you address the whole continuum of emotionally challenging situations, from the mild (e.g., how you feel when your teen doesn't do his chores) to the high-voltage variety (e.g., how you feel about the beer you find in your kid's daypack). This differs a bit from emotion coaching (discussed in chapter 2), because the RULER approach is about regulating and expressing your own emotions, while emotion coaching also includes guiding your child. Although you want your child to identify feelings, connect those feelings with cognitive systems, express himself clearly and effectively, and control outbursts, that probably won't happen until he sees you model it. In addition, teens are fanatical about not being pushed (as they see it) to participate in exploratory talks about feelings unless they are in the mood. So, it is a humble and skillful move on your part to prioritize modeling excellent emotional intelligence and trust that, over time, your teen will start to model it, too. Of course, if your teen is willing to try the RULER approach himself, wonderful. But don't push it!

Practice builds the emotional-intelligence muscle, so consider posting the RULER approach on the refrigerator. That way, you can refer to it when you need to address an emotionally complex situation. These moments may include a sibling dynamic, your own stress at work, a family member's new diagnosis, your feelings about your tween's peer struggles, your regrets about marital squabbles, or your desire that your teen bathe more regularly. Our lives are constantly offering upsetting new challenges, providing us with many opportunities to exercise this EQ muscle! It's a great way to put feelings into words and maybe even resolve a dilemma every now and then.

What follows is an example of the RULER approach in action, taken from a real-life scenario. At first, RULER skills are nowhere to be found, but you'll see them come into play later as the dad employs them as a means to reflect and repair after a damaging and upsetting fight.

Scene: *Dad comes home from work one day to find that his son, Jared, is not home—and not answering calls to his cell phone. Lately, this dad has been more anxious than usual about his thirteen-year-old. Jared has matured earlier than his friends and has been getting a lot of texts from girls (even older ones). Also, Jared has become friends with Sammy and a few other kids in the neighborhood who are older and a little on the wild side. Jared's parents are worried that things could be ramping up too fast, and that Jared could end up on the wild side, too, if something isn't done soon.*

So, when Dad can't find Jared, he assumes he's over at Sammy's house. Dad is mad, thinking there is some scam afoot and that Jared has let his cell battery go dead on purpose so he could go AWOL. Dad marches down to Sammy's. Sammy's little sister answers the door and acknowledges that Jared and a bunch of kids are upstairs in Sammy's room. Dad notes that Sammy's parents aren't home and thinks, "What kind of orgy is going on here?" His heart is pounding and he is about to scream "Jared!" (with expletives) when a tumble of boys and girls come hurtling down the stairs.

Dad yells at Jared in front of his friends and says all sorts of regrettable things: "You've manipulated me so you could do as you please. You basically lied to connive and come to this little party scene. What the hell were you doing in that room? You kids have no decorum at all these days, spending time in bedrooms all together. Jared, get home right now. Don't even try to defend yourself!"

Out they go and as Jared leaves, he starts crying, and he runs all the way home, screaming, "You won't even listen to me!"

At first, Dad thinks, "Good! Run home and think about your misdeeds. Maybe you'll learn." Then he walks around the block, checks his phone, and finds to his chagrin that Jared had indeed texted him about going to Sammy's. In his defensive conversation with himself, he thinks, "Why can't kids just answer the phone? What is wrong with this generation?" He bobs back to criticizing Jared: "Well, he didn't ask me whether he could go to Sammy's. Texts are stupid; he knows I never check for them. If he really wanted a conversation about whether something was a legitimate plan, then he would call. It's so manipulative."

As he blows off more steam, he starts to really think about the situation. In truth, he and his wife have never explicitly said that Jared can't use texts to inform them of his whereabouts, and he's been doing it for quite some time. They have also never made rules about bedrooms being off-limits for pubescent boys and girls. This was all new! He probably jumped the gun and thought the worst. He was pretty out of control at Sammy's and probably humiliated himself, and, more importantly, Jared. Now that he has calmed down, thought about the big picture—including his anxious feelings about girls coming on to Jared (and the other way around)—he is withering with regret and embarrassment.

He knows he needs to apologize. He wants to use this opportunity to share deeper feelings, as well. He wants Jared to be the kind of guy who can both apologize and connect feelings, thoughts, and insights. He gets home, glances at the RULER steps posted on the fridge, and decides to give it a go. He knocks on Jared's door. Jared looks wary but relieved when he sees his dad's softened expression. Dad gives his pitch.

Recognize the emotion:
> *"I was upset when you weren't home as I had expected."*

Understand the cause of the emotion:
> *"First, I was angry that you didn't leave a note or answer your phone when I called. Then, I was worried about your hanging out with kids who were older."*

Label the emotion accurately:
> *"Because you are a very attractive thirteen-year-old, and girls are interested in you, I am anxious about you and your sexual behavior. I worry that you could get in over your head with girls before you even know what's happened."*

Express the emotion appropriately and use feelings to facilitate thought:
> *"I know that this will disappoint you, but we are going to have stricter rules about guys and girls socializing in bedrooms. I know we need to have some more talks about sex and attraction to girls, but I've been avoiding it because it makes us both feel awkward."*

Regulate the emotion successfully:
> *"I'm sorry I lost it at Sammy's. Afterward, I walked around the block to calm down. I thought about this situation from your perspective—I realize that my reaction seemed to come out of left field. I wished I'd calmed down before I rang Sammy's doorbell."*

Let's assume that Jared threw some zingers at Dad during this presentation. After all, he no doubt saw an opening for agreeing that Dad had been a jerk, and that it was Dad's mistake that he didn't look at the texts, and that Dad's stupid behavior made him look like a third-grader in front of his friends. So we have to give Dad extra credit for nodding and validating those feelings, as well as regulating his defensive emotions, while he plowed on with this elegant and emotionally intelligent presentation.

ESSENTIAL
ACTIVITY

Practice the RULER for Yourself

The next time you find yourself facing an emotionally loaded moment with your child, try to employ the RULER steps. Complete the activity below (use your journal if you need more space).

1. Think of something going on with your tween or teen right now that feels negative and describe it below (e.g., you've been nagging them about their grades; you feel angry over their poor treatment of a sibling; you're upset by the bad attitude they've been displaying at the dinner table).

_____

_____

_____

2. Using the RULER format, write out a presentation of your feelings, your thoughts, and your wise-minded insights about what is going on that makes this issue tough for you.

Recognize the emotion:

_____

_____

_____

Understand the cause of the emotion:

_____

_____

_____

Label the emotion accurately:

_____

_____

_____

Express the emotion appropriately and use feelings to facilitate thought:

_____

_____

_____

Regulate the emotion successfully:

_____

_____

_____

3. Review your RULER with the following guidelines in mind as you imagine talking to your child:
- Make sure you only talk about your feelings, without focusing on or judging their behavior.
- Don't succumb to defensiveness or hostility, no matter what your child says in response to your statements.
- If you refer to their behavior, it should only be with empathy about the validity of their feelings, considering:

_____

_____

_____

(e.g., something they are going through in their life; or adolescence makes it understandable that he hates homework, dinners, his sibling, your face, your agenda).
- Now ask yourself: Do you need to edit your RULER?

4. Remember, you are not doing this to make a point about your child's need to change a behavior, thought, or feeling. This exercise is about you modeling emotional intelligence. Do you need to edit further?

5. Deliver your RULER presentation with as much humility as possible and then record your impressions about how you felt, how your child received it, and whether you think it enhanced your relationship (even if he made fun of you, said "Whatever," or rolled his eyes).

_____

_____

_____

One of the hardest jobs of parenting is modeling behaviors a zillion times and then patiently waiting for the payoff: your teen demonstrating those behaviors on their own. You have to trust that they're internalizing the behavior, and that someday in the future, you'll see it shine through, whether in the form of good manners, empathy, generosity, tolerance, or just doing chores—without being asked! With all the complicated dynamics of cognitive, social, emotional, and neurological development, it takes a long time for teens to develop sophisticated emotional intelligence skills and then spontaneously and consistently display them.

Remember, if you deliver your RULER without reacting or going negative, you get an A, regardless of your teen's response. The goal is not to have some rosy Disney Channel breakthrough with your tween or teen, but for your child to observe emotional intelligence in action. Those rosy moments happen by accident; we can't control them. What we can do is set up as many opportunities as possible for that magic to happen.

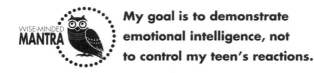

My goal is to demonstrate emotional intelligence, not to control my teen's reactions.

The RULER approach to enhancing emotional intelligence has been incorporated into a school-based curriculum with telling success (Brackett et al. 2010). A randomized study design was used to evaluate the effectiveness of the program in twenty-eight diverse schools. The program focused on the core skills of the RULER approach—recognizing, understanding, labeling, expressing, and regulating emotion. In addition, teachers received extensive training in using the curriculum in a positive learning environment. For instance, the RULER Feelings Words Curriculum helps children develop emotion skills through an exploration of terms such as "commitment," "elation," and "empathy." They learn to identify their own and others' thoughts, feelings, and behaviors, understand the emotions and points of view of characters in stories, and develop strategies to manage emotions in real-life situations. When compared with fifth- and sixth-grade students who did not receive the training, students who participated in the program received higher grades on their report cards and higher ratings from teachers for their social and emotional competencies (such as leadership and study skills).

The RULER curriculum addresses skills similar to those in the more extensive Collaborative for Academic, Social, and Emotional Learning (CASEL) programs described in chapter 3. An analysis of more than 300 CASEL studies shows that the average student enrolled in these programs ranks *at least 10 percentage points higher on achievement tests* than students who do not participate in such programs (Zins et al. 2004). Students in these programs also have better attendance records, classroom behavior, and grade-point averages.

The CASEL programs start at the preschool level, and include the whole family and school community in the curriculum to prevent adolescent adjustment problems among high-risk youth. A family-wide improvement in emotional functioning creates feedback loops of positive feeling among the families, teachers, and children, which improves the emotional climate in home and school settings. When children learn to "use their words" to express negative emotions more effectively and avoid behavioral outbursts, there is a synergistic effect. Boosting the emotional competencies of the most important people in a child's world—their parents—is the key to CASEL's success. Any child who comes home to depressed, stressed, or angry parents—who are not managing their own negative emotions—loses ground in maintaining their own mental health. Emotions, negative and positive, are contagious.

Programs that support emotional intelligence help children feel effective, confident, and safe, both with respect to their own feelings and the feelings of others. In turn, these children behave better and acquire the strengths of positive emotional adjustment. A focus on emotions seems to contribute to skills and security, leading to wide-ranging and long-term positive effects on children's and teens' lives. While the results from these studies suggest that every school could benefit from the CASEL curriculum, the teacher training and time requirements add yet more economic and academic demands on top of our already overwhelmed educational system. Still, the benefits of these programs make a good argument for widespread implementation. In the meantime, you can promote these emotion skills in your own family and home.

Mirror Neurons and Our 'Emotional Wi-Fi' System

It happened by accident: Neuroscientists who were mapping the brains of monkeys stumbled onto a discovery that illustrates the great degree to which brains interact with each other (di Pellegrino et al. 1991). While monitoring the monkeys' brain scans, researchers noticed a spike in activity when a research assistant raised an ice cream cone to his lips. The monkey's brain reflected the experience as if he was raising the cone to his own lips. Since then, neuroscientists have discovered "mirror neurons" at work in the brains of humans, as well. If you see someone receive a pinprick, your own brain will register it, too.

THE EVOLUTIONARY BENEFITS OF MIRROR NEURONS

Like the reflection in a mirror, mirror neurons allow humans to feel what others are feeling, which creates the basis of empathy. When we sense the vulnerability of others, especially infants, we feel it, not just know it, and we are compelled to nurture. This makes sense from an evolutionary standpoint. As humans evolved, our brains grew until it became essential for babies to be delivered before they were even close to maturity. Our empathetic attachment system developed at the same time, motivating adults for that long-term care project known as parenting.

Just as Daniel Goleman popularized the concept of emotional intelligence, he also decoded the work around mirror neurons and what he dubbed "social intelligence" (Goleman 2006). Goleman used the apt metaphor of "Wi-Fi" to describe the open circuitry we have for picking up each other's emotions, even going so far as to call the human brain an "interpersonal organ." That's a powerful concept, and there has been an explosion of research over the past two decades using brain scans to document the connectivity between people. Although developmental scientists are just beginning to investigate how emotional processing of information varies in children, teens, and adults, research on adult emotions offers insights about the Wi-Fi system.

Tuning into others' fears became an adaptive ability for humans and their ancestors millennia ago. As scrawny hominids, dependent on one another for survival in a world full of predators and natural adversities, humans could rely on each other as sentinels. A clan member registering fright at the sight of a lion or crocodile could be someone else's savior on the savanna. We modern humans tune into others' faces and expressions to interpret signals, too. If you hear but can't see someone scream, and everyone who *can* see the screamer smiles, your brain will intuit that it must be a scream of joy (a touchdown), rather than a scream of danger (witnessing an act of violence). Mirror neurons have protected us from danger for thousands of years.

They've also helped us bond socially. We smile when others smile. If someone looks stricken, we're alerted to find the cause. Mirror neurons are located near the premotor cortex—the area of the brain that governs activities ranging from speaking to movement to simply *intending* to act—so when these neurons fire, we don't always spring into action. For instance, when we watch someone play soccer, we might squirm around in synchrony, but we stop short of chasing down the ball. Neurons are fired when we practice a lecture in our head or rehearse a tennis serve. It's the same pattern of neurons we use for action, only the actual execution is blocked.

MIRROR NEURONS AND EMOTIONAL INTELLIGENCE

Mirror neurons not only help us sense another's actions, but they help us understand another's feelings *and their intentions*, which allows us to develop all kinds of theories about their motivations. While our emotional intelligence skills help us use the information gathered from our mirror neurons for hunches, we can be wrong. The workings of the entire brain—including the emotional (limbic) and conscious analytic (prefrontal cortex) systems—help integrate the information coming from within and outside of ourselves to formulate ideas about interpersonal situations and effective ways to respond to them.

Will your fourteen-year-old assert or ingratiate himself with his alpha peer, whose confident swagger seems aggressive? A lot goes into that decision. Emotionally, your boy will be tapping into his past experience, his innate reactivity, recent history with this peer, feelings about his relative status—and data from his mirror neurons. Additionally, he'll note how his friends and the popular kids are responding to Alpha Boy. In short, peer conformity is about teens wanting to join the peer tribe, but mirror neurons do a lot of the radar work to pick up information about how it might be done.

Mirror neurons are essential to children's learning. Babies mimic other humans almost from day one, opening and closing their mouths in response to their parents, and then later returning the smiles of those around them. Children learn from mere observation, too. They might watch a parent, a peer, or even a TV character get what they want by yelling or threatening, which inspires them to try the same thing. They will also see and feel the results of kindness and generosity and, hopefully, mimic that rewarding pattern as well.

When parent and child are playing with each other and enjoying one another, the parallel circuitry in their two brains creates a fond memory, tightening their bond. With the moodiness of adolescence and the developmental task of individuation, those moments are likely fewer. Since it's a teen's developmental job to forge a unique self and identity, they may accentuate differences with their parent, attempting to counteract this mimicry. Just because the parent smiles lovingly every morning when the teen comes to breakfast, it does not mean the teen will respond in kind. Negative attitudes, moods, and oppositional tendencies often trump a teen's mirror neurons. You can also see this phenomenon at work in the board room during hostile negotiations.

THERE'S MORE TO A SMILE THAN MEETS THE EYE

Whether there's a dearth of smiles in your home now or not, the human brain recognizes and responds more readily to smiles over all other emotional expressions, something that neuroscientists have described as the "happy face advantage." Humans have historically been primed for positive exchanges with others, because making allies is an advantage in social groups. Some neuroscientists suggest that this priming might be why people, short of dire circumstances, usually report they are mostly happy with their lives.

Additionally, psychologist Paul Ekman's research has demonstrated that emotions are primarily communicated through facial expressions, which are both universal and bio-logically innate (Ekman et al. 1982). Over the last thirty years, Ekman has identified eighteen kinds of smiles, involving combinations of fifteen facial muscles, including fake smiles, smiles to cover up unhappiness, cunning smiles, and more (Ekman et al. 1990). He also has shown that culture influences these expressions, adding complexity to form and function. Other experts have even categorized genuine smiles from yearbook pictures and found that these predict happy lives and happy marriages decades after the pictures were taken (Harker and Keltner 2001).

Teens actually smile plentifully and genuinely—just not necessarily around their parents—so parents are often surprised to learn that in large studies, most teens report being happy most of the time (Offer and Schonert-Reichl 1992). Daniel Offer—who conducted surveys on thousands of teens in the 1960s and 1980s, and then combined his mountain of data with others' research on nonclinical samples—has concluded that 80 percent of teens are emotionally stable, relate well to their families and peers, and are comfortable with their social and cultural values.

One of Offer's most valuable contributions to the field has been in emphasizing that a negative mood, so common in adolescents, is not indicative of a teen's general satisfaction with themselves, their parent and peer relationships, or their future lives. Busy days and the individuation business give us small and biased samplings of our teens' lives, so we need to remember Offer's research and consider that these negative or grumpy mood "moments" do not accurately reflect our child's happiness with their lives, selves, or families. In short, research suggests that most teens are happy with their lives, whether they smile easily and often, or not.

FACT

Teen Well-Being

Eighty percent of teens are emotionally stable, relate well to their families and peers, and are comfortable with their social and cultural values.

Interestingly, adolescents are more prone to misreading facial expressions than adults are. Using functional magnetic resolution imaging (fMRIs), researchers at the University of Pittsburgh found that children and teens use the neural pathways in their amygdalae to interpret emotional expressions, while adults use their prefrontal cortices (Todd et al. 2011). In viewing images of fearful and happy faces on standardized photographs, adults demonstrate activation of neurons in the "thinking" parts of their brains to figure out the meaning of emotions. Earlier research from this lab suggests that teens are more likely to misread fearful faces as angry and hostile. This research just confirms what parents experience regularly: Teens often react (and overreact) negatively to the facial expressions of others.

The fact that we adults are primed for positivity explains why we sometimes like a stranger instantly after we share a little joke on the bus together. Even *total strangers* return our smiles, so it's frustrating when our teens won't do the same. We are wired to expect a positive response to all our geniality, and in many cases we do—until we come home to our moody and rebuffing teens. It can feel hurtful and irritating. But remember, teens have their own agenda: individuation, displacement of the day's stress, and privacy. And they almost seem compelled to stymie the natural social duet of positivity with their parents, even though the parents are often transmitting love and kindness. Of course, teens mirror parental warmth sometimes—and on occasion, a lot—but they have significant incoming data from their internal moods and thoughts to contend with.

Sometimes, the whole parent-teen duet can be too intimate for our kids, and we, as parents, tire of all the rejection, too. When you get to that point, consider orchestrating a gathering of friends and/or family members. Never before in history have we lived in such small families, with as little support from extended family and lifelong friends. This puts undue pressure on teens to please their parents and on parents to find emotional satisfaction from their ornery offspring. But teenagers almost always warm up when others are around and the pressure is off.

TIP

Family-Time Option

Make family time more fun for kids by inviting friends or family to join in. The positive parent-teen bonding is still there, with none of the pressure or intimacy that some tweens and teens dread.

Another game plan is to skip the face to face and just do an activity together. Enjoy something side by side, such as shooting some hoops, watching a favorite TV show, or making dinner together. The pressure's off, but the mutual pleasure is still there.

ESSENTIAL ACTIVITY

Make and Savor Positive Moments

Think of three fun and nonthreatening (and not overly intimate) ways to spend quality time with your teen and then put them into action in the next two weeks. Ideas can include suggesting an after-dinner walk or game of Parcheesi, watching a few music videos of the teen's choosing, inviting a couple of friends over for a sit-down dinner, or making a contest of finding the best animal videos on YouTube. Write down your ideas and when you intend to roll them out.

Activity	When
1.	
2.	
3.	

Then, reflect upon those good moments later. Record them in a mental file and push the "play back" button when you want to conjure those positive feelings about your teen. Since life is a jumble, especially with tweens and teens, we can lose track of the good moments—especially when they are upstaged by negative ones every day. Research shows that people who savor positive experiences are healthier, happier, and live more satisfied lives (Bryant and Veroff 2007). Who doesn't want to join that club?

THE POWER OF LAUGHTER

All emotions are potentially contagious, but laughter is particularly so. Teens giggle, laugh, and share their own private jokes with each other, creating strong social bonds along the way. Parents might enjoy and even envy the sounds of happiness emanating from the raucousness sleepover downstairs. Either way, there is something special about brains resonating together in friendship.

A study conducted at the University of California, Berkeley, found that new college roommates who viewed two films—a comedy and a tear jerker—had dissimilar emotional responses, just as random strangers would (Anderson et al. 2003). Seven months later, the roommates were showed a new pair of films and this time most exhibited remarkable convergence in their emotional reactions. This experiment suggests that cohabitation produces emotion osmosis. No wonder parents want happy and high-functioning roommates for their college-bound teens! But the pressure to produce good vibes is on mom and dad in the meantime.

Emotion osmosis can occur in any group, especially when a crowd is swept up in a single passion. Think about a religious revival, a high-stakes athletic event, or a powerfully emotional theater production. Brains loop together en masse. Teens are often particularly influenced by, and a conspicuous part of, these mass events, since they experience feelings intensely, especially as members of a group. Teens are particularly aroused in the presence of peers, with dopamine released and risk taking more likely, which explains why teens together often run amok. Brains looping together can make for the best and the worst of group action.

Since emotions are contagious in small and large groups, it's important to remember that in the intimate context of the family, positive and negative emotions spread quickly through genuine smiles as well as from scowls and glares. And when the negative emotion involves significant anxiety or anger, mirror neurons can help spiral the most loving of families into a tornado of stress.

The Science of Stress

When talking about emotional health, it's helpful to understand a bit about the body's response to stress, which can derail us at the best of times. It's chemical! Stress is controlled by the autonomic nervous system, consisting of two parts: the sympathetic and the parasympathetic systems, both of which do their life-maintaining business beneath our conscious awareness (the term for that is *subcortical*). The sympathetic system revs us up, and our parasympathetic system calms us back down again and keeps our vital organs stabilized. The stress response occurs when the sympathetic nervous system is aroused, either by internal or external events. This causes the release of a family of chemicals— neuromodulators called *catecholamines* (dopamine, norepinephrine, and epinephrine)—that charge up our systems for action. These chemicals set in motion a cascade of other physiological processes that give us a surge of energy. Our heart rate and blood pressure increase with the flow of adrenaline (another word for epinephrine) and our peripheral vision is narrowed so that we can focus on potential dangers.

At mild or medium levels, this "stress response" is desirable, because it energizes us to pursue goals, makes us alert, and focuses our attention. When we are understimulated, we are bored and uninvolved. When we are challenged and optimally aroused, we are more alert, decisive, creative, and effective. When demands and stressors exceed our ability to meet them, we become "stressed out." We become overloaded with stress hormones and physiological arousal, which makes it hard for us to concentrate, and then we become irritable, anxious, fatigued, and finally exhausted.

An important part of the parasympathetic system is the vagus nerve, which controls the calming of the heart after the stress response is triggered. When active, the vagus nerve is thought to be responsible for that "heart-warming" feeling in the chest that is associated with compassion, trust, and bonding. Children with high baseline activity in their vagus nerve are more cooperative and generous (Eisenberg and Sulik 2012). Since individual differences in vagal tone exist, some people are naturally more able to marshal kindness and self-soothing, while others are more prone to aggressiveness and reactivity. Kids of the latter variety are a lot more work for parents; their emotional regulation will need to be contracted out to their parents until they develop their own "top down" skills for managing emotional freak-outs.

"Top down" emotional regulation (or effortful control) occurs through cognitive effort, and "bottom up" regulation (or reactive control) happens through the parasympathetic system, which operates "beneath" our conscious awareness. When we use techniques like the RULER approach, we are *consciously* trying to calm ourselves down and think in a focused manner. When our stress management comes straight from the vagus nerve, it is reactive control via parasympathetic systems, which is not willful or conscious. Both effortful control and reactive control are related to emotional adjustment in children; the kids with high top-down and high bottom-up abilities to inhibit impulses are better adjusted (Eisenberg et al. 2005).

Why does this matter? If your child has frequent outbursts, throwing fits in response to mild stressors, it is easy to think, "What's your problem? All I did was ask you to empty the dishwasher!" or "So I can't take you to the mall. That is no reason to have a meltdown!" It's important to understand that he might have a weaker vagus nerve and parasympathetic system, which is supposed to naturally calm him down. These kids require patience and lots of practice with the RULER approaches, emotion coaching, and mindfulness so that they can learn effortful control over their emotions.

THE EMOTIONAL HIJACK

Humans inherited lightning-quick, extreme-stress reactions to perceived dangers from their distant pre-primate relatives. The emotional (or amygdala) hijack was explained at length in chapter 2, but it bears repeating here: When the amygdala is triggered, it "hijacks" or commandeers our entire biological system to respond to threats. When we detect danger, the response time of the amygdala is around thirty-three milliseconds— and for some people, half that time (Cozolino 2006). The prefrontal cortex (our "thinking" brain) requires at least ten times that amount of time to process information from the environment as a conscious thought. In metaphoric terms, on the elaborate highways of conscious thought, it's as if our amygdala activation is racing down the fast lane, while our cognitive system putters along in the slow lane.

For millions of years in human evolutionary history, the "fight or flight" reaction pattern triggered by the amygdala has survived because it saves lives. In the "tooth and claw" days of yore, this adrenaline-charged system allowed our ancestors to club the predator, or grab the baby and run. In modern life, the stress response still saves lives when we hit the brakes to avoid an oncoming car. However, since our hair-triggered reactions to extreme stressors do not include a "cognitive review," we also react to a lot of false alarms. Think of road rage as the adult equivalent of a two-year-old's (or twelve-year-old's) temper tantrum. Every day, in families all over the world, people yell, scream, curse, and take flight from loved ones when their buttons (amygdalae) are pushed.

Our emotional Wi-Fi system detects danger signals coming from all over the place—internally and externally, from the real world and the virtual world, from threatening events and from demanding people, and from small-, medium-, and large-decibel levels of emotional noise. And since the modern world is so fast, arousing, and loud, our emotional Wi-Fi detects alarms sounding most of the day. The stress response system, designed to release rapid bursts of cortisol for slaying the occasional tiger, is often saturated with stress hormones for dealing with everyday life. The physiological effects of chronic stress are legion, contributing to virtually every mental and physical illness.

ESSENTIAL
FACT

Stress in Daily Life
The human stress response system—which once helped us avoid predators—now saturates us with stress hormones for dealing with everyday life. The physiological effects of chronic stress are legion, contributing to virtually every mental and physical illness.

Leading researchers in the field of child health have found a substantial increase in severe psychological adjustment problems among children and adolescents over the last twenty years (Evans et al. 2005). A committee from the American Academy of Pediatrics has declared that toxic stress in early childhood is a threat to lifelong health (Garner et al. 2012). And children across all income groups are more at risk for psychological problems from our society's ubiquitous stressors.

Given that our biological systems evolved to respond the way they do, and that few of us are going to be moving to Tahiti any time soon, what can be done about this chronic stress in our lives? How can we help families—children, adolescents, and parents—better manage and reduce stress? How do people create positive emotions to compensate for the negative ones that inevitably occur? Do positive emotions really enhance mental health? And how can we move from emotional health to emotional flourishing? All of these concerns relate to the burgeoning field of positive psychology.

The Role of Positive Emotions in Mental Health

In the study of emotion, not all feelings are equal. Negative feelings hold greater sway than positive ones, and from a neuroscientific point of view, this makes sense. By focusing our narrowed, heightened attention on negative events, we are sure to address them. When we feel positive and comfortable, we let our guard down, and our minds wander. Our biological predisposition to focus on negative feelings, our "negative affectivity bias," makes worrywarts of us.

Louis Cozolino, a psychologist at Pepperdine University who writes widely about neuroscience, referred to negative feelings as Velcro—sticky—and positive ones as Teflon—

not sticky (Cozolino 2006). Hanging onto negative thoughts and feelings is adaptive in truly dangerous situations that require solutions, but it can also be destructive when we get stuck in chronic worry or depression loops. Smiles may be powerful facial expressions, but positive vibes can't compete with negative ones when the fast lane to freak-out is activated, whether the trigger is a real threat or a false alarm. Our ancestors' brains learned that they could always pursue positive stuff tomorrow (e.g., food, sex, play), but they had to save themselves from predators today. Thus, the fast lane for dangers and fears took precedence in brain circuitry.

While negative stress creates tunnel vision, positive feelings broaden our perspective, making us more open-minded, flexible, creative, and adaptable. We all know what it feels like to have a really good day. We are kinder, more generous, and resourceful in managing all kinds of problems when we approach them with a positive attitude.

Psychologist Sonja Lyubomirsky and her colleagues conducted a meta-analysis of 250 studies (which included a quarter-million subjects) to calculate the benefits of positive feelings (Lyubomirsky et al. 2005). They estimated that about 50 percent of an individual's happiness originated in their "set point" personality, 40 percent from intentional activity, and 10 percent from circumstances. Significantly, the researchers found that life satisfaction and happiness preceded markers of success in people's lives, including relationship quality, occupational achievement, and health. In other words, happiness appears to make people successful, not the other way around.

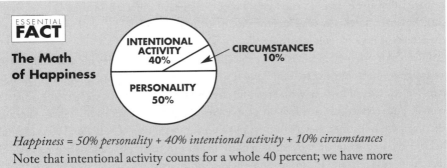

Happiness = 50% personality + 40% intentional activity + 10% circumstances
Note that intentional activity counts for a whole 40 percent; we have more control over our own happiness than most of us realize!

Many people imagine that they will be happy when they achieve success or other goals (e.g., admission to a certain school, losing weight, getting a girlfriend), but that is actually backward. While those events might elicit happiness, it's important to realize that many of those good things happen in the first place due in great part to our positive emotions and the role they play in our lives.

Recent research seems to indicate that positive emotions *create* pathways to success. Whether they are optimism, hope, or enthusiasm, those positive emotions are certainly advantageous building blocks of success. Connected to these positive emotions are character strengths such as resilience, perseverance, and self-control, which really help emotionally flourishing individuals reach their goals.

Seminal research conducted by trailblazers Ed Diener and Daniel Kahneman documented that having at least three positive emotions for every negative emotion predicted subjective well-being (Diener 2000; Kahneman 1999). Expanding on this research, Corey Keyes broke ground in developing the concept of "flourishing," and described mental health as ranging from flourishing at one end to psychological impairment at the other end (Keyes 2002). As mentioned earlier, flourishing has been defined as living within an optimal range of human functioning—one that connotes goodness, growth, purpose, meaning, and resilience. Think of some of the people you admire for their contributions to society, their family relationships, their spirit, values, and purposeful life, and they probably embody these features of flourishing.

> ESSENTIAL
> **FACT**
>
> **The Math of Happiness, part 2**
> 3 positive emotions : 1 negative emotion = well-being

Based on his research, Keyes estimated that fewer than 20 percent of adults are flourishing, meaning that they have high levels of psychological, social, and personal well-being and an absence of mental problems. The opposite of flourishing has been called "languishing," which study participants describe as a feeling of emptiness. About 27 percent of Americans are languishing, or suffering from mental health problems that negatively impact their quality of life, including emotional distress, restricted daily activities, failure to meet life goals, and lower psychosocial functioning across the board (Kessler and Wang 2008). With all the stressors of modern life, along with the biological bias toward negativity, it's a challenge for many to infuse their days with enough positive emotions to compensate for this plight. And kids are no exception.

Keyes studied one thousand children between ages twelve and eighteen and found that those who were flourishing experienced fewer conduct problems and less depression, and had higher psychological assets, including management of responsibilities, positive relationships, and feelings of community connectedness (Keyes 2006). About 50 percent of the twelve- to fourteen-year-olds were flourishing in this sample, dropping to about 40 percent by the time these kids entered high school.

Barbara Fredrickson, another pioneer in the study of positive emotions, developed a "broaden and build" theory, which demonstrated that flourishing not only has immediate benefits, but leads to future health and well-being (Fredrickson 1998). Her theory maintains that positive feelings also have been adaptive over thousands of years, since they widen the array of thoughts and actions made available for such options as play, affiliation, and exploration—thereby facilitating flexibility and creative problem solving.

Lab studies support these claims, showing that negative emotions (i.e., the stress response) narrow the subjects' thoughts and problem-solving abilities, whereas positive emotions broaden these abilities (Fredrickson and Branigan 2005). In other words, we are wired to feel positive emotions, because positivity increases our chances of survival in different ways than negative emotions do.

ESSENTIAL
ACTIVITY

Keep a Positive Emotion List

For one week—or even just one day—keep a positive emotion list. We've included Barbara Fredrickson's top ten positive emotions as a prompt. You can invite your kids to do this, too, but if they are older than about eight, be ready for a brush-off. No matter; your attention to positive emotions may prove contagious. In your journal, write down where and when you experience the following:

1. **Joy**—an unexpected delight, when things feel wonderful. What created joy for you today?

2. **Gratitude**—somebody did you a good turn, something moved you deeply; you are aware of good things in your life.

3. **Serenity**—a sense of peacefulness; a time when you can let go and be.

4. **Interest**—a heightened state that pulls your attention to something intriguing and makes you want to dig in and discover.

5. **Hope**—a belief that things can change for the better and turn out well in spite of being in a difficult situation.

6. **Pride**—the sense of satisfaction after reaching a difficult goal that we worked hard for.

7. **Amusement**—things that make you laugh; often the best times are spontaneous and shared. In-jokes, shared memories, stories, and pet antics are common sources of amusement in families.

8. **Inspiration**—experiences that touch you deeply, whether it is a thing of beauty, kindness, feat, or athletic triumph over adversity.

9. **Awe**—experiencing wonder on a grand scale; feeling overwhelmed; having a "breathtaking" experience.

10. **Love**—this is a trick list because the first and most frequent positive emotion is listed last. Love encompasses all the emotions above and more. It can flood us with oxytocin (the "tend and befriend" hormone), make us feel rosy all over, and create a deep sense of well-being.

While positive feelings can be fleeting, they can also ignite processes that pay off down the road in personal growth and resilience. The broadened perspective gained by a teen who trusts, explores, and is open to social connections may lead to more knowledge acquisition and opportunity. While negative emotions can be adaptive in life-threatening situations, they encourage avoidance and distrust over the long haul. Ultimately, it's the positive feelings that build more accurate cognitive maps of what is good and bad in the environment. This greater knowledge becomes a lasting personal resource.

The Upside of the Downside

"Appropriate negative emotions" that are realistic can actually motivate people to solve problems, Fredrickson contends, including those that crop up in relationships. John Gottman—a psychologist at the University of Washington who has made a career of studying marriages—agrees that negative emotions can be healthy when they are part of productive conflicts, limited, and in a five-to-one ratio to positive emotions (Gottman 1994). Certain negative emotions, however, including contempt and disgust, were found to be particularly toxic in marriages.

Interestingly, Fredrickson argues that positivity is an asset only when appropriate and genuine. Studies have shown that smiles that are insincere backfire, and, in fact, subjects can distinguish between genuine and disingenuous smiles and trust the people with fake smiles less (Frank et al. 1993). Positive feelings must be meaningfully grounded in the reality of current relationships, rather than feigned or forced.

While this is a basic principle in the positive psychology field, teens seem to be especially resentful of phony "Be happy" coercions. In my work with teens over the years, I've been astonished by the acuity of their B.S. antenna. "Phony" is one of their greatest condemnations. Since they are struggling to establish their own authentic identities, as well as learning to protect themselves from people they can't trust, they invest a lot of energy in detecting genuineness. Teens enjoy positive emotions as much as anyone, but those emotions need to be read as "real."

ENHANCING HAPPINESS

Martin Seligman at the University of Pennsylvania led the charge in the field of positive psychology to understand how to *increase* happiness (Seligman and Csikszentmihalyi 2000). The goal of positive psychology is to move beyond studying mental illness to investigate how psychologists can help enhance mental health and flourishing. Seligman and his colleagues have published more than twenty studies on the research conducted through the university's Positive Psychology Center, which is aimed at enhancing mental health among children, adolescents, and college students. His research has shown that the program can reliably prevent or reduce depression and anxiety, even in classroom interventions (Seligman et al. 2009).

In one of the original studies, study participants (adults) logged onto a website (*authentichappiness.com*), completed an inventory to discover their "signature strengths" and received three assignments hypothesized to reduce depressive symptoms (Seligman et al. 2005). During the six months of the study, two assigned activities were found to increase happiness and decrease depressive symptoms. One was the act of writing about three good things that happened each day, every day, for a week; the other was using one's signature strengths in a new way. One other assigned activity—writing a letter of gratitude to someone and then hand-delivering it—made people happier for a shorter time (about one month). Given that the participants had no coaching other than what was provided on the website, it is remarkable that the study had the impact it did.

ESSENTIAL
ACTIVITY

Glass Half-Full Practice

Positive feelings make us feel better and set the stage for the happiness of others around us. Over the next week, do one of these exercises every day. Consider enlisting your child to do the same (writing about a parent for number three).

1. Write down three good things that happened and their causes that day.

2. Write a letter of gratitude to someone who has made a difference in your life (send it or read it to them).

3. Write down three things that you appreciate about your child.

Seligman believes that happiness should be further delineated into three distinct and better defined routes to happiness: positive emotion, engagement, and the creation of a meaningful life. The most satisfied people are those who orient their pursuits toward all three, with the greatest emphasis on the last two. Chapter 6 explores how teens can better develop character strengths and build a meaningful life. Here's a hint: Organized activities play an important role and, as a bonus, they boost moods as well. It is no wonder that adolescence specialists advocate the availability of after-school activities for all teens. Experiences such as volunteering at the Boys & Girls Club or at a senior center are far more meaningful than spending the afternoon updating your Facebook page or playing first-person shooter video games.

ENLISTING YOUR COGNITIVE RESOURCES TO COMBAT PESSIMISM

One of the most effective ways to combat pessimism and depressive thoughts is via "cognitive behavior therapy." Essentially, it consists of recognizing and then disputing distorted thoughts. Change your thoughts and you are on your way to changing your feelings—and then your behaviors. Thoughts and feelings are not the same as facts, and yet we often treat them that way. The truth is they are frequently inaccurate, especially when triggered by emotional arousal (yours or someone else's).

For instance, if someone told you that you were a crummy parent, you'd probably counter the allegation by listing all the things you do for your child, how much you love

FACT

Increasing Optimism
Thoughts lead to feelings which lead to behaviors.

and adore your child, and how you prioritize your parenting over most other parts of your life. However, if you were having a bad day, you might fail to dispute the claim, worrying there was some truth to it. The key is to distinguish between the facts and your feelings, and to be able to recognize pessimistic thoughts as negative assumptions or distorted thoughts. This is especially important for busy parents in challenging circumstances (e.g., raising any tween or teen).

Since we know tunnel vision is a symptom of stress, we also know that this impels us to dwell on negative events in our life and our child's life. The wise-minded parent focuses first on calming down and balancing cognition and emotion to develop an accurate understanding of the situation at hand. Given the power of negative affectivity bias, we also want to examine those thoughts as they arise. Are they extreme? All-or-nothing thinking? Catastrophic, overgeneralized, or worst-case-scenario thoughts? Then ask yourself three questions:

1. What evidence disputes this thought?
2. Is there a different way of looking at the thought?
3. What triggers might have distorted the thought?

Here are some real-life examples from parents in my practice:

Thought: "I am an inadequate mother."
Answers to the questions:
  1. "I have many loving times with my son. I take good care of him. I provide structure, show my love, and support him."
  2. "I'm having a bad day. Everyone has bad days. I only have to be a 'good enough' mom, and my overall ratio is that we have a lot more good days than bad."
  3. "My triggers were that I didn't do anything for myself today, feel overwhelmed by my 'to-do' list, and have a hard time with all of the intense negativity of my son's teen phase."

Thought: "My teen hates me."
Answers to the questions:
  1. "My teen shows appreciation occasionally, enjoys being around me when he's in a good mood, and loves having me scratch his back."
  2. "He is swimming in hormones. He has his own hard days. He probably experiences all kinds of stresses during the day, but because he is in his privacy stage, I'm not in a position to hear about them or appreciate them. I'm his mom, so he

feels safe expressing his grouchy moods with me. I need to trust in his love for me and trust that my love gets through to him. He's a normal teen, but my getting sick and tired of his negativity is reasonable, too!"

3. "My triggers were his yelling at his sister for the umpteenth time this week, his selfish hogging of the bathroom, and his snippy responses to me when I tried to remind him of his chores. It's no wonder that I feel a negative blast of negativity—but it doesn't mean he hates me. He's just spilling over with his own gush of negative feelings."

ESSENTIAL ACTIVITY

Reframing Negative Thoughts

Now it's your turn. The next time you catch yourself in a pessimistic, all-or-nothing, overgeneralized, or worst-case-scenario thought, work through the process on the chart below. Try to make this a practice by doing the same in your journal any time you can. This will help you "catch" yourself first and then challenge those negative thoughts before they take root. The goal is not positive thinking per se, but accurate thinking, and a wise-minded analysis of the big-picture view on hurtful, anxiety-provoking, or disturbing experiences.

The thought:
Evidence against the thought:
A different way of looking at the thought:
Triggers:
How I feel now:
Did my behavior change? How?

After you go through this process on a bad day, ask yourself, "How do I feel now?" And then later, notice whether your behavior has changed. The mother in the second example above completed her reflections as follows:

Feelings: "I feel less mad at him, less judgmental of myself, and less like a martyr. I appreciate that he has hard times and that I do, too. We were just having bad moments, not a bad relationship!"

Behavior: "I was less grouchy at him later in the evening. I was nicer to him and even had some tender moments. I think I nagged him less, too, because I appreciated how hard it is to be a teenager."

By disputing extreme negative feelings, you are actually increasing optimism, because you are reducing negative ruminations about yourself, your life, and your parenting. The net effect is that you've reduced negative feelings, which opens up the possibility of greater empathy, more appreciation, and more creative opportunities to "broaden and build" positive emotions and reach a wise-minded perspective.

'HAPPIOLOGY'

Is all this focus on positive emotions over the top? Is happiness overrated? Despite the empirical findings, some fear that positive psychology has oversold "happiology." It's true that some people benefit from "defensive pessimism" as a way to cope with anxiety. They think about everything that can go wrong and prepare by adjusting expectations and creating alternative goals (Norem 2008). Another complaint is that those who can't manage to scrounge up some optimism are blamed for the negative outcomes that may come their way—even those caused by illness or other circumstances outside of their control.

The trivialization of happiness, as seen on T-shirts ("Life Is Good" or "Don't Worry. Be Happy"), is one reason the field has shifted to an emphasis on satisfaction through living a meaningful, engaged, and purposeful life (more on this life essential in chapter 6). For adolescents, this shift syncs with research on youth engagement that has found a strong correlation between teen success and organized activities. In that research, kids from nineteen diverse high schools participated in a study that found that service activities were associated with the development of teamwork, positive relationships, and supportive social networks (Larson et al. 2006). As Eleanor Roosevelt said, "Happiness is not a goal; it's a by-product of a life well lived."

 **Happiness is not a goal; it's a by-product of a life well lived.**

As the field of positive psychology evolves, there is hope that research will uncover a model or system that can help individuals find the tools that work best for them for pursuing a meaningful, flourishing and good life. Especially for teens—who can be so persnickety about psychological interventions—one person's breakthrough exercise ("Name three good things that happened today") will just annoy another ("Nothing good happened today!"). Parents may be very enthusiastic about raising their teen's happiness ratio, but a happy-face crusade shoved down a teen's throat can result in disaster. Unless the teens are open to some of the ideas presented earlier in this chapter, it's less risky for parents to support school programs that address emotional and social health, and then commit to their own personal happiness crusades. Upping the family happiness quotient by your own self-improvement increases the chances of everyone's moods benefiting, thanks to emotion osmosis (and those mirror neurons!).

Happiness research findings do have some important implications for how we lead our lives—and how we parent.

TOP TEN HAPPINESS TAKEAWAYS:

1. **Think hard about the role of desire in your life and in your child's life.** Happiness is both a *feeling state* and a *values-based part of life experience*. Since our brains can be tricked into thinking that "more is better," it is essential that we put a check on our yearnings. The second piece of pie is never as good as the first.

2. **Face the fact that we are often driven by emotion, not reason.** We can be terrible judges of what makes us happy in the long run, so we squander lots of money, time, and energy on pursuing illusory or feel-good stuff, or giving into our personal weaknesses (e.g., food, media, toys, money, perfectionism, workaholism).

3. **Prioritize and savor healthy, loving, and meaningful experiences.** A happy life is composed of satisfying work, deep relationships with others, and a sense of purpose. Easy to say, harder to pull off.

4. **Be optimistic.** Children who are pessimistic or moody are at risk for limited life options, and parents need to learn how to help counter this. Counting blessings and assuming a "glass half-full" perspective can steel us for the truly hard stuff that comes our way.

5. **Practice positive thinking, talking, and doing.** Try to keep a three-to-one ratio of positive to negative emotions. It's often easier to be negative and ruminate, but people flourish by being open, curious, appreciative, and generous. But don't be insincere or excessive.

6. **Be realistic and accurate in your thinking.** The stress response and extreme negativity can distort our appraisals of ourselves, others, and events around us. Calming down enough to complete a cognitive appraisal may help you right your thinking, improve your feelings, and reveal options for optimistic action.

7. **Practice the attitude of gratitude and random acts of kindness.** Share gratefulness at the dinner table, send letters of appreciation, and look for ways to do kind things in your community.

8. **Surround your children with positive role models.** Our brains are interpersonal organs and open Wi-Fi systems. Research on obesity, school achievement, and happiness has shown there is a contagion effect for both good and bad influences.

9. **Limit screen time and media access.** We need to help our children avoid a sedentary lifestyle, negative social influences, and wasting time that can be spent in positive engagement (e.g., school activities, athletics, walking the dog, volunteering). Brain research reveals that what we say, do, feel, and experience affects neural growth. We should be mindful of our family "consumer" habits.

10. **Avoid bubble-wrapping your child.** Children develop many emotional, social, educational, and life competencies from exposure to some adversity and risk, and by being allowed the freedom to make mistakes. Ironically, a happy life seems to evolve out of many lessons learned from unhappy times.

MATERIALISM AND NARCISSISM

A barrier to enhancing happiness is the "hedonism treadmill," which causes people to inevitably adapt to good things by habituating to them over time (e.g., that new computer, a pair of designer jeans). As we gather more and more material possessions (or even accomplishments), our expectations rise. We reach for new goodies to get that fleeting boost of dopamine (the neurotransmitter associated with pleasure) we experience by acquiring these things initially. Inevitably, the high dissipates over time, so we keep looking for that next easy but short-lived boost; living our lives on a treadmill of materialism.

If you doubt such a treadmill exists, ask yourself this question: Are people who get the goodies much happier at their cores than those who do not? Research says no. After an initial, transient rise in happiness triggered by a good event, or a reduction in happiness caused by a bad event, people adapt (Wilson and Gilbert 2008). Obviously, there are limits on adaptation—some events, such as the loss of a loved one or another significant trauma—greatly challenge a person's ability to bounce back. But the adaptation phenomenon explains why we are resilient in the face of so many setbacks—and also why we so voraciously seek the next goody.

Despite the huge increases in American material wealth in the last half-century, people are no more satisfied with their lives overall (Diener 2000). Furthermore, some cross-cultural research has found that high material wealth is associated with lower psychological well-being in adults. Hungarian psychologist Mihaly Csikszentmihalyi, known for his writing on flourishing and creativity, among other concepts, has described how the pressure to work, acquire, and consume tends to deplete the energies that might otherwise be invested in friendships, art, literature, natural beauty, religion, and philosophy (Csikszentmihalyi 1999). In short, material consumption dulls our sensitivity to less-dopamine-saturated rewards.

Kids who regularly plug into electronic devices and consume high-voltage entertainment are likely to be bored by the pursuits of yesteryear, such as reading, chatting with friends, and walking in the park. And parental warmth seems to have an effect on materialism, too; one study found that the teens of cold, controlling parents later developed more materialistic orientations than those from warmer homes, whose parents valued more intrinsic goals, such as personal growth and close relationships (Kasser et al. 1995). Obviously, this phenomenon isn't limited to teens: The quest to acquire "stuff" to counter the effects of boredom, loneliness, emptiness, and insecurity is a society-wide problem.

Marketers know that people tend to buy stuff when they experience uncertainty about themselves or the world around them. There is even an acronym used by advertisers, FUD (fear, uncertainty, and doubt), which refers to the state they want to create, and *then help resolve* by selling you, or especially your children, their stuff! Since "self-doubt" is a teen's middle name during their identity-construction phase, corporations have come up with a zillion ways to "solve" the "problems" teens have with their hair, skin, style, status, and self-image—all the while contributing to that hedonistic treadmill.

Even though wealth does not create satisfaction, it is addictive. Recently, theories about the motivation for acquiring wealth and material possessions have been expanded to include the drive for accessing technology and social media in both adults and teens. In addition, materialism is no longer confined to the affluent; many of us, regardless of our financial status, are preoccupied with accumulating possessions and wealth. And given the correlation between digital media use and loneliness—just about anyone can be over-connected to the virtual world and underconnected to the real one—the dilemma for many Americans is that unlimited access to media has left us with inadequate time for pursuits that nurture and fill us, such as time in nature, relationships, and play.

Materialism has an evil twin: narcissism. The technical definition of narcissism goes well beyond self-absorption (the "It's all about me!" syndrome); it implies a core deficit of empathy. Jean Twenge has documented that today's college students score much higher on narcissism scales than did previous generations (Twenge and Foster 2010). Twenge and her colleagues argue that three cultural trends contribute to this problem: increased electronic communication, which reduces face time; increased violent and sexualized images in the mass media, which objectifies people; and our culture's saturation in consumerism and materialism. Interestingly, the research also shows that levels of self-esteem among teens have never been higher—and neither have depression levels! How is this possible? The answer may lie in the fact that while teens these days are constantly told they are superstars, when they look in the mirror that's not what they see. Remember, they have excellent BS radars. It's the problem of overpraise, all over again.

Teen Happiness

Levels of self-esteem among teens have never been higher—and neither have depression levels!

There are some who question this rise in narcissism, pointing to other statistics that run counter, such as the fact that volunteering by teenagers is at an all-time high. And even if they're really only volunteering to gain social approval or recognition, or because it's a high-school graduation requirement, does that mean kids today lack sincere empathy for others? A major study recently documented that empathy among college students has plummeted over the past forty years (Konrath 2011). It's enough to make you wonder if kids are losing one of the most important components in a civil society.

By now, you may have noticed the contradiction between the negative statistics about teenagers' emotional functioning ("Kids today have no empathy!") and the positive ("Most kids are doing well; almost a quarter are flourishing!"). It's impossible to reconcile, but it does underscore the messiness of adolescent emotional development. Even if you have a healthy, happy child, you may wonder what the future will bring, given all of the biological, social, and emotional changes that are inevitable in adolescence. Every parent wants their teen to flourish, but how to optimize the odds? Wise-minded parents brace themselves for the bouts of moodiness and stress, while they support their teens in building social and emotional competence in the myriad ways outlined in this chapter.

ESSENTIAL
ACTIVITY

The Spoilers of Materialism and Narcissism

What follows are some wise-minded parental policies that can head off materialism and narcissism. Which ones are firmly established in your house? And which are you ready to work on right now?

Policy	Doing now	Needs work
Regular chores are assigned—and enforced.	☐	☐
Children are expected to clean up after themselves.	☐	☐
Children do regular service work in the community *over and above that which is mandated by school.*	☐	☐
Parents do regular service work in the community.	☐	☐
Children do not regularly get advances on their allowances.	☐	☐
Children are expected to save up for the extra things, paying for those things themselves.	☐	☐
Parents practice restraint with respect to material acquisitions.	☐	☐
Parents reward good effort with genuine, appropriate praise, rather than "stuff."	☐	☐
Parents do not pay cash for good grades.	☐	☐
Dinner-table discussions sometimes center on the hardships of people in the world who are less fortunate.	☐	☐
Dinner-table discussions *of any kind* happen at least three times a week.	☐	☐

The Challenge of Emotions

Emotional intelligence determines how well children can use their other abilities (and that glorified IQ) to become successful and flourish. Life places enormous demands on our emotional systems, with stress from commutes, school expectations, economic difficulties, and constant stimulation from technology. The wise-minded parent appreciates the pressures on teens and the family as a whole, and prioritizes emotional wellness and thriving. Parental focus on providing for children—including those nice amenities, access to good schools, and help with homework—sometimes eclipses the importance of generating positive emotions at home. The research on stress and the fact that we absorb negative emotions from one another makes it clear that we should care about the way we treat each other as much as the quality of the air we breathe and the food we eat.

Parents are a child's primary model for emotional awareness and management. It takes three positive emotions to offset one negative one, and it's hard to imagine any family these days that doesn't want to improve its ratio. Often we lapse into seeking positive feelings through buying things or electronic entertainment, but the twin evils of materialism and narcissism should dissuade us from taking this easy route. Becoming good cooks and sharing meals, getting a neighborhood kickball game going, or taking a hike can increase the "joy and fun" quotient, but it takes concerted effort. And no matter how high your family's joy and fun quotient, those dark adolescent moods won't disappear altogether. Still, we can train ourselves to view these negative emotions as opportunities for offering empathy and solutions, not as bad feelings we must vanquish. These efforts may not change our child's mood, problem, or behavior in the moment, but the positive effects of skillful emotion management will help them flourish in ways that will resonate across many, many years.

CHAPTER 6

Strong Character

Scene: *Thinking ahead to summer, this dad is planning to sign his tween up for some volunteer work. His son's reaction to the idea is much as he expected, but Dad stays wise-minded while discussing this nonnegotiable family expectation.*

> **Chad:** *Why are you making me volunteer at that stupid day camp? I just want to chill out like all the other eighth-graders do in the summer.*
>
> **Dad:** *I get it. Full-time chill sounds great to you, I know. But I'm insisting on this because I know that you've got other weeks to chill, and I'm betting that you will like helping out with all the sports. A lot of these kids don't have big guys like you in their lives to play basketball with.*
>
> **Chad:** *That's your thing. You love that "do-gooding." But I know what's good for me, and that's chill time.*
>
> **Dad:** *It's part of our family's value system that we give our time to others. You know our creed, "From those who have more, more is—"*
>
> **Chad:** *Yeah, I know, "more is expected." Ugh. I wish I had parents who just let me do what I want.*
>
> **Dad:** *That sounds good to you, I know. Sorry. I'm playing the parent card on this one.*

Is Chad just a narcissistic brat? The kind of kid who only thinks about himself and his own needs and desires? No! He's a regular fourteen-year-old who wants to do whatever he wants in the summer. Because he can't understand the value of volunteering on his own quite yet, his dad plays "the parent card"—overruling his son's objections—because he knows that the only way to discover the benefits of volunteering is to do it.

Maybe Chad won't like teaching sports to younger kids; if that's the case, he can help out at the local science center, aquarium, or nursing home next summer instead. In the end, *where* and *how* Chad donates his time is not the important part; what matters is that he does *something* to help others.

Helping kids develop strong moral character requires parents to make these practices a priority and to model them as well. Luckily, parents have help in doing this; there is a wide array of positive institutions, including schools, religious organizations, and youth and community clubs, that provide myriad opportunities for tweens and teens to volunteer, be inspired by respected mentors, and practice virtuous behaviors.

Character building involves a lot more than just "do-gooding," as Chad calls volunteering. It involves practicing virtuous behaviors of all kinds, from being honest and fair to helping the less fortunate, to finding the courage to do the right thing—especially when it's not the easy thing. This chapter will introduce you to the six major virtues that researchers have pinpointed as vital in helping children develop strong character, along with dozens of character strengths that support these qualities. You'll also read about ways to identify your child's existing strengths and areas of potential growth, and learn some practical methods for encouraging the development of virtuous behavior.

Why It's Good to Be Good

A virtuous character keeps kids from breaking laws and harming others, but the benefits go much deeper than that. Developing and practicing virtuous traits prompts children to reach out to others with compassion, empathy, and a sense of fairness, building bonds with peers and with those less fortunate than themselves. In return, children gain acceptance and admiration from society, which they internalize, providing a foundation for self-confidence based on goodness and true accomplishment.

People who give to others are mentally and physically healthier than those who do not. A review of more than thirty studies that analyzed the link between health and volunteering in adults found that volunteers live longer, are happier, and have lower rates of depression and heart disease (Corporation for National & Community Service 2007). The many benefits of virtuous and charitable behavior will be explained at greater length throughout this chapter, but for now, suffice it to say that in its most "meta" form, virtuous behavior is essential to individual happiness and world peace!

THE SIX VIRTUES

Building strong character is the one essential that is not often highlighted in parenting literature. Yet many of us know intuitively that having a tween or teen with a strong sense of what's right and wrong and a deep-seated compassion for others is important, even essential, to their creation of a satisfying and purposeful life. So, to this end, what specific qualities should we be encouraging in our kids? Psychologists Christopher Peterson and Martin Seligman combed the cumulative work of moral philosophers, religious thinkers, and psychologists in their documentation of the qualities and traits that consistently emerge across history and cultures that support the pursuit of the good life (Peterson and Seligman 2004). They identified six major virtues that are vital for the development of the "whole" child and for the good of society:

- **wisdom**
- **courage**
- **humanity**
- **justice**
- **temperance**
- **transcendence**

The character strengths that make up these virtues will be presented in a later section; they include such characteristics as kindness, honesty, love of learning, optimism, and teamwork, which are then reflected in thoughts, feelings, and behaviors. For instance, for Chad to develop the virtue of humanity (compassion for others), he'll need to practice the character strengths of kindness, love, and social intelligence (being aware of the motives and feelings of others). He'll get some help in doing that from positive relationships with parents, peers, institutions, and youth-development programs. There is much more information on how to help your child build these strengths later in the chapter, but first, take a moment to consider the 10,000-foot view of your child's best character strengths—and possibly identify a few you'd like to help him develop more fully.

ESSENTIAL
QUIZ

Checking in on Character Strengths

Think about your child's overall character and answer these questions the best you can. Mark "true" if the statement is mostly or usually true (nobody's perfect!).

True False

1. ☐ ☐ My child is open to new ideas and usually doesn't dig in and refuse to hear people out.

2. ☐ ☐ When the going gets tough, my child gets going, working through challenges.

3. ☐ ☐ In group school assignments, my child does her fair share and will even go a step further if it helps the team.

4. ☐ ☐ When in a dispute with someone, my child truly tries to understand his opponent's point of view.

5. ☐ ☐ My child is willing to forgive and usually doesn't hold a grudge.

6. ☐ ☐ My child shows gratitude for the good things in her life.

If you answered "false" to one or more of the questions above, congratulations! You probably have a normal adolescent who is still building up her store of character strengths. Think of each of those "false" answers as an opportunity— a potential area for growth. Before we go into the various exercises and tools that will help you grow these strengths in your tween or teen, let's first look at the nuts and bolts of character development.

How Character Strengths Develop

In a sense, developing every other essential covered in this book contributes to building character and a purposeful life. Here's how:

• Securely attached children are more cooperative, obedient, and self-controlled.

• Practicing virtuous behaviors requires self-control; doing the "right" thing requires that teens control their impulses, think through consequences, choose appropriate behaviors, practice willpower, and avoid risk taking.

• Good schools transmit societal values through academic curricula (ranging from literature to health education), an ethical atmosphere, and the moral orientation of the teachers.

- Positive social values are modeled and supported throughout childhood by parents, teachers, religious leaders, youth-development program leaders, and coaches. Children also learn character strengths from positive social experiences with other children—strengths such as sharing, helping, responsibility, and honesty.
- Emotional learning and emotional competence, which emphasize empathy and interpersonal skills, are modeled in authoritative homes, in which parents are responsive to and respectful of children's perspectives while guiding and supporting responsible behaviors.
- Physical health (the essential that's discussed in chapter 7), athletic teams, and healthy lifestyles support the practice of good habits and ethical behaviors.

Since wise-minded parenting models empathy and thoughtful, discerning action, it's ideal for supporting adolescents as they develop character strengths.

MORAL REASONING

Fifty years ago, Lawrence Kohlberg conceptualized stages of moral development that described the logic children use for reasoning in moral dilemmas (Kohlberg 1963). In his research method, subjects are asked to comment on written scenarios that depict moral dilemmas. Here's one classic scenario:

> *Heinz needs medicine for his wife, who suffers from a life-threatening illness. Heinz has raised half the money for the medicine, but can't afford the full fee. The druggist charges ten times the amount that he paid for the medicine and refuses to discount the fee or let Heinz pay him later. Should Heinz steal the medicine? Why or why not?*

Kohlberg discovered that as children mature, they gradually progress through stages, from obedience ("How can I avoid punishment?") and self-interest ("What's in it for me?") to mutuality ("I'll be good to you if you are good to me"), to social order ("People can't just do what they want"), to law and justice ("I should follow laws, and laws in a civil society are usually based on systems of justice"), and finally to universal principles ("All humans should have certain human rights and live according to the Golden Rule").

In analyzing the responses to Heinz's situation, Kohlberg found that children in their older teen years usually reason at the higher stages of moral development, understand the importance of law and order, and respect that laws organize and regulate our society, but some would even reach the final stage, arguing for the universal rights of the individual to protect human life and defending Heinz's stealing of the drug.

There were problems with Kohlberg's moral development stages, not the least of which was that they were standardized initially on male samples and represented moral reasoning and not moral behavior. Carol Gilligan noted that they also overlooked the ethic of caring, which influences responses to ethical dilemmas, especially among females (Gilligan 1993). For instance, some would respond that Heinz should not risk going to jail because he might have other children to take care of at home. Doesn't this answer also reflect a valuing of human life above all else? In fact, the ethic of caring for and nurturing the vulnerable was not represented in Kohlberg's system of individual rights, nor were values that elevated

ESSENTIAL
ACTIVITY

Discussing Moral Dilemmas

Here are a few scenarios to kick-start family discussions of values and virtues. Try posing one at the dinner table and engaging in an analytic conversation using the Socratic method.

1. Jeremy had a copy of last year's Spanish final. The teacher is known to give the same (or very similar) test every year. Jeremy presents a copy to Aidan, but Aidan declines to look at it. When the principal finds out about the breach, he threatens to cancel the big end-of-year dance unless someone comes forth to reveal the identity of the test thief. Should Aidan reveal his knowledge for the good of the school community? Would Aidan's decision change if his confidentiality was assured? Why or why not? Why do so many teens cheat? What are some reasons not to cheat, even if "everybody" else does?

2. Bobby offers to sell a bike to Tom on the cheap. Tom buys it, but then the police come to his school and confront him; the bike was stolen. Should Tom tell the cops it came from Bobby? What if Tom is going to be arrested for theft? What if Bobby is poor, from disadvantaged circumstances, and going to college on a full scholarship next year? Should this make a difference? Why or why not?

3. Yolanda's sister's diary is on her desk. Yolanda is curious and concerned because her sister has been acting sad lately and starting to retreat from family and friends. Is it OK for Yolanda to read the diary? If she found a poem inside the diary that included the line "There is no reason to live," should she say something to an adult? Is it ever OK to read someone else's diary or personal writing without permission?

4. You saw your neighbor lightly bump another neighbor's car and then drive away. Later, the owner of the bumped car asked you point blank whether you saw his car get bumped. What do you do?

5. You are attending a party where a lot of kids are drinking heavily, but you are not. You notice one kid has passed out and you try to turn him on his side in case he starts to vomit. At one point, somebody yells that the police are coming and everyone runs out the back door. Do you run, too? What do you think would happen to you if you decided to stay with the inebriated kid?

one's responsibility to one's community over one's individual rights, which are found in other cultures.

Moral development research has since evolved to include the study of the practice of virtuous behaviors. Still, even on its own, moral reasoning does guide behavior and reflect a teen's ability to analyze moral dilemmas, think through consequences, understand implications of actions, and weigh principles such as obedience, the law, loyalty, obligations to the community, and social justice. Reasoning is good exercise for the prefrontal cortex, conditioning teens to thoroughly think through moral dilemmas, whether in history class or at the dinner table. But it's quite another thing to transfer that thought into action on a Saturday night when the beer comes out at a party or at school on Monday when a peer is being bullied.

Even though reasoning does not necessarily determine behavior, it certainly influences it, and discussion of moral dilemmas can still kick-start some fascinating dinner table talks. You can do this in a way that encourages critical thinking by asking Socratic questions (see page 125). Following this method ensures that you will engage your child without evaluating or lecturing. If your teen asks your opinion, try to be humble, and remember the DBT assumption from chapter 1: There is no absolute truth.

In fact, there are many truths to be examined to help us acquire a deep understanding of the complexities of life. Your goal is only to stimulate thinking. To that end, your questions should focus on clarification ("Can you describe what you mean specifically by that statement?"), assumptions ("What is the evidence for that assumption?"), reasoning ("What would be a counterargument for that?"), and gaining perspective ("What would be another way of looking at that?" "What would be the consequences of going with your judgment call?").

WISE-MINDED **MANTRA** **There is no absolute truth.**

CHARACTER EDUCATION AND YOUTH PROGRAMS

Character education became a popular mission of schools in the late 1990s, ushered in by a demand for the integration of moral education with intellectual education (Damon 2002). Efforts were made to promote character strengths, such as respect, compassion, responsibility, and self-control, to name a few. But questions have been raised about the effectiveness of these programs and about which virtues should be taught. Some parents wanted to prioritize the promotion of tolerance, and others thought the focus should be on the respect for authority. Teaching values can be touchy business.

At the same time that schools were grappling with how to promote strong character, intervention researchers were emphasizing the importance of character strengths in protecting against the negative effects of stress and trauma, and minimizing the harm of psychological disorders. Social intelligence, self-control, and spirituality are also character strengths, and all of them play a role in preventing or mitigating problem behaviors such as risk taking, substance use, and school failure (Elias et al. 2008). As discussed in chapter 4, "developmental assets" (which include a commitment to learning, positive values, social competence, and sense of purpose) were found to contribute to social thriving, as well as protecting against psychological disorders (Leffert et al. 1998). Although these researchers operate in different fields, they are finding similar positive results for the relationship between character strengths (also known as assets or traits) and well-being.

A common practice among schools these days is to require students to participate in volunteering or service learning, the goal of which is to help children build the character strengths of kindness, altruism, empathy for the less fortunate, and responsibility. In fact, in a review of various youth-development programs, character building was among the most frequently cited goals, mentioned by 81 percent of the forty-eight programs (Roth and Brooks-Gunn 2003).

A comparative study of nineteen diverse high schools documented the distinctive qualities that a variety of youth programs enhanced (Larson et al. 2006). In this research, sports and arts programs were found to provide more experiences related to developing initiative than the other activities, although the sports teams were also associated with high stress. While sports offer kids opportunities to apply effort and to deal with excitement and disappointment, competition can also be taxing (although no more stressful than school classes or friendships). Youth in faith-based activities reported higher rates of experiences related to identity ("thinking about who I am"), emotional regulation, interpersonal skills, and connections to adults. Service activities stood out as providing opportunities associated with the development of teamwork, positive relationships, and social capital (community connectedness). Overall, organized activities appear to fulfill an important function in providing experiences that enhance teen development, and in ways that are often different than those provided in school classes, unstructured leisure time with friends, and jobs. Certain strengths, such as teamwork, initiative, and social responsibility, are particularly bolstered by youth programs. According to one researcher, such programs promote positive development by emphasizing the following five C's (Lerner et al. 2000):

- **competence** (problem solving)
- **caring** (empathy)
- **connection** (relationships)
- **character** (morality)
- **confidence** (identity)

The premise is that teens contribute to and benefit from experiences with the group, the activity, and the participation and leadership opportunities these programs offer. They also profit from the program's emphasis on life skills and the supportive relationships with adults (Ramey and Rose-Krasnor 2011). In addition, the hope is that teens become motivated by the challenges these activities provide, develop a sense of purpose, and become more actively engaged in their own personal development. As a bonus, many of these activities take place after school and on weekends, filling time that teens might otherwise have on their hands to get into trouble.

Another approach to studying the benefits of youth programs has been to measure the engagement and absorption of teens involved in these activities (Froh et al. 2010). Researchers took the concept of "passion" (already associated with positive emotions and flourishing in adults) and linked it to initiative and absorption to measure engagement among teens involved in organized activities. Engaged living, defined as teens having a passion for helping others and being completely immersed in activities, was examined across five studies and three samples of middle school and high school students. Higher levels of engaged living (as determined by teen, peer, and teacher reports) were related to well-being, academic achievement, gratefulness, hopefulness, happiness, life satisfaction, positive emotions, and self-esteem—and lower levels of depression, envy, and delinquency.

So, volunteering is great for building character, but if you have a tween, you may have already noticed how difficult it is to find volunteer opportunities for middle schoolers. Faith-based youth programs, scouting, and other service clubs are available, but most opportunities at nursing homes, pet shelters, science centers, and similar organizations have age limits that exclude younger kids. This means that parents often have to volunteer with their tweens to provide this valuable experience. Access to these programs usually depends on parent initiative and availability, which puts rural, overburdened, or impoverished families at a disadvantage. Given how stressed the average family is these days, this to-do item can easily fall off the priority list.

It takes extra effort, true, but it's well worth it. There is a significant relationship between happiness, engagement, and a passion for helping others. Character seems to have a direct link with psychological wellness. In addition, up to now, much of the conversation around living a purposeful life has been confined to adults. Yet the research reviewed above indicates that we should be just as focused on meaningful lives for tweens and teens. The second decade of life is not too early to emphasize the importance of helping others, practicing initiative in service activities, and deriving positive emotions from interpersonal engagement and full absorption. Furthermore, given the many pressures that tweens and teens suffer during these years, these enriching activities often offer stress relief and fun.

VALUES IN ACTION

All of the character strengths discussed so far help develop the six major virtues (listed on page 180), but there are many others. Nansook Park and Christopher Peterson, two psychologists in the brigade of researchers studying character and its relationship to personal strengths, developed a "Values in Action Inventory" (Park and Peterson 2006), which identifies twenty-four character attributes organized by the virtues they foster. They are paraphrased here:

wisdom
- *creativity:* thinking of novel and productive ways to do things
- *curiosity:* taking an ongoing interest in many experiences
- *open-mindedness:* thinking things through and examining them from all sides
- *love of learning:* mastering new skills, topics, and bodies of knowledge
- *perspective:* being able to provide wise counsel to others

courage
- *honesty:* speaking the truth and presenting oneself in a genuine way
- *bravery:* not shrinking from threat, challenge, difficulty, or pain
- *persistence:* finishing what one starts
- *zest:* approaching life with excitement and energy

humanity
- *kindness:* doing favors and good deeds for others
- *love:* valuing close relationships
- *social intelligence:* being aware of the motives and feelings of self and others

justice
- *fairness:* treating all people the same according to notions of fairness and justice
- *leadership:* organizing group activities and seeing them through
- *teamwork:* working well as member of a group

temperance
- *forgiveness:* forgiving those who have done wrong
- *modesty:* letting one's accomplishments speak for themselves
- *prudence:* being careful about one's choices; not saying or doing things that might later be regretted
- *self-regulation:* controlling what one feels and does

transcendence
- *appreciation of beauty and excellence:* noticing and enjoying beauty, excellence, and/or skilled performance in all domains of life
- *gratitude:* being aware of and thankful for the good things that happen
- *hope:* expecting the best and working to achieve it
- *humor:* laughing and joking readily; bringing smiles to other people
- *religiousness:* having coherent beliefs about the higher purpose and meaning of life

Research has replicated the original findings that document the relationship between character strengths and psychological health among youth (Toner et al. 2012). Certain character strengths have emerged as more important than others, though; for instance, the strength of self-control is predictive of well-being. In addition, teen well-being has been particularly associated with hope, zest, and leadership. In the high school sample that Emily Toner and her colleagues surveyed, curiosity and capacity for love were linked to greater happiness. And kids who possessed "other-directed" character strengths (e.g., forgiveness, kindness, teamwork) at the start of high school experienced fewer symptoms of depression by the end of tenth grade (Gillham et al. 2011). Researchers also found that character strengths such as hope, gratitude, and meaning (all aspects of the virtue of transcendence), when combined with curiosity and love for learning, predicted well-being over time. Given the moodiness that accompanies puberty and the psychiatric difficulties that can emerge during adolescence, these research findings suggest that character-building activities are not only important for long-term happiness and satisfaction, but are an important way to protect and bolster psychological health in the short term, too.

ESSENTIAL ACTIVITY

How Engaged and Altruistic Is Your Child?

Reflect upon your tween or teen, and then fill out this chart to get an idea of your child's attributes related to engagement, altruism, and connectedness to the community. Remember, this is not a formal instrument—it's just a way for you to think about important qualities you might want to promote by getting your child involved in meaningful activities. Don't enlist your child to help you complete this exercise; this one's just for you. The next section has a validated survey for your child to take.

For each item below, list a recent example or two here or in your journal, or take notes about where you'd like to see growth.

Attribute	Example(s) or comments
Enjoys helping others	
Gets totally absorbed in activities	
Feels a sense of purpose	
Likes to be physically engaged	
Feels a sense of social responsibility	
Has hobbies that he or she truly enjoys	
Prays, meditates, or practices mindfulness	
Enjoys relating to others	

Attribute	Example(s) or comments
Likes volunteering	
Prefers building friendships to buying things	
Feels grateful for many things	
Likes to be part of a team	
Wants to make the world a better place	
Would rather be engaged in an activity than doing nothing	
Feels part of something bigger	
Uses personal strengths for helping others	
Feels like a member of the community	
Appreciates good things that happen	
Cooperates as a member of a team	
Would rather be close to people than have a lot of money	
Has a sense of personal spirituality	

ESSENTIAL
ACTIVITY

The 'Values in Action' Quiz

If you're curious about how your child is progressing in building character strengths and virtues, here's a fun family activity to inspire all kinds of self-awareness. Even teenagers love to take quizzes that reveal interesting things about themselves. Set aside an evening to go online and register, then take the "Values in Action" survey (it's confidential and anonymous, and the basic results are free) at *viacharacter.org*. Ask your tween or teen to take the "youth" survey (validated for eleven- to seventeen-year-olds), while you take the adult version. Answer the 240 questions; upon completion, you'll instantly learn all twenty-four of your character strengths ranked in order. Compare notes with your child and discuss how you think you display these strengths in your day-to-day lives. Tell stories that reflect when you exhibited one of these strengths. Warning: The older your teen is, the less agreeable they may be to join in on this activity—remember, they are individuating from you! Try to get them to take the survey anyway, even if they don't want to share the results. Teens love finding out about their own personalities and character—and this one is all about their strengths!

Practicing the character-building skills of helping others, emotional intelligence, and teamwork contributes greatly to mental health, but there are probably many more nuanced ways that organized activities benefit teens. When kids find engaged activities that are a good match for their interests, it stands to reason that the amount of time they have for ruminating on negative emotions decreases significantly. Furthermore, an upward spiral of positive experiences can occur, in which teens enjoy interpersonal exchanges, receive feedback about their attributes, and challenge themselves.

TEEN EMPLOYMENT AND CHARACTER STRENGTHS

What role does teen employment play in the development of character strengths? While this question has not been comprehensively examined, a link has been established between high-intensity employment of teens during the school year (more than twenty hours a week) and negative outcomes, such as poor academic performance, delinquency, and substance use (Greenberger and Steinberg 1986). At lower levels (fewer than twenty hours per week), proponents often assert that employment contributes to self-reliance and self-esteem, but it also seems to be linked to more permissive parenting and autonomy among the teens (Monahan et al. 2011), which can lead to a lack of monitoring, substance use, and counterproductive purchasing choices (i.e., kids spending their hard earned money on junk food and partying). Ellen Greenberger and Laurence Steinberg found that it's the rare teen who is really "saving for college," like in the good old days. In my practice, I've found that it's far more common for immigrant teens to be savers; they see college as a truly American gateway to success.

All told, the development of character strengths probably varies among employed teens. And another reason for this may be the fact that the jobs most teens hold offer poor mentorship opportunities, questionable role modeling among adult coworkers, and nonengaging work responsibilities.

In my clinical practice, I sometimes see teens who put forth enormous effort at school, but will never be at the top of their academic classes because of learning and attention problems. For these kids, investing *all* of their energies in academics can be discouraging, because they don't get much reward in the way of grades for a lot of effort (at least not in high school; some do get there later). However, these same kids may have all sorts of strengths in emotional and social competence that allow them to excel at and enjoy organized activities, such as athletics or volunteering—or a well-selected job at a restaurant, town newspaper, or other small business. The right engaging activity (with restricted hours) may make them a star performer in a nonacademic setting. And that activity or job may supply the teen with a sense of integrity and confidence that translates to resilience and persistence in the school setting.

Adults in your child's youth programs or employment setting can be the mentors who see your teen's best assets and become their greatest fan and advocate for the next opportunity. Parents need to be resourceful to help kids find that meaningful setting or job—perhaps working as an assistant to a family friend, the leaf-removal king for everyone in the neighborhood, or the cool T-shirt producer for class service projects. Enterprising parents are like scouts, always looking for ways to match their teens' talents, interests, and needs to new experiences that will provide opportunities to build or enhance character strengths.

ESSENTIAL
TIP

Tapping into Teen Talents
Act as a "scout" for your child, seeking out the best match of activities for your child's talents and interests. This can open doors to opportunities that build character strengths.

HOW SHOULD YOUR TEEN SPEND HIS TIME?

A crucial job of every parent of an adolescent is to decide how that child should spend his time. When it comes to after-school, weekend, and summer activities, are you proactive about matching your child's interests and skills to character-building activities, or do you let things flow? Are you careful not to overschedule your kid, leaving him no time to relax and learn to structure his own life?

Seeking character-building opportunities should not stray into "designer parent" syndrome, in which parents engineer their children's lives based solely on what looks best on a college application. This syndrome is the bane of psychologists who work with stressed-out kids. During the writing of *The Launching Years*, I was made painfully aware of the damage designer parents can cause. Some of the most important parts of identity development happen within those unstructured and random experiences that unfold because parents aren't engineering those résumés. Fly-fishing, fire-twirling, and hula-hoop contests can be great for the spirit and an awful lot of fun, but they won't happen if parents are trying to map a stairway to the Ivies. And without leisure time and time for individual interests, how can teens learn to have balanced lives?

Would a struggling and stressed-out student who feels burned out at school really benefit from a summer spent at a name-brand college taking AP classes and SAT prep? Probably not. Instead, he might benefit more from the opportunity to run the summer art program at the Boys & Girls Club. Or maybe she would flourish at an outdoor leadership program. Or how about saving money for college by spending the summer working on cousin Gail's dairy farm? Not only can these kinds of experiences energize kids, but they may kindle their passion to reach out for more engaging activities—for more "character building." As an added benefit, those college admissions officers have laser-sharp eyes for authenticity. They'd rather hear about genuine, poignant life lessons learned over a summer spent working on a farm than about the experience of taking three months of AP classes, any day.

Making decisions about activities can be maddening for parents, even for those who have the means to buy any experience they want for their kids. Research on decision making shows that when people are overwhelmed by lots of options (for cookies, mutual funds, colleges, jeans, you name it), they are more likely to regret their choice, not make a choice, or blame themselves for poor decision making if the outcome isn't wonderful (Schwartz 2004). This dynamic applies to parents choosing character-building activities for their kids. You can go bonkers wondering about the "right" school, camp, athletic team, youth program, job, or service experience.

Some parents make it look easy. They funnel all their kids into public schools, encourage them to be lifeguards at the local pool during the summer, and sign them up for Scouts as their extracurricular activity, with little to no hand-wringing about "what else." These are the lucky ones; fewer choices can be bliss! On the other hand, teens (especially the ones who are failing to thrive) are lucky if they have parents who look high and low for experiences that engage them in helping others, or help them find work settings they will enjoy and gain self-confidence from. Maybe you're not that into fashion, decal creation for skateboards, or prayer flags at football games, but if it gets your couch potato engaged, it's worth considering.

Challenges to Building Character Strengths

THE EFFECTS OF ADVERSITY

For many kids, developing character strengths happens in the context of some pretty severe life challenges. Physician and researcher Vincent Felitti, of the Kaiser Permanente Medical Care Program in California, and Robert Anda, an epidemiologist at the Centers for Disease Control and Prevention, conducted a study of more than 17,000 (mainly middle-class) patients and documented the long-lasting effects of what the researchers called "adverse childhood experiences" (ACE). Along with the subjects' comprehensive medical information, they collected data on ten different categories of stressful experiences, including physical and sexual abuse, neglect, household chaos, and parental dysfunction—ranging from drug abuse to incarceration (Felitti et al. 1998).

One of the most noteworthy findings was the surprising level of childhood trauma: More than one-quarter of the participants grew up in homes with an alcoholic or a drug-abusing parent, and another quarter reported being beaten as children. Two-thirds of the patients had experienced at least one adverse experience, and twenty percent—one out of five—had experienced four or more. Most startling of all was the correlation between ACE scores and health outcomes: The higher the ACE score, the worse the subject's health later in life. This was true in every measure, from addiction problems to psychological disorders to chronic disease. The conclusion after many years of analyzing this data and more data like it is that stressful events experienced early in life can alter your body's systems and your health (an area of study called *psychoneuroimmunology*) for life. The fact that the original study was conducted with a middle-class sample shifted the focus beyond the rubric of poverty and onto the biological pathways that affect health, the upper limits of tolerance for natural resiliency, and particular character strengths that can help mitigate future health consequences of traumatic events in childhood.

What this research tells us is that adverse childhood experiences result in changes to kids' biological systems, including reduced volumes of the prefrontal cortex and hippocampus, greater activation of stress responses, and elevation in inflammation levels (Danese and McEwen 2012). The extraordinary stress caused by these experiences hurts children—it gets into their bodies and brains—and it can stay with them throughout their lives. However, research on resilience offers some hope and points to the ways that a child's inherent character strengths and certain environmental advantages in the family and community (referred to as "protective factors") can help kids tolerate stress and bloom despite the trauma they experienced.

Forty years of research on resilience has demonstrated that certain protective factors (one researcher, Ann Masten, calls them "ordinary magic") can help children adapt to negative circumstances and thrive (Masten 2001):

- **Individual level:** good intellectual functioning, sociable and positive temperament, self-confidence, talents, and faith
- **Family level:** bonds with family members, authoritative parenting, socioeconomic advantages, and connections to extended supportive family networks
- **Community level:** bonds with positive adults outside the family, connections to youth programs, and effective school settings

How do these "protective factors" compare with the character-strength benefits cited earlier for this population? For a start, children in these studies on resilience who possessed faith, sociable temperaments, and positive connections with adults, schools, and organizations would probably have measured sky high on character strengths in the "Values in Action" survey (if it had existed then). In addition, intervention researchers, who provided services to high-risk youth in early childhood, found that enhancing protective factors for all kids, regardless of their character strengths, resulted in preventing or reducing mental health problems, risky sexual behavior, substance abuse, and crime—up to fifteen years after the intervention (Hawkins et al. 2008). These findings, along with the CASEL interventions described in chapter 3, make a spectacular case for the importance of enhancing protective factors and character-building opportunities for all children.

Does the list of protective factors sound familiar? Over and over, you are reading pretty much the same list of essentials for optimizing your child's adjustment to adversity of all kinds, whether poverty, a learning disability, a childhood trauma, or the loss of a parent. But one caveat is offered by researchers of all stripes, from backgrounds as diverse as public health, child development, clinical psychiatry, and sociology: The magic of those protective factors only goes so far. A child subjected to a great deal of adversity will suffer the consequences, no matter how many protective factors you put in place. We need to eliminate the source of the trauma, not just build resiliency.

Although particularly resilient poor children can develop many character strengths through coping with hardships, no one would wish for a child to develop valor by defending a sibling from bullies, perspective through hunger, or hope from multiple evictions. For poor children, organized youth-group opportunities and after-school activities are sorely lacking. Low-income parents can't afford to pay for many of these options, nor can they manage to provide transportation during the afternoon hours they are working. While we've all read the stories of valiant achievers who rise out of poverty to become amazing contributors to society, in most cases these individuals are fortunate enough to possess a bumper crop of character strengths that help to protect them from the usual consequences of extreme hardship.

THE BURDEN OF AFFLUENCE, OVERPROTECTION, AND INDULGENCE

You read that right: There's trouble to be had on both extreme ends of the economic spectrum. In the same way that poverty creates stressors that tax character building, so can affluence. Whether you call them the overscheduled, hot-housed, helicoptered, hyperparented, or entitled, the victim of "overparenting" will suffer, too. As discussed in chapter 3, Suniya Luthar has documented the compromised well-being of affluent children and related it to academic pressures and parent-child disconnection (Luthar and Latendresse 2005). Parents can harm their children with a preoccupation with grades and a disregard for the importance of the parent-child relationship. Well-meaning but anxious parents may stunt their child's growth by trying to protect them from difficult experiences; children who are never given the chance to be challenged or make mistakes lack the opportunity to develop the character strengths of zest, originality, and perseverance. And you don't have to be rich to fall into the trap of buying your child's love—substituting time and connection with material goods—or protecting them from the discomfort of high expectations, or solving problems for them.

The Story of 'Prince' Charles

A fifteen-year-old patient of mine—let's call him "Charles"—once said, "I wish my parents had another hobby besides me." Charles felt like he was responsible for his mother's happiness, and he resented it. His father complained that Charles' mother practically praised their son for breathing. The mother said she brushed her teeth before she breastfed Charles as a baby so her breath wouldn't offend him; she felt guilty that his depressed demeanor must mean she was a bad mother; and she dreaded college admissions because she was certain that the process would crush her son's spirit.

Anxiety suffused Charles' childhood from early on. He wasn't allowed to deal with daily stressors on his own, and he wasn't trusted to develop some rigor by trial-and-error learning. Anticipated difficulties at school or in sports were preempted by his parents. They let him quit every activity when it got tough. They worried relentlessly about his self-esteem. Parental hovering prevented Charles from learning how to fall down, pick himself back up, dust off, and carry on.

It was difficult but necessary for me to tell Charles' parents, "Your perceptions of your child's fragility are hurting him more than any failure would. He needs to struggle, so that he can learn to develop resilience and perseverance." I advise indulgent or overprotective parents to find some character-building experiences, preferably in collaboration with the child, and then insist that they stick it out. I recommend organized activities outside of the parents' observation, because scrutiny is so suffocating for these kids. Also, if the parents aren't on site, they're also not in the position to bail their kids out.

Eventually, Charles' parents were able to back off, but it wasn't easy. At one point, Charles joined an improvisational acting group, but refused to perform if his parents were in the audience. His parents were hurt, of course (who wouldn't be?), but they needed to understand the history of "overfocus" that led Charles to this point. Unlocking his talent for improv put in motion his motivation for working hard on pursuits he enjoyed. He completed college and now manages a successful bike store. He told me recently that he works like a demon, and believes he really benefited from the way improv taught him to roll with the punches and bounce back from failure. Charles went from having little perseverance to having a lot. His parents deserve credit for developing some, too!

TRUE GRIT

Perseverance is one of the character strengths that builds courage, as is zest. Put them together with the dogged ability to pursue a very challenging goal despite setbacks, and you get "grit," a term popularized by University of Pennsylvania psychologist Angela Duckworth. In her study of West Point cadets, Ivy League students, and National Spelling Bee finalists, she and her colleagues found that grit predicted educational success above and beyond IQ (Duckworth et al. 2007). While grit is correlated with one of the main traits studied by personality researchers—conscientiousness—it is also a strength unto itself. Grit involves working assiduously toward challenges, sustaining effort and interest over years despite failure, and coping with adversity and setbacks. As Duckworth says in her study, "The gritty individual approaches achievement as a marathon; his or her advantage is stamina. Whereas disappointment or boredom signals to others that it is time to change trajectory and cut losses, the gritty individual stays the course."

One implication of the research on grit is that children who have shown an exceptional devotion to developing a particular skill—whatever their natural talents—should be given the same support for pursuing their dreams as those deemed "gifted" or "prodigies." One oft-cited study of 120 world-class pianists, neurologists, mathematicians, swimmers, chess players, and sculptors found that only a handful of them had been regarded as child prodigies (Bloom 1985). Instead, they seemed to personify the very essence of grit. They may also have believed in their own capabilities and assumed an optimistic attitude about their future potential. Grit, resilience, and optimism help us stay in the game despite the inevitable curveballs that come our way.

ESSENTIAL
ACTIVITY

Does Your Child Have Grit?

How does your child demonstrate grit? Parents often fail to appreciate this asset, because they may see certain activities as "child's play" and not related to academic or career-relevant endeavors (e.g., DJ spinning and organizing playlists, fashion blogging, collecting Magic cards).

Take note of a time your child has shown perseverance, tenacity, and unwavering commitment to a long-term interest. Remember that this interest does not need to appear useful to you!

_____

_____

_____

_____

Now note the character strengths and skills this demonstrated. You can use the list on page 186–87 for inspiration.

_____

_____

_____

List a "gritty" interest you had as a child that may be linked with valued life pursuits now.

_____

_____

_____

If you, like most parents, would give your eye teeth to see your kids develop the character strengths of courage, grit, and resolve to cope with difficult situations, here's the place to start: yourself. After all, modeling character strengths is one of the greatest gifts we can give our children.

Grit involves overcoming setbacks while mastering important challenges, staying with a commitment in spite of distractions, working hard, and being diligent while pursuing long-range goals. Sometimes, passionate kids will demonstrate these qualities on their own. But at other times, especially when kids seem apathetic about everything or are always quitting, authoritative parenting must prevail; parents should insist that the child choose some activity or goal. "None" is not an option. Dealing with complaints and protests is usually the downside for parents who take this approach, especially with a child who has an anxious, avoidant, or negative tilt to their temperament, but this is where the character strengths of parent perseverance and patience come into play.

Let's listen in as a wise-minded single mom insists on a little grit from her tween daughter.

> *Mom:* I know how much you want to quit orchestra since your friend Roxie won first chair in your violin section, but since you've opted out of other activities at school, I want you to stick it out through eighth grade.
>
> *Celia:* This should be my decision. And Roxie is not my friend anymore. And it's not just that. I haven't enjoyed it ever since I started at this school. I hate living here. If you hadn't divorced Dad and moved here, my life wouldn't suck like this.
>
> *Mom:* You've had to adjust to an awful lot of changes. I wish it were less stressful for you. But I'm convinced that music and staying in orchestra is good for you and that you will pull through this. I have faith in you, Celia.
>
> *Celia:* You don't care how I feel about it. You wrecked my life and now you won't let me have a say about anything.
>
> *Mom:* There are certain values I'm going to stick with—chores, bedtimes, media use, and after-school activities. I understand your point of view. I do insist on a lot of stuff around here.
>
> *Celia:* Yeah, I wish I could boss you around and see how you liked it.
>
> *Mom:* You've told me many times how immersed you can get during orchestra. You called it bliss. Does that help you live with my insistence that you stick it out?
>
> *Celia:* Maybe, I don't know.
>
> *Mom:* What hugs you the most? I know how much you like the music.
>
> *Celia:* I like all of it and none of it, depending on my mood. And right now, I hate that Roxie got first chair. It should have been me.

This mom is sticking with her plan to support her daughter's development of grit. And for a pubescent tween of twelve, Celia is showing remarkable insight to realize that her attitude about youth orchestra is dependent upon her mood. Her mom wanted to say all sorts of reassuring things about how many times Celia returned home in an exuberant mood from orchestra, proclaiming that Bach was her favorite person ever born. But as a wise-minded parent, Celia's mom knows that reminding her daughter of these times would be dismissive of her current mood. Right now, Celia feels that orchestra is demanding, difficult, and even humiliating with Roxie winning first chair.

Mom is also wise to stay on topic, since going around and around about the divorce and anger about the move might throw them off course (although, if this was a new disclosure on that topic, she would want to dive in to validate her daughter's feelings, and fast). Also, she knows that if she pushes too many of the positive parts, they could end up in a power struggle (e.g., "You love orchestra!" "No, I don't!"). And finally, Mom appreciates that Celia's reflective moment about her ambivalent (positive and negative) attitude and reluctant acquiescence might be the best resolution she can get right now.

WHEN GOOD KIDS DO 'BAD' THINGS

While character strengths contribute to psychological well-being and good behavior, even the most high-functioning kids are still kids (not to mention human, which means flawed). Good character does not guarantee good behavior full-time! Given the fact that the majority of teens will display moodiness, argumentativeness, and risk taking, inevitably they also occasionally appear to lack the very character strengths that they are regularly praised for. Kids—especially tweens and younger teens—can be stellar citizens at school and other activities, and then come home and lay down some serious disrespect, selfishness, and defiance. As you'll recall from chapter 4, teens aren't individuating from adults in those other settings, but when they get home, they are engaged in battle with the controller of resources and rules—you. You are the secure base; so secure that they know they can afford to sacrifice a little of the rapport with you that they work so hard to maintain in other social groups.

Good character does not guarantee good behavior full-time.

Where are the virtues of justice, temperance, and prudence on Saturday night when teens take off on a scavenger hunt that includes the stealing of a stop sign? A lark like this one can tempt even an Eagle Scout. If he gets arrested for this prank, does this mean his character is damaged irrevocably? What if he gets caught cheating on a test? A wise-minded parent soon learns, with the help of some calming techniques outlined in chapter 1 and a wide-angle appraisal of the situation, that his son can have many admirable character strengths—and still make big errors in judgment.

Most of the literature on moral development and character focuses on positive strengths and behavior. But you know from your own experience that many of our most character-defining moments came at times when we did the wrong thing and learned from it.

A strong character doesn't emerge from an easy, trouble-free life; quite the opposite. Likewise, treating children as if they are fragile does not build strength. And reacting to their big mistakes with vilification inflicts shame, sending the message that they are a bad person, rather than a person who did a bad thing. Guilt, which is feeling bad and regretful about a behavior, can be productive when it is short-lived, generates reflection, and results in a behavioral change. Parents can better help their teens learn from their mistakes by transmitting acceptance even after they do really bad things, like stealing a stop sign and getting arrested.

In difficult times, when your tween or teen has made a big mistake, consider this quote from Robert Coles, a psychiatrist who has written widely on the moral lives of children: "First, ascribe the best motive" (Coles 1997). When your child makes mistakes, even premeditated ones, such as shoplifting, cheating, or lying, they aren't aiming to screw up their lives or to hurt you. They're usually overwhelmed by temptations and impulses. The child still needs to accept responsibility for the crime, but the wise-minded parent thinks calmly and clearly about their child's motivations. Begin by giving your child the benefit of the doubt.

Let's imagine it's your son who's been caught stealing a stop sign. Now imagine you are driving to the police station, pondering how you'll react. In what ways can you ascribe the best motive to this escapade? (Hint: What might be going on with your son that led him to this? What lessons do you want your son to learn from this mistake? How can your son best develop character from this crisis?)

Try this:

This was a terrible, impulsive act that occurred, but the fact that he was arrested instead of causing a fatal accident is extremely fortunate. Many forces were in play, which resulted in his impulsive act, because he did not slow down enough to use good judgment and think through potential consequences. This crisis does not detract from all of the character strengths my son has exhibited elsewhere in many parts of his life. He needs to think about his zeal for competition and hubris, which may blind him to similar risks in the future.

This is an exercise in a powerful practice: choosing the attitude you will use in approaching adversity. Choosing an effective attitude requires a calm, wise-minded state in which you consider all sides of a situation, rather than reacting off the cuff. The attitude you choose when dealing with all manner of teen blowups and screwups can have a profound effect on how well your child learns from his actions. It also puts you in the driver's seat, more in control of your own reactions and better able to influence the outcome.

Choosing the right attitude about adversity not only affects your ability to control your own reactions, but it can turn a crisis into a character-building experience. In many of these situations, the best course is to deal with the immediate emotional fright of the evening first, and leave a lot of the reflection for days to come. The ideal goal is to generate discussions in which your son can reflect on his personality and character weaknesses, and commit to self-awareness as he goes forward. He may be an Eagle Scout, but he is still, as we all are, a flawed person. He is also a teen with an immature brain, competitive spirit, and excessive enthusiasm for social escapades.

A teen can have many character strengths—and make many errors in judgment. With inexperience, hormones, social excitement, and immature impulse control, good teens can do bad things. The goal is to learn from mistakes and build those character assets, through good actions and bad ones, one experience at a time.

Caring About Character

One of the best definitions of character is "the way people act when no one is looking." But when people aren't looking, who amongst us doesn't jaywalk, let our dog off the leash, take pens home from work—or worse? And why should kids be any different, considering their immature brains, lack of experience, and raging hormones? Parents can sound pretty self-righteous with "kids these days!" comments about drugs, sex, and selfish or entitled behavior. But we're all flawed, and teens—like the rest of us—are still works in progress. We should remember that none of us is perfect, and though we might be *right* about a particular situation, the goal is to be *effective* as we address conduct issues with our teens.

Research shows that good character is cultivated by good parenting, positive school experiences, healthy engagement in after-school activities, and virtuous habits. In addition, an important "pathway" to good outcomes in late adolescence (academic achievement, positive identity, healthy psychological functioning) is positive emotion. Feeling good about one's experience with others while engaged in activities allows teens to feel important, needed, and connected, which energizes them to engage more. It also builds trust and wisdom, as children figure out the right things to do in various situations. When we practice wise-minded parenting, we are dipping into the well of our past experiences and using our intuition to guide us in complicated parenting dilemmas.

When a child learns to help others through volunteering, develops grit by sticking to a difficult task, and develops character strengths through healthy pursuits, she is building the foundation of a happy, purposeful, and meaningful life. And when teens encounter difficulties, like the loss of a loved one, an illness, or the consequences of a big mistake, they are challenged to adapt to these circumstances and build resilience. Part of building character is going through challenging times and creating a positive identity of oneself as hardy and able to withstand adversity—and even finding some meaning in the experience. A child who suffers a serious injury and has to give up playing sports may turn to running for school office, sparking an interest in politics. A child who takes care of a disabled sibling may feel that she has gained a deeper sense of empathy from the experience. Even a young tween can begin to understand the importance of living with a sense of meaning and giving to others, and this sense will serve him well later.

It's an elegant, spectacularly beautiful cycle, and one that truly makes the world go 'round: *I give of myself to others, and in return, I am given tenfold.*

CHAPTER 7
Physical Health

Scene: *It's a glorious autumn Sunday afternoon, and you return from running errands to find your son holed up in his room playing first-person shooter games on his Xbox.*

    Mom: *Honey, what are you doing inside? It's a beautiful day.*

    Thanh: *My homework is done. I'm just relaxing.*

    Mom: *Have you been playing video games all day? Honey, I hate to be a nag, but I'm concerned—you were on that thing all day yesterday. And then you just watched movies and videos on YouTube last night. Don't you want some fresh air? Maybe find some friends to hang out with?*

    Thanh: *God, Mom! It's just a hobby. I'm playing with someone right now. You're so out of it. This is how kids hang out in the 21st century. Get with it.*

    Mom: *Honey, I know. But it is excessive. It's my job to worry about your health. And look at all the candy wrappers and empty soda cans on the floor!*

    Thanh: *I'll pick them up when I'm done. Geez! You're messing up my concentration. Stop worrying so much.*

But this mom *is* worried, and with good reason. Like so many other parents these days, she's concerned about her son's inactivity and the other negative consequences that can be related to a passive lifestyle and screen addiction. The truth is, Thanh has become sedentary and overweight. His mother knows she needs to put limits on screen time, but that problem is really a symptom of a bigger one that's all too common among adolescents today: obesity. At this point, just talking about it won't cut it. The solution lies in overhauling routines, policies, and activities in the whole family's lifestyle.

Every parent wants physically healthy children, but many do not have them. According to the Centers for Disease Control and Prevention (CDC), obesity rates in children ages six to eleven in the United States increased from 7 percent in 1980 to almost 20 percent by 2008. During that same time, adolescent obesity rates have gone from 5 percent to 18 percent—that's nearly one in five teens. These kids are well on their way to being among the 35.7 percent of adults who are obese (CDC 2012). And those numbers are projected to get much worse, *reaching at least 44 percent by 2030* (Levi et al. 2012).

Obesity in adolescents is a huge public-health concern, but this group is also increasingly at risk for other health-zapping factors, too, such as excessive stress, poor nutrition, and sleep deprivation. Our kids are drowning in sedentary activities and high-calorie temptations, but there are practical, wise-minded ways you can turn the tide. It's critically important to your child's health—both physical and mental—that you do.

FACT

Healthy Behavior is Contagious
Both healthy and unhealthy behaviors can spread as far as three degrees of separation—to the friends of one's friends' friends.

Why Physical Health Matters

The data is unequivocal: Good physical health is vital to all kinds of tween and teen thriving. Exercise benefits all body systems and reduces the risk of everything from cancer to diabetes to depression. Its boost to brain functioning enhances school performance and overall adolescent health outcomes; kids who are physically fit are also less likely to use alcohol or drugs.

Healthy sleep habits play a big role in tween and teen thriving, too. Forgoing sleep in favor of studying is a common teen practice, but it's a bad plan: Sleep deprivation has a negative impact on school performance, as well as emotional health, stress management, and friendships. It also contributes to everything from acne to obesity to automobile deaths (National Sleep Foundation).

Further, research shows that physical health and mental health are vitally interconnected. A spectacular argument has been made to focus public-health efforts on lifestyle factors for everyone, since health-enhancing habits foster psychological and physical health, as well as optimize cognitive capacities and neural functions (Walsh 2011).

Healthy habits can also help prevent some of the leading causes of death for American teens, including homicides, suicides, and motor vehicle crashes, as well as reduce some of the other biggest risks to teen health, such as nicotine use, substance use disorders, obesity, violence, and problems related to sexual behavior.

Given all that's at stake, it's clear that insisting upon habits that contribute to physical health is crucial. Parents can have a big influence, too—from having an impact on obvious factors, such as lifestyle choices, to supporting less obvious ones, such as the degree to which we influence each other through our wide-ranging friendship networks. Did you know that both healthy and unhealthy behaviors can spread as far as three degrees of separation—to the friends of one's friends' friends (Fowler and Christakis 2010)? Are your friends the cheerful type? If so, chances are that it will rub off on you! Likewise, you have a probability of weighing a tad more if you have friends on the heavier side.

This chapter focuses on wise-minded ways to help parents address emerging health concerns with their kids and establish habits and routines that promote good physical health.

The 10 Building Blocks of Physical Health

By now, you've learned much about the six other essentials for successful tweens and teens, but physical health isn't just essential number seven, it's the essential that makes all of the others possible—and vice versa! Physical health is part of a continuous feedback loop that includes self-control, academic success, social thriving, emotional flourishing, strong character, and even maintaining a secure attachment. Build on essential number seven, and you build on 'em all!

There's much more to physical health than diet and exercise; in fact, boosting your child's potential for good health requires a focus on ten different factors:

1. exercise
2. nutrition
3. time spent in nature
4. sleep
5. technology management
6. sexual health
7. limits on risk taking and substance use
8. stress management
9. religious or spiritual involvement
10. recreational and leisure activities

This glorious list probably reads like an impossible dream to many parents. After all, insisting on even half of the list will take considerable time and effort. But remember: We are aiming for "good enough" parenting. These ten building blocks are intended to serve as guidelines for health; it's not an all-or-nothing endeavor. A commitment to pay attention to even one building block can set you and your family on a path toward better health.

ESSENTIAL
QUIZ

The Physically Healthy Teenager
Test your knowledge of teen health issues.

True False

1. ☐ ☐ Most teens need about eight hours of sleep every night.
2. ☐ ☐ If they have to cram for a big exam, kids can make up for lost sleep by sleeping in on the weekends.
3. ☐ ☐ If my kid is stressed out but making A's and doing sports, she's probably still basically healthy.
4. ☐ ☐ Teenagers need about twenty minutes of physical exercise every day.
5. ☐ ☐ Sleep-deprived kids tend to be skinnier than kids who sleep a lot.
6. ☐ ☐ My teen's diet should contain less than 20 percent fat.
7. ☐ ☐ If my son is unhappy and overweight, I should put him on a diet.

The correct answer to all of the above is "false," which might surprise you. But as you read on, you'll learn the truth about tween and teen health, as evidenced by an ever-growing body of research. And, more importantly, you'll learn strategies for avoiding common parental mistakes and for ramping up your family's commitment to physical health.

Building Block No. 1: Exercise

What if you had a magic potion that guaranteed your child would have a better chance of thriving emotionally, intellectually, socially, and physically? You do! Regular exercise, in its most basic form, is free, readily available, and indisputably proven to be effective in the vast majority of cases. Although the emphasis is usually on aerobic exercise for its contributions to overall physical health, weight training is also greatly beneficial for both adults and kids ages six and older (Behringer et al. 2010). And research suggests that exercise is not only good for the body, it's also both preventive and therapeutic for depression and anxiety in children and adolescents. Its beneficial effects have even been found to compare favorably with pharmacotherapy (prescription drugs) and psychotherapy (Larun et al. 2009).

THE SCIENCE OF EXERCISE

How does exercise work its magic on emotional health? It is thought that exercise improves serotonin (the "well-being" neurotransmitter), sleep, and endorphin release (the "runner's high"). Kids and adults who establish a regular exercise regimen experience enhanced self-esteem, reduced worry, and a stronger ability to short-circuit negative thought preoccupations. In adults, neuroscience research has found that exercise actually increases brain volume (both gray and white matter) and blood flow (Hamer and Chida 2009)! Animal studies indicate that exercise induces changes in the hippocampus (the memory station), increases brain connectivity between neurons, and releases the same brain-growth substance that antidepressants unleash (Cotman and Berchtold 2002).

If exercise results in positive effects on brain functioning, it must also improve academic performance, right? Right! A review of fourteen studies determined that participating in physical activity is positively related to good academic performance (Singh et al. 2012).

> **ESSENTIAL FACT**
>
> **The Benefits of Exercise**
> Participating in physical activity is positively related to good academic performance—and just about every other good thing you want for your child.

The American Academy of Pediatrics recommends that teens engage in sixty minutes of moderate exercise per day. That's a benchmark that most teens are far from reaching. In fact, a study of obesity revealed that only 34.7 percent of teens exercise five to seven days a week (Li et al. 2010). And with obesity rates tripling among U.S. youth between 1976 and 2004, there is speculation that the trend might be due in large in part to increased inactivity among young people, caused by slashes in physical education programs, the rise of the screen-addicted couch potato, or both.

But what Stan Li and colleagues found when they analyzed data gathered from 16,000 high school teens suggests something different. Teen activity patterns haven't actually changed much over the last couple of decades; what has changed is food consumption. Exercise has many important benefits, but in the fight against obesity, it's not the be-all and end-all. Eating habits are the front line in this battle—and we'll get to that in building block number two—but these findings should not dissuade parents from putting physical fitness on their agenda.

> ESSENTIAL
> **FACT**
>
> **Teen Physical Activity**
> The American Academy of Pediatrics recommends that teens engage in sixty minutes of moderate exercise per day for adequate physical fitness.

The easiest way to make sure teens get the exercise they need—and hit that sixty-minute-a-day target—is by insisting they take part in physical education, either during school PE programs (if they exist) and/or after school. According to the CDC, only 28 percent of high school students are enrolled in daily physical education classes, and this rate has not changed since 1995. If PE classes don't exist at your child's school, find an after-school or weekend PE program; the effort will pay off in more ways than you might imagine.

There are five benefits of participation in sports during middle school and high school:

- **enhanced physical fitness;**
- **improved mental health;**
- **increased contact with positive peers;**
- **tightened bond with the school; and**
- **increased time spent in adult-supervised settings (which reduces opportunities for afternoon risk taking).**

Neighborhood and community sports teams and other organized after-school fitness activities provide almost the same advantages for adolescents as school-sponsored teams (minus the school bonding). Either way, a single decision on the part of parents—to prioritize the participation in athletics throughout adolescence—has many cascading benefits for physical, academic, and mental health.

Some kids will try to bargain with their parents, promising to exercise on their own if their parents let them out of participating in organized activities. Avoid agreeing to this if you can! Kids who exercise on their own miss out on the benefits of peer and school bonding, not to mention adult supervision. Also, tweens who drop out of school sports usually don't get back into them later on. And kids who pledge to work out on their own rarely follow through.

MODEST BEGINNINGS

Unless you and your kids really love exercise, that one-hour-a-day goal may seem daunting, if not undoable. And when goals seem unreachable, people often give up altogether. That's when Chinese philosopher Lao-tzu's famous line can put things into perspective:

A journey of a thousand miles begins with a single step.

In other words, begin where you are, with acceptance in your heart, and take that first single step. Make sure that your child's fitness needs are being met through school, teams, and classes—not by you and at home, which can trigger nagging wars, and result in shame and blame. Set your child on a path and then turn your focus on yourself, so you can offer an example of healthy habits. If you are really lucky (and act casual, even somewhat indifferent), your kid may join you for a walk, yoga class, or dance workshop—this fitness stuff can actually be fun!

Research on habit change suggests that success is more likely if you commit to fitness activities with others, enjoy it (or at least reward yourself in some way), and are accountable, either by keeping records or with a support group of some kind.

Building Block No. 2: Nutrition

It's a well-documented fact: The diets of American adolescents have been getting steadily worse. The prevalence of processed convenience foods—combined with the multimillion-dollar marketing machine that pushes them—has too many kids eating too many chemicals, and too much sugar and unhealthy fats (and too few fruits and vegetables).

Healthy eating is simple in theory. "Eat food. Not too much. Mostly plants," according to journalist Michael Pollan (author of *The Omnivore's Dilemma*, among other books). Another Pollan gem: "Don't eat anything your great-grandmother wouldn't recognize as food." (*Even ready-made whipped cream?* Ah, c'mon! All advice in moderation!)

Multiple research studies have shown the health advantages of Pollan's approach, which is essentially the Mediterranean diet: high in fruits, vegetables, and whole grains. Only 14 percent of American adults and fewer than 10 percent of teens eat five or more servings of fruits and vegetables per day, a recommendation set by the CDC (Hannley 2012).

Pollan's words are meant to emphasize the dangers of too much processed food, excessive consumption of calories, and the old debunked food pyramids of yore that favored copious amounts of grains over all other food groups. These days, we know we need to eat a diet that emphasizes vegetables and fruits, then proteins, and de-emphasizes those plentiful, prevalent grains or simple carbs. Processed foods, sugary drinks, junk food, desserts, and animal products are in the "careful moderation" category.

THE FAMILY DINNER

The benefits of the family dinner go way beyond good nutrition. It brings the family together for what might be the only face time of the entire day, building the communal good feelings that spring from enjoying food, looking into each other's eyes, and sharing the day's events. As discussed in previous chapters, establishing regular family dinners

ESSENTIAL
ACTIVITY

Teen Nutrition and a Food Competence Agenda

With so much conflicting nutritional information coming in from all corners, it's hard to know what to teach your teen. To make things easier, we've included a list of nutrition-related activities for the teen years. Note that this list takes the long view; you'll implement and practice each one over months or even years, depending on your child.

1. Plan and cook nutritious meals together at first, then gradually let your teen take over for a few meals a month.

2. Discuss your teen's food intake during the day. Does she have access to fruits and veggies at school, or at the store she visits after school or soccer? If not, figure out how she can integrate healthy snacks into her day.

3. Understand how to evaluate food basics. Read and then don't read labels. Estimate and then don't count calories. Although it's good to know the basics, you don't want to overdo a food focus (unless there is an illness, including obesity, and you are under a specialist's care). There is a balance to strike here: Awareness is good; obsession is bad.

4. Model healthy eating and attitudes. Do you sit down and eat with your kids? Do you eat well-balanced meals? Do you talk negatively about your body? Do you share anxieties about weight? Do you talk about other people's body size?

5. If your teen declares a desire to go on a vegan, vegetarian, or other specialty diet, make sure she does her homework. Investigate your teen's knowledge and the diet's nutritional implications, and consider consulting a physician together. Sometimes, parents cave to these new plans without ensuring that teens have the competence to take responsibility for their health. Many eating disorders started with fad diets camouflaged as "healthy eating."

6. No matter how busy you or your teen are, missing meals is never OK. Low food intake can result in binge patterns. Three meals a day is the norm, with snacks figured out according to exercise patterns.

also sends a strong message that connection is a priority. It increases and nurtures the parent-teen bond, and anything enjoyed with another person brings that good feeling to the relationship. But with tweens and teens (and parents) ever on the run, getting the entire family around the table can take a Herculean effort.

But here's another reason meals eaten together are worth it: Multiple studies have documented that teens who share family meals have healthier eating habits and body weights, higher academic achievement, and a lower risk of substance abuse and delinquency (Fiese and Schwartz 2008). Teens who share fewer than three family dinners per week are nearly twice as likely to smoke, drink, and get poor grades as compared to teens who eat five to seven dinners with their families per week. Studies have tried to tease out which elements of a regular meal are critical in predicting these positive outcomes. Since many family factors can be overlapping and mutually reinforcing, it seems safe to assume that the family meal is just one part of a larger package of good routines and rituals that reflect parenting priorities (Musick and Meier 2012). Children thrive with routine and stability, to say nothing of the merits of good nutrition. Granted, this all gets trickier in adolescence, with competing priorities and complicated schedules, but still, we need to do our best to prioritize family dinners.

ESSENTIAL
FACT

The Importance of the Family Dinner

Teens who share fewer than three family dinners per week are about twice as likely to smoke, drink, and get poor grades as compared to teens who eat five to seven dinners with their families per week.

Weight-related problems, including obesity, eating disorders, and disordered eating (such as fad dieting and skipped meals), are major health concerns for teens. While obesity is getting a lot of media attention these days, some of the public-health campaigns that promote "healthy eating" can run the risk of triggering restrictive eating habits, especially with tween and teen girls. Many well-meaning families that start "healthy eating" crusades unwittingly trigger restrictive dieting, which can be the beginning of an eating disorder.

One study surveyed approximately two thousand teens about their eating habits and weight, and found that a staggering 44 percent of the girls and 29 percent of the boys had weight-related problems (Neumark-Sztainer et al. 2007). About 40 percent of the overweight girls and 20 percent of the overweight boys engaged in at least one disordered eating behavior, such as binge eating; use of laxatives or diet pills; or vomiting. If you ever discover that your child is engaging in any of these behaviors, consult a specialist.

Nutritionist Ellyn Satter, an expert on healthy eating and child development, has spent her career helping parents understand that it is their responsibility to put healthy food on the table at regular intervals, and it is the child's responsibility to choose what to eat from that table. When parents pressure and persuade, cave to "à la carte" grazing instead of meals, and fail to provide regular and reliable eating opportunities, real problems can result (Satter 2000).

PLANTING THE SEEDS OF DISORDERED EATING

When it comes to your teenager's body, there is reality, and then there is body image. By now, you probably have some inkling of just how much daylight there is between the two for your child. If you've ever stood aghast after your normally shaped tween daughter exclaimed, "I'm so fat!" while pinching an imaginary inch, you know that body image does not always reflect reality. The opposite can also happen; it's just as disturbing when your child's weight gain has accelerated and he refuses to see it as a problem. Obesity is a clinical problem, and, as with psychiatric illness and other physical illnesses, parents must consult professionals. However, short of a diagnosis of some kind, there is an enormous amount of disordered eating among youth, placing them at risk for serious eating disorders.

Why do so many kids end up with harmful eating habits? How do kids get such mixed messages about what constitutes a healthy body size and shape? The answer lies in that confusing, nonstop onslaught of messages kids receive from media, peers, and even parents. Fashion is a multibillion-dollar industry with vast marketing power, and the psychological obsession of teens to be accepted and attractive makes them tremendously vulnerable. Parents are misguided by marketing messages, too. Negative messages from parents can be overt, they can be subtle, and they can certainly be unintended, but they can still do harm. Here are some of the seemingly benign but actually harmful things people commonly say to kids that contribute to body-image difficulties, problematic dieting, and eating disorders.

"You look so great since you lost all that weight!" What a nice compliment! Or is it? This declaration means "You'll look bad when you gain it all back," which is more likely to happen than not if the weight loss was quick and substantial. Feeling bad about the failure to maintain weight loss can result in more extreme dieting, and a "yo-yo" pattern may ensue—sometimes for life. The unintended consequences of extreme dieting are many and they can be serious.

"If you feel so bad about your body, why don't you just lose some weight?" The tricky word here is "just." If it were that simple, there would be no obesity crisis.

"Honey, if you want to lose weight, you shouldn't have had that second helping of mashed potatoes . . . or the butter." As well intentioned as a parent's advice might be, these kinds of messages can create shame in kids, with overeating as a possible consequence. Here again, you might be right, but are you effective?

And one of the worst . . .

"We're going to cut out carbs and fats from our diet from now on, so we can be on a healthy eating campaign." "Healthy?" "Cutting down" would be fine, but cutting out carbs and fats is an unbalanced and unrealistic meal plan. Many parents mistakenly believe that restrictive dieting is a good idea if weight is a problem. But sugar, fats, and carbs should be eaten in small, healthy quantities, not banned all together. Demonizing certain food groups can trigger cravings and backfire by provoking bingeing. The goal is balance, which contributes to genuine good health, satiety, and successful weight management.

One of the most difficult types of consultations I engage in is with parents who have a tween or teen who has recently gained weight. Parental panic often results in an attempt to overcontrol food intake. While unhappiness and the threat of poor health in the future make the concern understandable, parental efforts at control usually make things worse. My advice is to read Satter's book *Your Child's Weight: Helping Without Harming* (2005), and seek help from a specialist who works with adolescents and has a background in treating disordered eating.

A strategy that can help parents reduce eating-disorder risks for their kids includes providing balanced meals, encouraging physical fitness, modeling good nutritional habits, avoiding diet talk or criticism of body types (yours or theirs), valuing aspects of your kids that do not relate to appearance, supporting emotional intelligence, and discouraging an obsession with the "perfect girl" stereotype (i.e., thin, beautiful, accommodating, always good, and never angry), or "perfect boy" stereotype (i.e., thin, muscular, athletic, and stoic). About 10 percent of those with eating disorders are boys, so don't overlook their eating habits if they should become restricted or otherwise out of balance. With any child, the most well-intentioned parents can end up cluelessly collaborating with our media-saturated culture, supporting dieting, perfectionism, preoccupation with appearance, and superficial values.

ESSENTIAL ACTIVITY

Family Media Inventory

Consider the media your family consumes and the messages it is sending. Inventory the magazines you and your kids subscribe to. Write down every magazine and then jot down the values you think each promotes (e.g., "fashion sense," "good looks," "exploring the world," "good dental heath"). What is the ratio of fashion magazines (e.g., *Vogue, Cosmopolitan, Glamour*) to magazines that promote health, fitness, adventure, politics, literature, and exploration (*Backpacker, Outside, National Geographic, Popular Science, The Economist, Discover, Sports Illustrated*)? Consider adjusting your subscriptions—by canceling some and starting others—to achieve at least a three-to-one ratio that favors adventure, physical health, and intellectual and physical exploration. Note: Many "fitness" magazines are actually fashion magazines in disguise.

Magazine title	Values it promotes	Action needed?

Building Block No. 3: Time Spent in Nature

Much of the national conversation about child health centers on exercise and nutrition, often overlooking the vital connection between contact with nature and good physical health (Kuo 2010). Psychologist Frances Kuo's review of a number of rigorous and diverse studies found evidence that regular contact with nature promotes healthier social behavior and lessens social dysfunction, helps alleviate stress, improves resilience, promotes optimal psychological functioning, speeds recovery from physical trauma, and reduces mortality rates. Studies have even shown that patients recovering from gall bladder surgery do so more quickly if they are assigned rooms with views of trees instead of a parking lot!

Nature is a therapy that has no negative side effects (besides the occasional foray into poison ivy), is free and often readily available, and can improve cognitive functioning and overall well-being (Berman et al. 2008). Most parents instinctively know this; that's why they pay big money to send their kids on wilderness experiences and to outdoor leadership courses and camps. Yet most of us find it difficult, if not impossible, to shut down the screens and venture into the forest on a regular basis.

Time spent in nature is often viewed as part of an overall healthy lifestyle that some children have and some children don't (Pretty et al. 2009). On the "have" side, children are active and engaged in nature, and as a result, tend to live longer and have a better quality of life. The "have-nots" lack these assets, and tend to be from urban, low-income homes, where they have little access to outside activities and spend a lot of time indoors.

Another review of the research focused on the specific benefits of nature to mental health, especially over the last decade (Townsend and Weerasuriya 2010). It found that exposure to specific kinds of landscapes, local parks, forests, and gardens improve our well-being. By contrast, environments devoid of nature, with an excess of noise and artificial lighting—composed of nonnatural spectra and artificial day/night rhythms—take a toll on us, resulting in disruptions of mood, sleep, and nutrition, short-term impairment of attention and cognition, and reduced academic performance among youth over the long term.

Several years ago, journalist Richard Louv gathered compelling scientific data and then sounded the alarm about today's wired generation: There is a strong link between the dearth of experiences in nature and huge upticks in obesity rates and diagnoses of attention deficit disorder and depression (Louv 2008). There is nothing like creating a new deficit disorder to grab public attention, and Louv's "nature deficit disorder" did the trick. He founded the nonprofit organization The Child and Nature Network, kick-started the "Leave No Child Inside" campaign, and started the New Nature Movement, all with the goal of connecting more kids and families with the outdoors.

Despite these efforts, there has been relatively little quantifiable change in the amount of time kids spend in nature. With a hefty agenda to improve schools, create better access to health care, and address economic problems, it seems like parents, educators, and mental health professionals often consider contact with nature a fluffy luxury at the bottom of the "to-do" list—and who can blame them? Where on a college application do "weekend family hikes" come in?

Prioritizing Nature in Daily Life

Get out your calendar and have a family meeting. Talk about a nature and health agenda. Decide together on the simple ways you can get into nature, and when, and then put it in ink on the calendar. Will you spend a Saturday afternoon hiking, biking, or strolling in the park? Will you volunteer to work on a local trail? Go skiing or snowshoeing? You could let each family member choose one activity. Mark it in ink and refuse to bump it without rescheduling.

But those hikes actually *are* relevant to that college application. They are reflected in your child's grade point average; in his interest in and pursuit of extracurricular activities and volunteer work; and in his overall physical and mental health. In the messy, crazy business of daily life, don't dismiss regular contact with nature. It doesn't have to be a full-day assault on a local peak or even a weekend family camping trip. Encourage your child to take the dog (or a neighbor's dog) for a walk in the park. Find an easy local trail and go for a leisurely family trundle one weekend morning a month. Get a favorite uncle to take your child fishing. There are as many ways to be out in nature as there are benefits to doing so.

Building Block No. 4: Sleep

Dear Parent,

Your child is not getting enough sleep. This is harming
his ability to do his best academically, socially, and physically.
Please do something immediately.

Love,
Twenty years of research

The odds are better than 50-50 that if you have a teenager, you have a sleep-deprived teenager. You've no doubt heard rumblings about the effect of too little sleep on all kinds of tween and teen functioning—heck, you've lived it yourself! If you suspect that your adolescent is not getting enough sleep on a regular basis, you're probably right.

Sleep is nature's way of soothing and resting all kinds of mental and physical systems. It is a vital activity, crucial to a healthy heart and lungs, and to overall bodily health. Because sleep research has only recently taken off, the science of sleep has yet to enter the mainstream, but the coming few years will surely produce even more compelling evidence of the essential nature of a good night's sleep.

WHY TEENS ARE VULNERABLE

During early adolescence, melatonin—the hormone that regulates sleep/wake cycles—is released up to two hours later than it is during childhood. That's why many teens complain about wanting a later bedtime; it's not just to sneak in more social media time! But biology is not the only thing wreaking havoc on teen sleep; some of it is self-inflicted. Teens just like to stay up late, especially on Fridays and Saturdays, and then sleep late on weekend mornings. This might seem like a logical plan, but the truth is that "makeup" sleep never really makes up for lost sleep. Paying off a "sleep debt" can feel good, but regularity is key for the circadian rhythm cycle. What is needed—what is optimal for teens—is a regular bedtime seven days a week that allows for a full nine to ten hours of sleep.

If you're thinking that's a tall order, consider this: Inadequate sleep limits your child's ability to concentrate, learn, listen, remember, and solve problems. It can contribute to acne, mood problems, weight gain, cravings for junk food, sensitivity to the effects of alcohol, and increased use of caffeine and nicotine (Mahowald and Schenck 2005). It also makes teens prone to illness and causes drowsiness, which contributes to 100,000 motor vehicle accidents a year (National Sleep Foundation). Teen drivers who get less than eight hours of sleep per night are 33 percent more likely to crash a car than are their better-rested peers.

One study investigating the effects of sleep on school performance divided a sample of fourth-, fifth-, and sixth-graders into two groups: one that extended their sleep by an hour, and one that restricted their sleep by an hour (Sadeh et al. 2003). The results? Researchers found that losing one hour of sleep was the equivalent to losing two years of mental age on tests of neurobiological functioning (e.g., memory, concentration, reaction time) given in the days immediately following sleep deprivation.

You might wonder how a few hours of sleep can have such an enormous effect on cognitive functioning. Sleep impacts memory by consolidating those memories, prioritizing the ones that are relevant to future plans, and even producing changes in memories and the ability to recall knowledge from implicit, subconscious memories (Born and Wilhelm 2012). Tired children won't have this advantage, because fatigue translates into tired neurons. Sleep impairment results in less plasticity in the neurons, which makes them less able to form the synaptic connections necessary for encoding memories and recalling information. Learning and memory consolidate during sleep.

ESSENTIAL
FACT

Teens and Sleep

Inadequate sleep limits your child's ability to concentrate, learn, listen, remember, and solve problems. It can cause acne, mood problems, weight gain, cravings for junk food, sensitivity to the effects of alcohol, increased use of caffeine and nicotine, increased illness, and dangerous driving. Teen drivers who get less than eight hours of sleep per night are 33 percent more likely to crash a car than are their better-rested peers.

The Teen Sleep Myth

Sixty percent of teens in high school report extreme daytime sleepiness, even though 90 percent of their parents think that their kids are getting enough sleep.

Sleep loss also takes a toll on our body's ability to extract glucose from the bloodstream. Remember the research on willpower in chapter 2: Mental energy requires glucose. The prefrontal cortex, the part of the brain responsible for analytic functions, problem solving, setting goals, and impulse control, also gets tired when it is not fed glucose—and doesn't get sleep. A well-rested brain is a functioning brain, which is more nimble and creative with those problem sets in algebra, essays in language arts class, and conversations at lunch.

According to surveys conducted by the National Sleep Foundation, 60 percent of high schoolers report extreme daytime sleepiness, even though 90 percent of their parents think their kids are getting enough sleep. Half of all adolescents sleep less than seven hours on weeknights (most need nine hours), and by their senior year, they get only about six and a half hours of sleep on average. Only about 5 percent of seniors get an average of eight hours of sleep. The foundation recommends nine and a quarter hours of sleep each night for teens to function at their best, with some doing OK with eight and a half hours.

ESSENTIAL
ACTIVITY

Practices to Improve Your Child's Sleep

Here are the best practices for families who want to prioritize adequate sleep. Check off those that you have well in hand; circle a few to work on.

1. ☐ Consider enforcing a family bedtime (easier with tweens than teens).
2. ☐ Take screens of all kinds out of the bedroom an hour before bedtime.
3. ☐ Don't drink caffeinated drinks close to bedtime.
4. ☐ Establish sleep/wake times, and keep them as regular as possible.
5. ☐ Keep naps short and not too close to bedtime.
6. ☐ Don't drive when drowsy, and don't ever let your teen do it, either.
7. ☐ Make bedrooms into sleep havens—cool, quiet and dark at night, and open to sunlight in the morning.
8. ☐ Make all-night study sessions off-limits.
9. ☐ Go online with your child and search for "sleep hygiene." There is a lot of information on reputable websites that may help convince your child of the importance of sleep.

Mary Carskadon, a pioneer researcher of adolescent sleep cycles at Brown University Medical School, has documented the problems stemming from sleep deprivation in teens, including depression, anxiety, and school-related issues. In one study, she and a colleague found that kids lost forty to fifty minutes of sleep per night between the ages of thirteen and nineteen, right at the time when they need more sleep (Wolfson and Carskadon 1998). Furthermore, students who described themselves as struggling or failing at school (getting C's, D's, and F's) reported going to bed about forty minutes later and sleeping an average of twenty-five minutes less on school nights than their peers who were doing well in school (getting A's and B's). In fact, most of the teens in the study got inadequate sleep, which interfered with their daytime functioning due to drowsiness, depression, and difficulties falling asleep and waking up. This landmark study has been cited and replicated, but here's the big question: With the academic demands and entertainment pursuits teens experience, is it any wonder they're not changing their sleep habits?

The evidence that teens would benefit from more sleep is irrefutable. The concern about sleep deprivation has led to a push for schools to delay start times. One study showed that even delaying start time by a mere forty-five minutes made a significant difference in the amount of time that the high schoolers slept and in their subsequent mood and behavior (Owens et al. 2010). Those students reported more satisfaction with sleep, improved academic motivation, and less daytime fatigue and depression. Class attendance increased, and fatigue-related complaints at the health center decreased. Other studies on the benefits of delayed school start times have found the same positive results, but the upheaval to school, family, and transportation systems have made this difficult to implement in many communities.

ESSENTIAL
ACTIVITY

Reality Check: Your Teen's Sleep—and Yours

It's time to get a reality check on just how much sleep is actually happening in your house. For one week, keep track of your sleep, and ask your teen to do the same. Depending on your teen, you might want to promise that you will not ask him to share his notes (he may fear nagging and fudge the numbers!); you just want to raise his awareness of sleep deprivation.

Building Block No. 5: Technology Management

The importance of limiting electronic entertainment and social media is a recurring theme of this book. It comes into focus time and again as a "best practice" for boosting your child's functioning on many levels. Pursuing the seven essentials takes time, as do the healthy-lifestyle building blocks; one way to get that time is to snatch it back from the digital void.

Since the invention of the television in the 1950s, time has been sapped from family activities and community connections and transferred to more electronic entertainment and communication devices. Fast-forward through fifty years of technological growth, and many people live in their separate rooms, entertained by their separate devices. They no longer know their neighbors. They don't even have to fight over the remote anymore, because everyone has their own. "Remote" pretty well sums it up, actually.

There's no doubt that technological advances have been a boon in many ways—for education, business, communications; for connecting fragile or alienated social groups; and for leveling the playing field for those in less advantageous situations. Many meta-analyses have documented the benefits of digital media to kids, including social-skills training, spatial and response-time enhancement, and even altruism (Preiss et al. 2006). As the saying goes, you can't put the genie back in the bottle, and you wouldn't want to, anyway. But it's time to address the very real dangers of that magic.

A 2010 survey by the Kaiser Family Foundation found that kids are in front of screens of one kind or another for fifty hours a week. Tweens and teens spend on average seven and a half hours a day engaged with television, video games, and the Internet; add cell phones and multiscreening (viewing multiple screens at the same time), and the number goes up to eleven hours a day. Video gaming consumed nine hours a week. And the heaviest media users were more likely to be obese, depressed, and performing poorly in school.

The American Academy of Pediatrics recommends no more than one to two hours of recreational screen time per day (yes, including social media). Excessive screen time has been associated not only with obesity, depression, and poorer school performance, but also with irregular sleep, behavioral problems, and less time for positive and creative pursuits.

There is a causal link between gaming and academic performance. Controlling for relevant academic factors, a study examined the effects of video game use by comparing two groups of boys who had never owned gaming systems (Weis and Cerankosky 2010). The researchers introduced a gaming system into the homes of one group and delayed the introduction to the other group until after the study period. Compared to homes with no video games, the boys who received the video games had more teacher-reported learning problems and lower scores in writing and reading. The researchers concluded that gaming had indeed supplanted the academic learning that had occurred when gaming was not available.

DIGITAL MEDIA AND THE BRAIN

Research has also shown that digital media has a neurological impact. The current explosion of digital technology is actually *changing our brains*. All of that daily connecting with computers, smartphones, video games, and entertainment centers releases neurotransmitters and hormones, which strengthen some neural pathways and weaken others.

In one study, the brains of computer-naive volunteers changed after just five days of using the Internet for online searches (Small and Vorgan 2008). While the subjects had almost no activity in the dorsolateral prefrontal cortex at the beginning of their Internet

ESSENTIAL
ACTIVITY

Guidelines for Limiting Screen Time

If you, like many parents, feel unsettled or unhappy about your family's screen usage, reform can come in a series of baby steps from each of the three categories below.

1. Set an example. If you text on your smartphone in restaurants, check e-mail in the grocery store, and stay up late updating your Facebook status, you are not modeling balanced media usage. Pay attention to the message you are sending to your kids. *I pledge to break my following bad media habits:*

_____

_____

_____

2. Set time limits. Create an actual schedule for electronic media usage. If you need help figuring out what's reasonable to expect and enforce, visit Common Sense Media's website. Here's a basic chart to get you started; note how many minutes you'll allow for each screen during the times listed.

Time	Video games	Social media	Television	Texting
Before school				
After school/ before dinner				
During dinner				
After dinner				

3. Set content limits. Not all screen time is equal. Know what your kids are up to when they go online; have them walk you through their favorite games; and watch their favorite YouTube videos and television shows with them. Before you let your child use Facebook, insist upon knowing their login information, so you can keep "training wheels" on their social-media use at first. Review the cyber safety guidelines on page 131. The more conversations you have with your child about their media preferences, the more you will understand how best to guide their usage. Make a note of your child's favorites below or in your journal:

Favorite video games	Favorite TV shows	Social media site logins	Favorite websites

search training, as the training progressed, the subjects' brains were rewired as their neural circuitry became activated in that area. Their brains began to resemble those of an Internet-savvy comparison group. Why is this relevant? The dorsolateral part of the brain is involved with our capacity for complex decision making, integrating thoughts and sensations, and working memory. It helps us to remember things for a short amount of time—such as the time it takes to recall a phone number or manage a Web search. Going online actually strengthens our scanning skills and short-term attention span.

Sounds like a good thing, but there is a flip side: Those same researchers warn that our high-tech world has plunged us into a state of "continuous partial attention." We want to stay continuously busy, keeping tabs on everything while focusing deeply on nothing. Peripheral attention on multiple gadgets allows us to scan for novelty and interesting stimuli, and the next contact, no matter where it comes from. And teenagers—whose developing brains are open to any stimulation that produces dopamine—are especially vulnerable.

The partial attention created by a multiplicity of stimuli carries a heavy price: stress. Because texts, games, calls, pokes, and pings zap the brain into registering "Alert!" and "Attend *now!*" both stress hormones (norepinephrine and cortisol) and the pleasure-cuing dopamine are released. The buzz combination is pricey; we are stressed, but we like it.

All of this connectivity poses another serious danger for teens and tweens: All it takes is one incident of poor judgment to upend your child's entire life. An impulsive posting on a classmate's Facebook page, and your child could be accused of sexual harassment ("Hey, nice boobs!") or bullying ("Your acne is soooooo ugly!"). Young children and tweens are all but guaranteed to stumble upon porn, unhealthy attitudes about sexuality, and images of violence on the Internet. In addition, there is a documented relationship between violent video games and aggressive thoughts, feelings, and behaviors.

Screen addiction is a real and growing phenomenon. And the gendered patterns that have emerged are disturbing, too, with more boys drawn to violent games, and girls gravitating to websites about clothes, beauty products, dieting, and celebrity gossip. For all these reasons, teens and especially tweens need adult Internet supervision for a while (and kids with thrill-seeking personalities need it for longer). Parents should utilize filters and lay down some rules and a system for tracking compliance until they are confident their mature teen is a responsible consumer. There is information all over the Internet about its dangers, and plenty of superb guidelines for parents. Take a look at a few of the excellent (and wise-minded) guidelines on Common Sense Media (*commonsensemedia.org*).

Building Block No. 6: Sexual Health

Since romance and relationships were addressed in chapter 5, this section will focus exclusively on sexual health. Start kids with regular checkups by health care practitioners, who should provide information in a manner called "anticipatory guidance," which means that they will attempt to talk to your kids before they have experiences with their bodies and the social world that leave them worried or confused. Parents can do this, too.

By the time your child is a tween, you can assume he has heard just about everything that's true about the mechanics of sex (and a lot that is false!); you should discuss information about sexuality or sexual maturation whenever you see an opening. In addition, if you hear of a new romance on the horizon for your child or a sexually related incident in her peer group or school (e.g., sexting, sexual harassment, relational violence, date rape), use the opportunity to strike up a conversation. This constant, ongoing approach is vastly more effective than having a single, sit-down "birds and bees" talk, because it establishes an open line of communication that will hopefully become more comfortable over time.

While parents want their teens to be sexually well adjusted, most have a hard time communicating positive attitudes about sex without also delivering lectures about safety, delaying sexual activity, and dangerous consequences—for good reason. The social and public health consequences of teen sexual activity are huge. Half of the eighteen million sexually transmitted infections diagnosed in the U.S. each year occur in teens. Teens get pregnant at the rate of about 750,000 per year; 80 percent of which is unintended. While the rates of teen pregnancies and childbearing have gone down in recent years—thanks to better contraceptive practices and fewer teens having sex—the U.S. still has the highest pregnancy rate among the industrialized countries. Comprehensive sex education—which includes information about abstinence and contraception—reduces teen pregnancy. But there are many regions of the country that still insist on abstinence-only education, which has been shown to be ineffective and, in fact, results in higher rates of pregnancy and childbearing (Santelli et al. 2006).

Parental involvement plays a big role in teens' sexual attitudes and behaviors. In a large review of studies, strong parent-teen relationships, good communication, and parental monitoring of teens' whereabouts were all associated with delayed sexual initiation and reduced risk of teen pregnancy (Miller et al. 2001). But parents often underestimate the degree to which even fifth- and sixth-graders are interested in romance and sex (O'Donnell et al. 2008). Since supervision is a key part of reducing risk, parents need a reality check on their children's romantic and sexual interests.

Authoritative parenting, with its emphasis on warmth, limits, and regard for psychological autonomy (see page 62), is associated with lower risk for early sexual initiation, as well as lower pregnancy rates and sexual-health problems (DeVore and Ginsburg 2005). While unsupervised time with other kids increases the probability of sexual activity, that risk is offset in homes where high-quality parent-child communication is in force.

According to a study on parent-child communication about sexuality, parents show greater skill when they do not dominate the conversation, listen more than talk, are less directive, and respond nonjudgmentally (Akers et al. 2011). In short, when they act like wise-minded parents! Not only do adolescents whose parents engage in these behaviors report greater comfort discussing sex with their parents, but teens who even *recall* that a parent has talked to them about sex are more likely to report delaying sexual initiation.

Fathers have a tougher time talking about sex than mothers do (Kirkman 2002). Although dads perceive it to be partly their responsibility, many find talking about sex distressing and feel that puberty disrupts their relationships with their children. But it's been my experience when working with teen boys and girls that when dads do take an active role—even when they stutter and stammer—if they avoid lecturing, their kids appreciate their efforts. I conducted some teen focus groups about sexuality for a local PBS documentary, and most of the girls I spoke with said they missed the closeness they felt with their dads in the preteen years. Here are some of the messages they wanted to send to their dads: "We will sneer at your attempts to hug us. We will recoil at your invitations to hang out more. We'll roll our eyes if you try to talk about guys. But don't give up! We want you to pursue us. We want to feel important to you. It's just awkward!" Remember that attempts at connection, no matter how awkward, translate as caring.

ESSENTIAL
TIP

Talking to Tweens and Teens About Sex

Here are a few of the best practices for parents as they make a plan to address the crucial issue of teen sexual health:

- Instead of just saying, "You can ask me questions anytime," keep up a running dialogue about sexuality issues throughout childhood and adolescence. Having "the talk" is so last century! You should be having hundreds of interesting conversations about sex and sexual-health issues through the tween and teen years.

- Having lots of sex talks will not result in more sexual behavior; if anything, it is the other way around. Kids who have parents who talk to them (respectfully) about sex are usually closer to their parents than kids from homes without this kind of communication. And teens who are secure and close to their parents are rarely the ones having sex in middle school.

- Most sexuality chats should not be about questioning your child about his/her personal life. The goal is to make kids knowledgeable about this important part of life, so that they can take responsibility for it. Grilling them for information is not a good way to open up lines of communication.

- Use natural opportunities to start conversations, such as news, gossip, and celebrity stories. There are plenty of lurid and cautionary tales to choose from. But no wagging fingers! Be "intellectual" in your analysis of the sociological, psychological, and situational factors. Look for opportune moments when something is going on with your child or in their school or peer group. Does your tween or teen have a new love interest? It's probably time to talk about your values, his or her safety, sexual decision-making, and responsibility.

• Consider talks about sexuality to be a form of psychological immunization. Giving them knowledge and stimulating their thinking brains is like administering a vaccine that can help keep them safe from toxic experiences, by helping them anticipate and work through complicated and emotionally charged scenarios intellectually.

• Persevere despite rolling eyeballs, groans, and "please don't" messages. Teen surveys reveal that parents should talk about sex more, not less, but teens acknowledge that they give "go away" messages because of acute awkwardness.

• Check out sexual-health websites built just for teens. Find the ones you like. Ask your teen to view them with you (or alone). The National Campaign to Prevent Teen and Unplanned Pregnancy's site (*stayteen.org*) features information, games, polls, and graphics on everything from how to deal with sexual pressures to definitions of healthy relationships to reasons for not having sex in high school. (The "Myths" section is superlative!) Let cool sites present information so that you and your teen can get closer by responding to it together, instead of putting you in the role of sex educator. This technique works best with twelve- to sixteen-year-olds; older teens will probably think this approach is silly.

• Watch out for overkill. While all of these points are solid and important, finesse is needed in the parent/child sex-education dance.

Building Block No. 7: Limiting Risk Taking and Substance Use

Andy, age twelve, loves to watch things blow up. He likes violent computer games, fireworks, and paintball. He's already been caught purchasing M-80s online. His parents wonder what Andy's obsession with explosives is all about.

Jayne, age fifteen, is one of those girls who liked to act like a teenager when she was six years old, especially the sexy ones depicted on MTV. She loves makeup, shopping, and suggestive dancing. It was all her parents could do to keep her from starting a secret online dating service at her high school.

Conrad, age thirteen, is a regular guy who loves sports, his buddies, and having fun. Early maturation, good looks, and popularity landed him invitations to parties and dates in middle school. Conrad seems kind of oblivious to the attention at this point, but his parents feel like they need to police his phone and computer—and even his bedroom windows.

The biological drive for risk taking is influenced by the genes that determine temperament and by the brain/hormonal changes of early adolescence. Andy's, Jayne's, and Conrad's attraction to excitement originates in their brains, and is hard-wired and genetically programmed. Unless they are extremely shy, anxious, or avoidant, tweens and teens seek increasingly more social and independent experiences that are exciting and novel. With these new experiences come opportunities for building competence, and also for taking risks. A parent's job is to encourage the competence agenda and limit the risk. Since risk taking is part and parcel of the teenage years, the challenge is to harness the abundant energy available for arousal seeking and channel it into productive and relatively safe goals.

Although the relationship between high parental monitoring and lower levels of risk taking among teens has been documented for decades, recent research has emphasized the role that personality plays in determining delinquency and substance use (Elkins et al. 2006). Traits such as impulsivity and negative emotionality—common in risk-taking teens—have strong links with substance use, but these same traits make these kids particularly hard to monitor. Still, the correlation between monitoring and positive outcomes is so strong that parents with kids hardwired for risk taking need to be ever vigilant.

It's no wonder that parents often rush to sign their kids up for sports, clubs, and volunteering: The more time spent in activities, the less time there is for risk taking. Plus, these highly engaging pursuits help teens develop skills, values, and character. Not surprisingly, research has demonstrated a link between extracurricular activities and positive adjustment in teens, especially for teens who may be having mood problems or struggle with their parents (Mahoney et al. 2002).

Families that suffer from poverty, unemployment, or illness will frequently lack the resources for securing these pro-social opportunities. Additionally, when teens move into the "I don't want to, and you can't make me" phase, it can require a particularly wise-minded and tenacious parent to impose the mandate that teens participate in sports, school clubs, and service.

HEALTH-RISK BEHAVIORS

Teens (ages fifteen to nineteen) who have done any of the following during the last month—and those who have ever had sexual intercourse—are said to be engaged in health-risk behaviors:

- had an alcoholic drink on three or more days;
- had five or more drinks within the span of a couple of hours (binge drinking);
- smoke cigarettes regularly;
- used cocaine, crack, or hallucinogens
- smoked marijuana;
- engaged in a physical fight;
- carried a weapon; or
- taken prescription drugs for recreational use.

A loud alarm should be sounded for any teen who has engaged in health-risk behaviors with regularity (and more than a couple of times with behaviors such as cocaine use or fighting). Professional advice should be sought for almost any child younger than the age of fifteen who is engaged in any of these health-risk behaviors. Parents should err on the side of caution. Dismissing the importance of substance use of any kind is a mistake, because research has consistently documented that the earlier a child starts using substances, the more progressed the abuse and dependency is likely to become during high school.

A national longitudinal research program called Monitoring the Future has tracked substance use among teenagers since 1975. The most recent summary, spearheaded by Lloyd Johnston of the University of Michigan's Institute for Social Research, has documented the most recently analyzed data available (Johnston et al. 2009). About one-third of all high schoolers report using marijuana and alcohol in the month previous to the data collection, with the percentages increasing over the four years of high school. About three-quarters of teens have consumed alcohol (more than a few sips) by the end of high school, and two-fifths of teens have done so by the end of eighth grade. (There is a bit of good news there; alcohol consumption and binge drinking are down from their peak levels in the early 1980s.) Nearly half of teens have tried an illicit drug by the time they finish high school. Prescription drugs are the second-most-abused drug, behind marijuana. About one in twenty high school seniors report having taken the painkiller oxycodone (without a prescription). One-third of high schoolers participate in multiple risk behaviors, and they are responsible for most of the total risk taking. Since this chapter cannot do justice to a comprehensive review of drug-use patterns, parents are encouraged to go online and peruse the government websites listed in the Parent Resources section.

Parents often wonder about the definitions of substance abuse and addiction. While some authors (including me) have sketched out the continuum of use from experimental to recreational to excessive to abusive to addictive, these labels are often unhelpful. I've seen middle schoolers begin "experimental" use of alcohol, marijuana, or prescription pills and plummet into compulsive, drug-seeking behavior within months. Often, these kids have underlying depression or anxiety. In such circumstances, clinicians don't focus merely on the quantity or kind of substances being used, but on how they are being used. Is the child using the substance by herself? Does he drink to become inebriated? Does he self-medicate so that he can relax? Again, if you have any concerns about the use patterns of your child, seek an evaluation from a licensed therapist who has experience with adolescents and drug abuse. As with any other serious health problem, your child deserves to be assessed by a skilled professional, not via a checklist in a book or online.

As profoundly damaging as many adolescent risk-taking behaviors may be, nicotine dependency will take the most lives. About 20 percent of twelfth-graders smoke. Each year, about a half-million Americans die from smoking tobacco, and the huge majority of these smokers became addicted as teenagers. One out of every five deaths in the U.S. is a result of tobacco use, making it more lethal than all other addictive drugs combined. One of the most important things parents can do to prevent their children from starting to smoke is to not smoke themselves.

Adolescent Health

One of the most important things parents can do to protect their children's physical health is to not smoke themselves.

MANAGING RISKS

Whenever parents think of risk taking, they think of peers (a topic addressed at length in chapter 4), and it's true that peers have a powerful influence on a teen's risk-taking behaviors. But peers are only part of the equation, and they're probably easier to focus on than all of the other family and individual factors that play a role, such as parenting style, the child's temperament, their history with school and disciplinary problems, and psychological maladjustment. The wise-minded parent knows to widen the lens and look at this complex array of factors, rather than focusing solely on friends. Kids are loath to give up friendships just because their parents take issue, and anyway, risk-proofing your child is far more complicated than just attempting to pick your child's friends.

Andy's, Jayne's, and Conrad's parents worried about sex, drugs, and violence, as do virtually all parents of teens. They wanted to limit risks while allowing their kids to develop unique identities and build competencies. But remember: Limiting health-compromising risk taking is the goal, not preventing *any* exposure to risk (which would require putting teens in a protective gulag somewhere). Childhood is never devoid of risk, and kids develop competencies by being out in the social world, making mistakes, watching others make mistakes, and feeling the sting of negative consequences. They also develop the muscle of self-control and curbing risk through lots of practice over time.

The trick is to manage the level of risk. If the teen is a born adrenaline junkie, channel that tendency in healthful ways. It's better to encourage ski racing or velodrome cycling than leaving her free to find her "highs" in other ways. Andy, Jayne, and Conrad—actual former patients of mine—turned out beautifully, thanks to their parents' hard work in balancing their authoritative parenting, setting those healthy building blocks in place, and helping their kids develop the seven essentials. Andy completed a challenging university program in construction management. Jayne sells software to hospitals and is a rising star. And Conrad works in finance. These stories had happy endings mainly because the parents stuck by their teens, adjusted the guardrails when needed, and supported them in finding healthy outlets for their energies and evolving identities.

Truth be told, life was hell for those parents when they were dealing with teen mistakes and risks. But they prioritized building competencies, parental monitoring, and the delicate dance of limiting risk taking, all while maintaining their loving relationships. The reward of producing high-functioning young adults came later.

Even if we do figure out ways for our kids to have fun, build skills, and limit access to

ESSENTIAL
ACTIVITY

Analyze Your Comfort Level with Risk

As you consider how to manage and monitor your child's risk taking, pause for a moment to reflect upon your comfort level with risk. This exercise can give you insight into your motivations as you plan your parenting approach.

1. Describe a personal experience in adolescence when you learned about the negative consequences of taking risks.

_____

_____

_____

2. Describe a risk that you took as a child that you hope your child never takes.

_____

_____

_____

3. Given your own adolescent experiences, what might be "hot buttons" for you as you parent your teen through risky experiences she or he might have?

_____

_____

_____

4. Describe a time when you know you did not address a risk experience effectively with your child.

_____

_____

_____

5. What might have been a more wise-minded approach?

_____

_____

_____

6. List some areas in your teen's life where you may need to allow for more independence, despite the risks?

_____

_____

_____

7. List some risk areas that you might need to monitor more closely or limit more.

_____

_____

_____

sex, drugs, and personal dangers, a parent will always worry about risk—it's in our DNA. Protective parents help their children survive adolescence, but there are disadvantages to overprotection and overcontrol. A child may rebel against hypercontrol or authoritarianism. Furthermore, a child who isn't allowed to bike to school, ride buses to a job, or travel internationally misses the opportunity to experience self-discovery and competency building.

Parents will do their own cost/benefit/risk analyses about what they will allow their child to do. There is no recipe for the right amount of freedom to give a child, because parents have different philosophies and tolerance levels for risk, and kids have different personalities.

Building Block No. 8: Stress Management

The latest Stress in America survey conducted by the American Psychological Association turned up some telling data: Tweens and teens reported experiencing high levels of stress, yet their parents estimated their kids' stress to be at much lower levels (Munsey 2010). Parents underestimated stressors in their eight- to seventeen-year-olds' lives across the board when asked about everything from school pressures to sleep to headaches. Nearly half of teens between the ages of thirteen and seventeen said that they worried more over the past year than they had the year before, but only 28 percent of parents thought that their teens' stress had increased. While 14 percent of tweens (eight to twelve years old) and 28 percent of teens reported stress in the extreme range, only 2 percent to 5 percent of parents rated their children's stress in this range. Forty-two percent of parents reported that their own stress worsened in the past year, and *two-thirds* of them reported that they had been diagnosed with a chronic condition in the past year, most commonly high blood pressure or high cholesterol.

Stress has harmful effects on physical, cognitive, emotional, and social health. As described earlier in the "stress response" section (chapter 5), the family of neuromodulators called *catecholamines* is released when we are aroused by stressful circumstances. This was handy in prehistoric times, when we needed to clobber a saber-toothed tiger every now and again, but nowadays, we swim needlessly in these chemicals all day long. This chronic stress, and the resultant release of hormones, contributes to health problems in every human organ system, and it's harming our executive functioning skills, including memory, concentration, planning, goal completion, and impulse control (Arnsten 1998).

A fascinating study conducted with an ethnically diverse group of ninth-graders in Los Angeles documented the spillover effects of stress from the home to teens' academic life, and vice versa (Flook and Fuligni 2008). Multiple measures of stress at home and at school revealed that difficulties at school resulted in more family stress the next day and for two days afterward. Likewise, when teens experienced family stress, they had more problems with learning at school the next day, with stress spillover lasting for days. Moreover, high levels of bidirectional stress in ninth grade resulted in declining academic achievement *four years later*.

Learning to manage stress is crucial for parents and children. There are many, many different ways to do this; the trick is finding the one that works for you. Many of the most effective stress-management skills originate from Far Eastern traditions, including tai chi, qigong, meditation, and yoga. Other self-management approaches involve guided imagery and progressive relaxation programs. Contemplative skills, such as meditation and prayer, are practiced by millions of people worldwide, and the research has demonstrated a wide array of positive effects, including psychological, physiological, and biochemical (Walsh 2011). Meditation and mindfulness practices also improve empathy, sensitivity, emotional stability, and psychological maturity while reducing distress and burnout (Shapiro and Carlson 2009).

WISE-MINDED **MANTRA** **There is no physical health without mental health.**

MINDFULNESS AND STRESS MANAGEMENT

The practice of mindful parenting is thriving, thanks to a greater understanding of emotions and our brains' sensitivity to family distress (Duncan et al. 2009). As first described in chapter 1, the root of mindful parenting is mindfulness, a form of meditation that has been used to successfully treat a multitude of mental health problems and reduce the pain and discomfort of chronic illness. Mindful parenting interventions have increasingly shown that they can both prevent and treat mental health problems in children, teens, and other family members (Thompson and Gauntlett-Gilbert 2008). Mindfulness is also a core component of many evidence-based treatments for stress reduction and emotional regulation.

Why all this emphasis on mindfulness? The biological responses to stress are elevated heart rate, release of adrenaline, and a narrowing of the mental focus in preparation for attack (fight or flight)—all of which are eased by the practice of mindfulness. Both teens' and parents' anger can be triggered during the tween and teen years quite easily, so we need ways to reduce this activation of our autonomic nervous systems. Moreover, since stress hurts our health and our children's, we need skills for lowering that heart rate and avoiding the release of all those harmful stress hormones. The practices of mindfulness, meditation, and paced respiration do the trick quite effectively. However, we need to exercise this "muscle," or it won't be available when we need it.

Mindfulness simply means focusing attention on the present moment, without passing judgment. If you can do this with an added sense of curiosity—an inborn trait of all human beings—you may also fire neurons in the positive-emotion part of the brain.

Here's an example, in which a father is dealing with a teenager who refuses take out the garbage, despite several requests. After his third request, the dad decides to practice some mindfulness, rather than blow up at his son, so he says to himself:

"I notice that my heart is racing. I notice that in my thoughts I am cursing my son. I accept this moment, my racing heart, and my angry thoughts. I will deal with my son's opposition later, when I settle down. I wonder what will happen if I just sit in the present moment without reacting. I'm curious about my anger and my son's noncompliance."

Right now, the father is focusing on calming his heart rate through deep breathing. He is taking steps toward empathy by being curious about his own emotions and those of his son. This is also a step toward an eventual wise-minded decision about his son's noncompliance: This dad is looking at the big picture of what is going on with his son's life, his feelings about chores, his son's incentives to do them, and perhaps even his son's incentive to rebel and push his dad's buttons.

Research shows that mindfulness modifies attention, so if you tend to be reactive by nature, practicing mindfulness can improve your emotional regulation skills (Jha et al. 2007). Another study, in which subjects were shown unpleasant pictures to trigger a reaction, found that the practice of mindfulness helped them more easily disengage their attention from the emotional stimuli and experience a subsequent decrease in emotional intensity (Ortner et al. 2007).

This research bodes well for parents: Practicing mindfulness can indeed help you disengage from negative parent-child patterns—but "practice" is the key word here. Just as we need daily exercise to maintain physical fitness, mindfulness "fitness" also requires practice, time, and discipline.

WISE-MINDED **MANTRA** — **A calm mind makes a wise mind possible.**

STRESS AND PARENTING

Stress affects parenting in myriad ways. We know that cumulative parental stress has a direct impact on mothers' positivity index—meaning the number of positive feelings and interactions —with their children. Since stress also negatively impacts marital quality, the black clouds of stress can ruin a family's emotional climate.

When a parent worries about her child, whether because of a temperament issue, emotional outbursts, or behavioral concerns, she may end up ruminating on that child's negative traits. It's only natural, but the contagious nature of emotions suggests that the child will pick up on these negative thoughts and feelings. Remember the research from chapter 5 showing that it takes three positive emotions to neutralize the impact of a single negative one? That emphasizes how important it is for a parent to learn to redirect her attention to positive (or at least benign) emotions, in order to reset or "reboot" the emotional atmosphere.

Moodiness and argumentativeness are so prolific during the teen years that parents may need to check their negative thoughts about their teen on a daily basis. A common negative thought such as "She always comes home so grumpy and uncooperative!" could be replaced by the mindful and wise "I will let her mood flow over me like water over a rock; I accept her completely as a fifteen-year-old with typical and normal emotions." Who knows what mood the teen might blow in with, but by practicing a little preemptive mindfulness, the parent can summon some blue skies to help deflect any approaching bad weather.

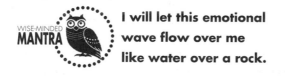

WISE-MINDED **MANTRA**

I will let this emotional wave flow over me like water over a rock.

In chapter 2, we discussed how high-stress family interactions can lead to "amygdala hijacks," those zero-to-sixty moments when conscious thought goes out the window and reactions barrel down the "fast lane" of emotion brain. For a refresher on coping with these hijacks, see pages 15 and 26, especially the several breathing techniques and the CALM technique for self-soothing and reflection. All of these tools are part of the art and science of mindful parenting. They help us calm down so we can review options, discern what's best considering our situation, and control our impulses. The goal is to reduce stress in the family in order to increase physical and mental health. Remember the wise-minded mantra: "My child is doing the best that he can, given his age and stage." We may not be able to change our kids' toxic moods, but we can use mindfulness to clean up our side of the street, setting an example for acceptance and emotional control. As Albert Einstein said, "The only rational way of educating is to be an example."

Building Block No. 9: Religious or Spiritual Involvement

About 90 percent of people in the world engage in religious or spiritual practices, and that appears to be a boon for mental health. One review of 724 studies found that in half of them, there was a significant link between religious involvement and mental health (Koenig et al. 2001). It appears that it's the focus on love and forgiveness—not on punishment and guilt—that is most beneficial.

Harold Koenig and his colleagues found that adults who attend religious services at least once a week tend to live approximately seven years longer than those who do not, even when they took into account the adults' health and health-maintenance behaviors. However, there is no way to parse the effects of communal giving, social support, positive emotions, and meditation—all of which may be part of the power of these services.

Practicing religion appears to have a powerful positive effect for teenagers, too. Using data from the National Longitudinal Study of Adolescent Health, the religious practices of teens in grades seven through twelve were examined and related to adolescent health measures (Nonnemaker et al. 2003). Both "public" religiosity (frequency of attendance at religious services and frequency of participation in religious youth group activities) and "private" religiosity (frequency of prayer and the perceived importance of religion in their lives) were generally related to fewer health risks. While different measures correlated with different health outcomes, the general pattern is that religiosity of *any kind* is associated with less substance use (drugs, cigarettes, and alcohol) and less violence, but only attendance at church and youth groups ("public" religiosity) was associated with delayed sexual initiation and fewer teenage pregnancies. This national data obscures regional trends and other demographics, but reveals a positive link, nonetheless. It would be interesting to know whether the health correlates would be the same for teens who did not engage in formal religious practices, but were from close families and considered themselves "spiritual," but since these indices were not measured, we are left to wonder.

As with the adult data, researchers are still uncertain about the causal pathway between religiosity and teen health. Are the positive outcomes related to family closeness and/or the transmission of values? Is it the health benefits of prayer, or the support of multiple adults, or the participation in communal activities? Is it positive peer influence of friends who also engage in religious practices? Given the extensive research, which documents the relationship between parent-teen closeness and health, the answers to these questions are almost impossible to determine.

ESSENTIAL
FACT

Teens and Religion

Teenage religiosity is associated with less substance abuse (drugs, cigarettes, and alcohol), less violence, less sexual activity, and less teenage pregnancy.

Defining spirituality is like falling into a linguistic briar patch, but a common description is the essence of being connected to something larger than oneself and to one's deepest values. Spirituality often includes an understanding of life's impermanence, and thus offers more meaning and intention to the choice to live with as much goodness as possible (Sheldrake 2007). Even Plato wrote about spirituality as a path to a higher state of awareness, wisdom, and communion with God or with creation. Spiritual practices may include prayer, meditation, and contemplative pursuits through reading of sacred texts. Love and compassion are common themes in spiritual practices.

Therapists have been slow to appreciate the role of religion and spirituality in overall well-being, but as a proven way to reduce vulnerability to illness, cope with stress, and enhance quality of life, religion is finally getting its due in the world of psychotherapy and medicine (Cloninger 2006). Since "psyche" is the Greek word for soul or spirit—and since research has documented the positive effects of meditation and spiritual practices—perhaps spiritual matters will be incorporated to a greater extent in the pursuit of physical and mental health in the coming years.

For those who seek to explore moral virtues and universal ethics outside of a traditional religious structure, there are many outlets and online communities to connect with. One example is Wisdom Commons (*wisdomcommons.org*), an organization that provides inspirational quotes, meditations, stories, and essays to encourage people to discuss the ways in which important virtues, such as generosity, compassion, and courage, can be practiced by families in everyday life.

Building Block No. 10: Recreational and Leisure Activities

There is yet another dangerous syndrome lurking within most families: "family fun deficit disorder." I'm only partly joking. With all that time demands of families, it's hard to fit in leisure time, yet research shows that it is associated with greater emotional bonding and less family stress (Zabriskie and McCormick 2001). Believe it or not, most teens report that they want to spend more time with their families, not less. Yet when parents kick-start the activity agenda, teens roll their eyes and try to wiggle free. It takes a huge commitment to overcome teen resistance and create family fun, but it's worth it.

And here's why: A lack of playful family interaction exposes your kids to all sorts of problems. Once the reservoir of good feelings in a family dries up, everything else starts shriveling up, too—children's cooperation, self-esteem, academic achievement, resistance to negative peer influence, and the effectiveness of your discipline, to name a few. A big part of the problem is that by the teen years, kids are not only naturally pulling away from their families, but with everything else they are doing (sports, community service, and homework), there is little to no time for family fun.

But do the math: If parents do the essential monitoring, managing, setting of limits, upholding of rules, and insisting upon routines, it adds up to a lot of negative interactions, subtractions from the bank account of good parent-child feelings. And there are more subtractions due to the stresses in your own life, and those from your teen's dumping of bad moods. It's no wonder the rapport between family members can run at a deficit.

Fortunately, family fun and joy can overlap with other healthy pursuits examined in this chapter, such as exercise, time spent in nature, and attending religious or spiritual services. In addition, research on play in childhood has shown that it enhances the development of social skills, adaptability, intelligence, creativity, and the ability to solve problems (Brown and Vaughan 2009). Curiosity and interest are hard-wired in our brains so that we learn, explore, and enjoy novelty. But what happens to play during adolescence? It gets transferred from jumping rope to bungee jumping, from board games to first-person shooter games, and from bicycles to cars. Luckily, it also transfers to activities with friends and immersion in many healthy outlets with sports, school, and hobbies.

Your best course of action is to establish a routine of family fun and recreation early on, and then hold onto it. Family traditions—such as annual camping trips, holiday celebrations, travel, and anything else that offers opportunities for shared fun—add variety to the mix, and up your family fun quotient. And don't underestimate the simple pleasures of sharing a joke. I'm often astounded by the effectiveness of a good doggy/kitty YouTube video in my clinical practice for resetting moods when children or teens suffer out-of-control emotional "dysregulation." Laughter can reduce stress, enhance mood, improve immune function and healing, and can even be a good way of off-loading negative feelings, as long as it's not at someone else's expense (Lefcourt 2002).

ESSENTIAL
ACTIVITY

Ideas for Shared Family Fun

Here are a few ideas that you can try for adding a little more laughter and fun to family time.

- **Dance, exercise, comedy.** Try exercise videos, Zumba, and Wii dance games. If you enjoy hiking, swimming, skiing, kayaking, get out there with your kids. Some comedy clubs schedule teen improvisation nights.

- **Game Night.** Board games anyone? Taboo is our family favorite. We love using the obnoxious buzzer frequently when family members make mistakes. If you have older teens, check out Charades, Salad Bowl, and Mafia. Also try Rummikub, Parcheesi, and Yahtzee. Need a little more action? Enlist the whole neighborhood to play Capture the Flag.

- **Cooking.** Prepare family meals together. Think about rotating the role of head chef; on your teen's night to be head chef, invite his or her friends over. You can even take a cooking class together.

- **Music tutorial.** Have your teen teach you about his or her music collection and load your favorites onto your iPod.

- **Volunteering.** Search the Internet for activities you can do together. Trail or park maintenance, kitchen work at shelters, and helping at food banks are always good options.

- **Back rubs.** Most teens enjoy a back rub or foot rub. Spa sessions are also fun; pedi or mani, anyone?

- **Movie night.** Watch a video together—while enjoying pizza and root-beer floats. OK, it's a screen thing. But Oscar Wilde had a point: "Everything in moderation, including moderation." Hey, at least you're sharing a laugh together.

Kids can deep-six our efforts to instigate good times, and they're so good at it that parents often simply give up. But don't! An agenda for fun might sound frivolous, but it's not. Parents must invest in efforts to deposit good feelings into the family emotional bank account, because kids (especially teens) will be making lots of withdrawals with their negative moods. Life brings many unanticipated challenges. As Mark Twain said, "The human race has only one really effective weapon, and that is laughter."

The Seven Essentials and 'Good Enough' Parenting

The list of good habits and tasks listed in this chapter—in this entire book, in fact—can seem overwhelming, until you remember the mantra "I am doing the best that I can right now, and I want to keep doing better." To do this, you need to strike a balance between accepting yourself as a "good enough" parent and striving for change. In achieving this balance, you avoid perfectionism, which is destructive, both to you and your child, and embrace the faith that your children will develop competencies precisely because you are *not* providing a perfect life for them, free of strife, disappointment, and challenge—and the many, many growth opportunities they bring.

Every single day in my family therapy practice, I sit with parents who are "right" when they say that failing grades are unacceptable, drug use is harmful, and cruel behavior is unkind and distressing. Many parents are also accurate when they state that their teens need to develop more self-control, emotional resilience, or physical fitness. But declaring these perspectives to a tween or teen is rarely effective, and in fact may make things worse by creating shame and driving a wedge between parent and child. What is needed is a wise-minded approach. Table being "right" and reach instead for communicating emotional calm and empathy, and work to understand and then validate the often complicated and conflicting feelings of your teen.

By applying a wide-angle lens and appreciating the many pressures and dynamics that impact a teen's chaotic—and sometimes apparently nonsensical—behaviors, we can more easily find empathy and then validate our child. We can also fully appreciate the finesse required in choosing the most effective strategy for coping with difficulties. Do you need a new policy? A clearly articulated consequence? Or emotion coaching in the form of a heart-to-heart talk, with feelings freely expressed, support freely given, and a teen's own eventual insight leading him to create his own solution?

One sacrosanct "essential" in parenting ties all the others together: the secure parent-child attachment. The wise-minded parent avoids lecturing, criticizing, and reacting to negative emotions in children, because these natural but hurtful responses undermine and degrade this precious relationship. It is the trust and positive rapport that exist within this secure attachment that make all of the nitty-gritty work on the other essentials possible.

Many of the "take-homes" in this book are standard maxims in parenting: be calm, listen, avoid power struggles, practice authoritative parenting, solve problems collaboratively when possible, establish healthy habits, and build a large social network of support. But none of that means much without the ability to balance emotion and reason as we interact with loved ones. Our intuition about what is truly effective, especially in challenging moments, can only shine through when we make the effort to calm our mind and deliberate carefully. Without a calm mind, a parent cannot possibly gain the big-picture perspective necessary to discern a wise-minded approach to building the seven essentials. And without personal health—mental and physical—a parent cannot broaden and build their wise-minded skills.

Self-care is vital; it gives us the immense fortitude and patience required for parenting. With enough self-love and self-acceptance, we can fully embrace one of the most challenging and rewarding endeavors of human existence: raising happy, loving, and ultimately successful teens.

Parent Resources

Technology

Center for Media Literacy: *medialit.org*

Pew Internet Project: *pewresearch.org*

Common Sense Media, a nonprofit organization that advises parents on media use by children: *commonsensemedia.org*

Rosen, Larry D. *iDisorder: Understanding Our Obsession with Technology and Overcoming Its Hold on Us.* Palgrave MacMillan, 2012.

Physical Health and Sexuality

American Academy of Pediatrics, topics of interest to parents: *healthychildren.org*

The National Institute on Drug Abuse: *drugabuse.gov/parents-teachers*

American Association of Child & Adolescent Psychiatry: *aacap.org/cs/forfamilies*

KidsHealth: *kidshealth.org*

Center for Young Women's Health: *youngwomenshealth.org*

Young Men's Health: *youngmenshealthsite.org*

Sexuality Information and Education Council of the United States (SIECUS): *SIECUS.org*

The National Campaign to Prevent Teen and Unplanned Pregnancy: *thenationalcampaign.org* and *stayteen.org*

Our Bodies, Ourselves: *ourbodiesourselves.org*

Richardson, Justin and Mark Schuster. *Everything You Never Wanted Your Kids to Know About Sex (But Were Afraid They'd Ask): The Secrets to Surviving Your Child's Sexual Development from Birth to the Teens.* Crown Publishers, 2003.

The Children and Nature Network: *childrenandnature.org*

Adolescent Development, Parenting, and Families

The Centers for Disease Control and Prevention: Visit *cdc.gov/ncbddd*, search for "child development," then select "positive parenting tips."

American Psychological Association: *apa.org/research/action/parenting.aspx*

Brooks, Robert and Sam Goldstein. *Raising Resilient Children: Fostering Strength, Hope, and Optimism in Your Child.* Chicago: Contemporary Books, 2001.

Kastner, Laura S. and Jennifer F. Wyatt. *The Seven Year Stretch: How Families Work*

Together to Grow Through Adolescence. NY: Houghton Mifflin, 1997.

———. *The Launching Years: Strategies for Parenting from Senior Year to College Life.* Three Rivers Press, 2002.

———. *Getting to Calm: Cool-headed Strategies for Parenting Tweens and Teens.* ParentMap, 2009.

Happiness and Well-being

Csikszentmihalyi, Mihaly. *Finding Flow: The Psychology of Engagement with Everyday Life.* Basic Books, 1997.

Fredrickson, Barbara L. Positivity: *Groundbreaking Research Reveals How to Embrace the Hidden Strength of Positive Emotions, Overcome Negativity, and Thrive.* Crown Publishers, 2009.

Seligman, Martin E.P. *Authentic Happiness: Using the New Positive Psychology to Realize Your Potential for Lasting Fulfillment.* Free Press, 2002. *authentichappiness.org*

———. *The Optimistic Child: A Proven Program to Safeguard Children Against Depression and Build Lifelong Resilience.* Mariner Books, 1997.

Emotional Intelligence, Emotional Skills, and Mindful Parenting

Gottman, John M., Lynn F. Katz, and Carole Hooven. *Meta-emotion: How Families Communicate Emotionally.* Mahwah, NJ: Lawrence Erlbaum Associates, 1997.

Gottman, John and Joan Declaire. *Raising an Emotionally Intelligent Child: The Heart of Parenting.* Simon & Schuster, 1998.

Harvey, Pat and Jeanine A. Penzo. *Parenting a Child Who Has Intense Emotions: Dialectical Behavior Therapy Skills to Help Your Child Regulate Emotional Outbursts and Aggressive Behaviors.* Harbinger Press, 2009.

Kabat-Zinn, Myla and Jon Kabat-Zinn. *Everyday Blessings: The Inner Work of Mindful Parenting.* Hyperion, 1998.

McKay, Matthew, Jeffrey C. Wood, and Jeffrey Brantley. *Dialectical Behavior Therapy Skills Workbook: Practical DBT Exercises for Learning Mindfulness, Interpersonal Effectiveness, Emotional Regulation, & Distress Tolerance.* New Harbinger Publications, 2007.

Siegel, Daniel J. *The Mindful Brain: Reflection and Attunement in the Cultivation of Well-being.* NY: W.W. Norton, 2007.

Stahl, Bob and Elisha Goldstein. *A Mindfulness-based Stress Reduction Workbook.* New Harbinger Publications, 2010.

Dweck, Carol S. *Mindset: The New Psychology of Success.* Random House, 2006.

Boy/Girl Development

Kindlon, Dan and Michael Thompson. *Raising Cain: Protecting the Emotional Life of Boys.* Ballantine Books, 2000.

Pollack, William. *Real Boys: Rescuing Our Sons from the Myths of Boyhood.* Owl Books, 1999.

Simmons, Rachel. *Odd Girl Out: The Hidden Culture of Aggression in Girls.* Harvest Books, 2003.

Wiseman, Rosalind. *Queen Bees and Wannabees: Helping Your Daughter Survive Cliques, Gossip, Boyfriends and Other Realities of Adolescence.* Three Rivers Press, 2003.

Levin, Diane E. and Jean Kilbourne. *So Sexy So Soon: The New Sexualized Childhood and What Parents Can Do to Protect Their Kids.* Ballantine, 2009.

Weight and Eating Issues

Neumark-Sztainer, Dianne. *"I'm Like, So Fat": Helping your Teen Make Healthy Choices about Eating and Exercise in a Weight-obsessed World.* Guilford Press, 2005.

Satter, Ellyn. *Your Child's Weight: Helping without Harming: Birth through Adolescence.* Kelcy Press, 2005.

Character

Values in Action Institute: *viacharacter.org*

The Wisdom Commons: *wisdomcommons.org*

Baumrind, Diana, Marvin W. Berkowitz, Thomas Lickona, Larry P. Nucci, Marilyn Watson, and David Streight. *Parenting for Character: Five Experts, Five Practices.* CSEE, 2008.

Tough, Paul. *How Children Succeed: Grit, Curiosity, and the Hidden Power of Character.* Houghton Mifflin Harcourt, 2012.

References

Chapter One

Ainsworth, M. et al. *Patterns of Attachment: A Psychological Study of the Strange Situation*. Lawrence Erlbaum, 1978.

Allen, J.P. et al. "Attachment and Adolescent Psychosocial Functioning." *Child Development* 69 (1998): 1406–19.

Allen, J.P. et al. "A Secure Base in Adolescence: Markers of Attachment Security in the Mother-adolescent Relationship." *Child Development* 74 (2003): 292–307.

Armsden, G. and M. Greenberg. "The Inventory of Parent and Peer Attachment: Individual Differences and Their Relationship to Psychological Well-being in Adolescence." *Journal of Youth and Adolescence* 16 (1987): 427–54.

Cassidy, J. and P.R. Shaver (eds.), *Handbook of Attachment: Theory, Research, and Clinical Applications*, 2d ed. The Guilford Press, 2008.

Collins, W.A. and B. Laursen. "Parent-adolescent Relationships and Influences." *Handbook of Adolescent Psychology*, eds. R. Lerner and L. Steinberg. Wiley, 2004.

Collins, W.A. et al. "Contemporary Research on Parenting: The Case for Nature and Nurture." *American Psychologist* 55, no. 2 (2000): 218–32.

Duncan, L., J.D. Coatsworth, and M. Greenberg. "A Model of Mindful Parenting: Implications for Parent-child Relationships and Prevention Research." *Clinical Child and Family Psychology Review 12*, no. 3 (2009): 255–70.

Grotevant, H.D., and C.R. Cooper. "Patterns of Interaction in Family Relationships and the Development of Identity Exploration in Adolescence." *Child Development 56*, no. 2 (1985): 415–28.

Harvey, P., and J. Penzo, J. *Parenting a Child Who Has Intense Emotions: Dialectical Behavior Therapy Skills to Help Your Child Regulate Emotional Outburst and Aggressive Behaviors*. New Harbinger Publications, 2009.

Kabat-Zinn, M., and J. Kabat-Zinn. *Everyday Blessings: The Inner Work of Mindful Parenting*. Hyperion, 1998.

Kagan, J. *The Temperamental Thread: How Genes, Culture, Time and Luck Make Us Who We Are*. Dana Press, 2010.

Kastner, L.S., and J. Wyatt, J. *Getting to Calm: Cool-headed Strategies for Parenting Tweens and Teens*. ParentMap, 2009.

Linehan, M.M. *Cognitive-behavioral Treatment of Borderline Personality Disorder*. Guilford Press, 1993.

Moore, K.A. et al. "Parent-teen Relationships and Interactions: Far More Positive than Not." *Trends Child Research Brief* (2004): Publication no. 2004-25.

Offer, D., E. Ostrov, and K.I. Howard. *The Adolescent: A Psychological Self-portrait*. New York: Basic Books, 1981.

Siegel, D. "Toward an Interpersonal Neurobiology of the Developing Mind: Attachment, 'Mindsight' and Neural Integration." *Infant Mental Health Journal* 22, nos. 1-2 (2001): 67–94.

Chapter Two

Barkley, R.A. *Executive Functions: What They Are, How They Work, and Why They Evolved.* Guilford Press, 2012.

Bates, J.E. et al. "Interaction of Temperamental Resistance to Control and Restrictive Parenting in the Development of Externalizing Behavior." *Developmental Psychology* 34 (1998): 982–95.

Baumeister, R.F., and J. Tierney, J. *Willpower: Rediscovering the Greatest Human Strength.* New York: Penguin, 2011.

Baumeister, R.F. et al. "Ego Depletion: Is the Active Self a Limited Resource?" *Journal of Personality and Social Psychology* 74, no. 5 (1998): 1252–65.

Baumrind, D. "Current Patterns of Parental Authority." *Developmental Psychology Monographs* 4, no. 1 (1971).

Cox, A.J. *No Mind Left Behind: Understanding and Fostering Executive Control—The Eight Essential Brain Skills Every Child Needs to Thrive.* New York: A Perigee/Penguin Group, 2007.

Dishion, T.J., and G.R. Patterson. "The Development and Ecology of Antisocial Behavior in Children and Adolescents." In *Developmental psychopathology.* Vol. 3, *Risk, Disorder, and Adaptation,* eds. D. Cicchetti and D.J. Cohen. New York, Wiley (2006): 503–41.

Gailliot, M.T., and R.F. Baumeister. "The Physiology of Willpower: Linking Blood Glucose to Self-Control." *Personality and Social Psychology Review* 11, no. 4 (2007): 303–27.

Giedd, J. et. al. "Brain Development During Childhood and Adolescence: A Longitudinal MRI Study." *Nature Neuroscience* 2 (1999): 861–63.

Goleman, D. *Emotional Intelligence: Why It Can Matter More Than IQ.* Bantam Books, 1995.

Gottman, J.M., L.F. Katz, and C. Hooven. *Meta-emotion: How Families Communicate Emotionally.* Hillsdale, NJ: Lawrence Erlbaum, 1997.

Graybiel, A.M. "Habits, Rituals, and the Evaluative Brain." *Annual Review of Neuroscience* 31 (2008): 359–87.

Hofmann, W. et al. "Everyday Temptations: An Experience Sampling Study of Desire, Conflict, and Self-control." *Journal of Personality and Social Psychology* 102, no. 6 (2012): 1318–35.

Kagan, J. *Galen's Prophecy: Temperament in Human Nature.* Westview Press, 1997.

Katz, L.F., and E.C. Hunter., "Maternal Meta-emotion Philosophy and Adolescent Depressive Symptomatology." *Social Development* 16, no. 2 (2007): 343–60.

Kiff, C.J., L.J. Lengua, and M. Zalewski. "Nature and Nurturing: Parenting in the Context of Child Temperament. *Clinical Child and Family Review* 14, no. 3 (2011): 251–301.

Larson, R.W. "Toward a Psychology of Positive Youth Development." *American Psychologist* 55, no. 1 (2000): 170–83.

Lieberman, M.D. et al. "Putting Feelings Into Words: Affect Labeling Disrupts Amygdala Activity in Response to Affective Stimuli." *Psychological Science* 18, no. 5 (2007): 421–8.

Mahoney, J.L., A.L. Harris, and J.S. Eccles. "Organized Activity Participation, Positive Youth Development, and the Over-scheduling Hypothesis." *Social Policy Report: Giving Child and Youth Development Knowledge Away* 20, no. 4 (2006): 3–30.

Mischel, W., Y. Shoda, and P.K. Peake. "The Nature of Adolescent Competencies Predicted by Preschool Delay of Gratification." *Journal of Personality and Social Psychology* 54, no. 4 (1988): 687–96.

Mischel, W., and O. Ayduk. "Willpower in a Cognitive-affective Processing System: The Dynamics of Delay of Gratification." In *Handbook of Self-regulation: Research, Theory, and Applications,* eds. R.F. Baumeister and K.D. Vohs. New York: Guilford, 2004.

Moffitt, T. et al. "A Gradient of Childhood Self-control Predicts Health, Wealth, and Public Safety." *Proceedings of the National Academy of Sciences*, January 24, 2011.

Oaten, M., and K. Cheng. "Improved Self-control: The Benefits of a Regular Program of Academic Study." *Basic and Applied Social Psychology* 28 (2006): 1–16.

Rothbart, M.K., and M.I. Posner. "Genes and Experience in the Development of Executive Attention and Effortful Control." *New Directions for Child and Adolescent Development* 109 (2005): 101–8.

Rothbart, M.K. et al. "Investigations of Temperament at Three to Seven Years: The Children's Behavior Questionnaire." *Child Development* 72, no. 5(2001): 1394–408.

Steinberg, L. et al. "Over-time Changes in Adjustment and Competence Among Adolescents from Authoritative, Authoritarian, Indulgent, and Neglectful Families." *Child Development* 65, no. 3 (1994): 754–70.

Steinberg, L. "We Know Some Things: Parent-adolescent Relationships in Retrospect and Prospect." *Journal of Research on Adolescence* 11, no. 1 (2001): 1–19.

Steinberg, L. et al. "Age Differences in Sensation Seeking and Impulsivity as Indexed by Behavior and Self-report: Evidence for a Dual Systems Model." *Developmental Psychology* 44, no. 6 (2008): 1764–78.

Vohs, K.D. et al. "Making Choices Impairs Subsequent Self-control: A Limited-resource Account of Decision Making, Self-regulation, and Active Initiative." *Journal of Personality and Social Psychology* 94, no. 5 (2008): 883–98.

Zimbardo, P.G., and S. Radl. *The Shy Child: Overcoming and Preventing Shyness from Infancy to Adulthood*, 2d ed. Malor Books, 1999.

Chapter Three

Asher, S.R. and J.D. Coie, eds. *Peer Rejection in Childhood*. Cambridge University Press, 1990.

Baumeister, R. F. et al. "Exploding the Self-esteem Myth." *Scientific American* 292, no. 1 (2005): 84–91.

Bersani, B.E. and C.L. Chapple. "School Failure as an Adolescent Turning Point." *Sociological Focus* 40, no. 4 (2007): 370–92.

Bryck, R.L. and P.A. Fisher. "Training the Brain: Practical Applications of Neural Plasticity from the Intersection of Cognitive Neuroscience, Developmental Psychology, and Prevention Science." *American Psychologist* 67, no. 2 (2012): 87–100.

Carpenter, S.K. et al. "Using Spacing to Enhance Diverse Forms of Learning: Review of Recent Research and Implications for Instruction." *Educational Psychology Review* 24, no. 3 (2012): 369–78.

Dornbusch, S.M. et al. "The Relation of Parenting Style to Adolescent School Performance." *Child Development* 58, no. 5 (1987): 1244–57.

Durlak, J.A. et al. "The Impact of Enhancing Students' Social and Emotional Learning: A Meta-analysis of School-based Universal Interventions." *Child Development* 82, no. 1 (2011): 405–32.

Dweck, C. *Mindset: The New Psychology of Success*. N.Y.: Random House, 2006.

Eccles, J.S., and R.D. Harold. "Family Involvement in Children's and Adolescents' Schooling." In *Family-School Links: How Do They Affect Educational Outcomes?* eds. A. Booth and J.F. Dunn, 3–34. Mahwah, N.J.: Erlbaum, 1996.

Eccles, J.S., and C. Midgley. "Changes in Academic Motivation During Adolescence." In *From Childhood to Adolescence*, eds. R. Montemayor, G.R. Adams, and T.P. Gullotta , 134–55. Newbury Park, Calif.: Sage, 1990.

Epstein, J.L., "School-initiated Family and Community Partnerships." *In This We Believe in Action: Implementing Successful Middle Level Schools*, ed. T. Erb, 77–96. Westerville, Ohio: National Middle School Association, 2005.

———. *School, Family, and Community Partnerships: Preparing Educators and Improving Schools.* Westview Press, 2011.

Epstein, J.L. et al. *School, Family, and Community Partnerships: Your Handbook for Action*, 2d ed. Thousand Oaks, Calif.: Corwin Press, 2002.

Fan, X. and M. Chen. "Parental Involvement and Students' Academic Achievement: A Meta-analysis." *Educational Psychology Review 13*, no. 1 (2001): 1–22.

Felner, R.D. et al. "Socioeconomic Disadvantage, Proximal Environmental Experiences, and Socioemotional and Academic Adjustment in Early Adolescence: Investigation of a Mediated Effects Model." *Child Development 66*, no. 3 (1995): 774–92.

Fine, C. *Delusions of Gender: How Our Minds, Society, and Neurosexism Create Difference.* W.W. Norton & Co., 2011.

Gonzalez-DeHass, A. R., P.P. Willems, and M.F.D. Holbein. "Examining the Relationship Between Parental Involvement and Student Motivation." *Educational Psychology Review 2* (2005): 99-123.

Halpern, D.F. et al. "The Pseudoscience of Single-sex Schooling." *Science 333*, no. 6050 (2011): 1706–7.

Halpern, D.F. *Sex Differences in Cognitive Abilities*, 4th ed. London: Psychology Press, 2012.

Hill, N.E., and S.A. Craft. "Parent-school Involvement and School Performance: Mediated Pathways Among Socioeconomically Comparable African American and Euro-American Families." *Journal of Educational Psychology 95*, no. 1 (2003): 74–83.

Hoff, E., B. Laursen, and T. Tardif. "Socioeconomic Status and Parenting." In M.H. Bornstein (ed) *Handbook of Parenting Volume 2: Biology and ecology of Parenting.* (2002): 231-252. Mahwah, N.J.: Erlbaum.

Hyde, J. S. "The Gender Similarities Hypothesis." *American Psychologist 60*, no. 6 (2005): 581-592.

Kohl, G.O., L.J. Lengua, and R.J. McMahon. "Parent Involvement in School: Conceptualizing Multiple Dimensions and Their Relations with Family and Demographic Risk Factors." *Journal of School Psychology 38*, no. 6 (2000): 501–23.

Kornell, N. and R.A. Bjork. "The Promise and Perils of Self-regulated Study." *Psychnomic Bulletin and Review 14*, no. 2 (2007): 219–24.

Linehan, M. *Cognitive-Behavioral Treatment of Borderline Personality Disorder.* The Guilford Press, 1993.

Luthar, S.S., "The Culture of Affluence: Psychological Costs of Material Wealth." *Child Development 74*, no. 6 (2003): 1581–93.

Mayer, R.E. "Does Styles Research Have Useful Implications for Educational Practice?" *Learning and Individual Differences 21*, no. 3 (2011): 319–20.

Mead, S. "The Evidence Suggests Otherwise: The Truth About Boys and Girls." June 23, 2006. *educationsector.org*

Mueller, C. M. and C.S. Dweck, C. S. "Praise for Intelligence Can Undermine Children's Motivation and Performance." *Journal of Personality and Social Psychology 75*, no. 1 (1998): 33-52.

Pashler, H. et al. "Learning Styles: Concepts and Evidence." *Psychological Science in the Public Interest 9*, no. 3 (2008): 105–19.

Perie, M., R. Moran, and A.D. Lutkus. "NAEP 2004 Trends in Academic Progress: Three Decades of Student Performance in Reading and Mathematics." Washington, D.C.: Institute of Education Statistics, 2005.

Posner, M.I., and M.K. Rothbart. "Research on Attention Networks as a Model for the Integration of Psychological Science." *Annual Review of Psychology* 58 (2007): 1–23.

Ramdass, D., and B.J. Zimmerman. "Developing Self-regulation Skills: The Important Role of Homework." *Journal of Advanced Academics* 22, no. 2 (2011): 194–218.

Rohrer, D. and H. Pashler. "Recent Research on Human Learning Challenges Conventional Instructional Strategies." *Educational Researcher* 39, no. 5 (2010): 406–12.

Rosen, L.D., N.A. Cheever, and L.M. Carrier. "The Association of Parenting Style and Child Age with Parental Limit Setting and Adolescent Myspace Behavior." *Journal of Applied Developmental Psychology* 29, no. 6 (2008): 459–71.

Rosen, L.D. *iDisorder: Understanding Our Obsession with Technology and Overcoming Its Hold on Us.* Palgrave MacMillan, 2012.

Spelke, E.S. "Sex Differences in Intrinsic Aptitude for Mathematics and Science? A Critical Review." *American Psychologist* 60, no. 9 (2005): 950–8.

Spera, C. "A Review of the Relationship Among Parenting Practices, Parenting Styles, and Adolescent School Achievement." *Educational Psychology Review* 17, no. 2 (2005): 125–46.

Spera, C., K.R. Wentzel, and H.C. Matto. "Parental Aspirations for Their Children's Educational Attainment: Relations to Ethnicity, Parental Education, Children's Academic Performance, and Parental Perceptions of School Climate." *Journal of Youth and Adolescence* 38, no. 8 (2009): 1140–52.

Topor, D.R. et al. "Parent Involvement and Student Academic Performance: A Multiple Mediational Analysis." *Journal of Prevention and Intervention in the Community* 38, no. 3 (2010): 183–97.

Chapter Four

Aron, A. et al. "Reward, Motivation, and Emotion Systems Associated with Early-stage Intense Romantic Love." *Journal of Neurophysiology* 94, no. 1 (2005): 327–37.

Barber, B.L., "To Have Loved and Lost: Adolescent Romantic Relationships and Rejection." In *Romance and Sex in Adolescence and Emerging Adulthood: Risks and Opportunities*, ed. A.C. Crouter and A. Booth. The Penn State University Family Issues Symposia Series, 29–40. Mahwah, N.J.: Lawrence Erlbaum, 2006.

Barry, C.M., and K.R. Wentzel. "Friend Influence on Prosocial Behavior: The Role of Motivational Factors and Friendship Characteristics." *Developmental Psychology* 42, no. 1 (2006): 153–63.

Benson, P.L. et al. *A Fragile Foundation: The State of Developmental Assets Among American Youth.* Minneapolis: Search Institute, 1999.

Boorse, C. "Health as a Theoretical Concept." *Philosophy of Science* 44, no. 4 (1977): 542–73.

Brechwald, W.A., and M.J. Prinstein. "Beyond Homophily: A Decade of Advances in Understanding Peer Influence Processes." *Journal of Research on Adolescence* 21, no. 1 (2001): 166–79.

Buhs, E.S., G.W. Ladd, and S.L. Herald. "Peer Exclusion and Victimization: Processes that Mediate the Relation Between Peer Group Rejection and Children's Classroom Engagement and Achievement?" *Journal of Educational Psychology* 98, no. 1 (2006): 1–13.

Cassidy, J., and P.R. Shaver. *Handbook of Attachment: Theory, Research, and Clinical Applications*, 2d ed. Guilford Press, 2010.

Cillessen, A.I.I.N., and C. Borch. "Developmental Trajectories of Adolescent Popularity: A Growth Curve Modelling Analysis." *Journal of Adolescence* 29, no. 6 (2006): 935–59.

Cillessen, A.H.N. and L. Mayeux. "From Censure to Reinforcement: Developmental Changes in the Association Between Aggression and Social Status." *Child Development* 75, no. 1 (2004): 147–63.

Connolly, J., W. Furman, and R. Konarski. "The Role of Peers in the Emergence of Heterosexual Romantic Relationships in Adolescence." *Child Development* 71, no. 5 (2000): 1395–408.

Connolly, J. et al. "Mixed-gender Groups, Dating, and Romantic Relationships in Early Adolescence." *Journal of Research on Adolescence* 14, no. 2 (2004): 185–207.

Dishion, T.J., and L.D. Owen. "A Longitudinal Analysis of Friendships and Substance Use: Bidirectional Influence from Adolescence to Adulthood." *Developmental Psychology* 38, no. 4 (2002): 480–91.

Duncan, S.C. et al. "Contributions of the Social Context to the Development of Adolescent Substance Use: A Multivariate Latent Growth Modeling Approach." *Drug and Alcohol Dependence* 50, no. 1 (1998): 57–71.

Erikson, E. Identity: *Youth and Crisis*. N.Y.: W.W. Norton, Inc., 1968.

Gardner, M., and L. Steinberg. "Peer Influence on Risk Taking, Risk Preference, and Risky Decision Making in Adolescence and Adulthood: An Experimental Study." *Developmental Psychology* 41, no. 4 (2005): 625–35.

Goleman, D. *Working with Emotional Intelligence*. Bantam Books, 1998.

Grotevant, H.D., and C.R. Cooper., "Patterns of Interaction in Family Relationships and the Development of Identity Exploration in Adolescence." *Child Development* 56, no. 2 (1985): 415–28.

Guyer, A.E. et al. "Probing the Neural Correlates of Anticipated Peer Evaluation in Adolescence." *Child Development* 80, no. 4 (2009): 1000–15.

Hawkins, J.D., and R.F. Catalano. *Communities that Care: Action for Drug Abuse Prevention*. San Francisco: Jossey-Bass, 1992.

Hawkins, J.D., R.F. Catalano, and J.Y. Miller. "Risk and Protective Factors for Alcohol and Other Drug Problems in Adolescence and Early Adulthood: Implications for Substance Abuse Prevention." *Psychological Bulletin* 112, no. 1 (1992): 64–105.

Kan, M.L., S.M. McHale, and A.C. Crouter. "Parental Involvement in Adolescent Romantic Relationships: Patterns and Correlates." *Journal of Youth and Adolescence* 37, no. 2 (2008): 168–79.

Kandel, D.B. et al. "Psychiatric Disorders Associated with Substance Use Among Children and Adolescents: Findings from the Methods for the Epidemiology of Child and Adolescent Mental Disorders (MECA) Study." *Journal of Abnormal Child Psychology* 25, no. 2 (1997): 121–32.

Kroger, J., M. Martinussen, and J.E. Marcia. "Identity Status Change During Adolescence and Young Adulthood: A Meta-analysis." *Journal of Adolescence* 33, no. 5 (2010): 683–98.

Luthar, S.S., and B.E. Becker. "Privileged But Pressured? A Study of Affluent Youth." *Child Development* 73, no. 3 (2002): 1593–610.

Marcia, J.E. et al. *Ego Identity: A Handbook for Psychosocial Research*. N.Y.: Spring Verlag, 1993.

Markiewicz, D., A.B. Doyle, and M. Brendgen. "The Quality of Adolescents' Friendships: Associations with Mothers' Interpersonal Relationships, Attachments to Parents and Friends, and Prosocial Behaviors." *Journal of Adolescence* 24, no. 4 (2001): 429–45.

Masten, A.S., and J.D. Coatsworth. "The Development of Competence in Favorable and Unfavorable Environments: Lessons from Research on Successful Children." *American Psychologist* 53, no. 2 (1998): 205–20.

Mayseless, O., and M. Scharf. "Adolescents' Attachment Representations and Their Capacity for Intimacy in Close Relationships." *Journal of Research on Adolescence* 17, no. 1 (2007): 23–50.

McDonald, K.L. et al. "Girl Talk: Gossip, Friendship, and Sociometric Status." *Merrill-Palmer Quarterly* 53, no. 3 (2007): 381–411.

Nansel, T.R. et al. "Bullying Behaviors Among U.S. Youth: Prevalence and Association with Psychosocial Adjustment." *Journal of the American Medical Association* 285, no. 16 (2001): 2094–100.

Orpinas, P., and A.M. Horne. "Creating a Positive School Climate and Developing Social Competence." In *Handbook of Bullying in Schools: An International Perspective*, ed. S.R. Jimerson, S.M. Swearer, and D.L. Esperlage, 49–61. Routledge, 2005.

Parker, J.G., and S.R. Asher. "Friendship and Friendship Quality in Middle Childhood: Links with Peer Group Acceptance and Feelings of Loneliness and Social Dissatisfaction." *Developmental Psychology* 29, no. 4 (1993): 611–21.

Perren, S. et al. "Bullying in School and Cyberspace: Associations with Depressive Symptoms in Swiss and Australian Adolescents." *Child and Adolescent Psychiatry and Mental Health* 4, no. 28 (2010).

Pettit, G.S. et al. "Dimensions of Social Capital and Life Adjustment in the Transition to Early Adulthood." *International Journal of Behavioral Development* 35, no. 6 (2011): 482–89.

Pew Research Center. "Teens, Kindness, and Cruelty on Social Network Sites," 2011. *pewinternet.org/reports/2011/teens-and-social-media/part-2/section-4.aspx.*

Phinney, J.S. "Ethnic Identity in Adolescents and Adults: Review of Research." *Psychological Bulletin* 108, no. 3 (1990): 499–514.

Pittman, K., M. Irby, and T. Ferber. "Unfinished Business: Further Reflections on a Decade of Promoting Youth Development." In *Trends in Youth Development: Visions, Realities, and Challenges*, ed. P.L. Benson and K.J. Pittman, 3–50. Boston: Kluwer, 2001.

Prinstein, M.J., J. Boergers, and A. Spirito. "Adolescents' and Their Friends' Health-risk Behavior: Factors that Alter or Add to Peer Influence." *Journal of Pediatric Psychology* 26, no. 5 (2001): 287–98.

Rodkin, P.C. et al. "Heterogeneity of Popular Boys: Antisocial and Prosocial Configurations." *Developmental Psychology* 36, no. 1 (2000): 14–24.

Rose, A.J. "Co-rumination in the Friendships of Girls and Boys." *Child Development* 73, no. 6 (2002): 1830–43.

Rose, A.J., L.P. Swenson, and E.M. Waller. "Overt and Relational Aggression and Perceived Popularity: Developmental Differences in Concurrent and Prospective Relations." *Developmental Psychology* 40, no. 3 (2004): 378–87.

Sandstrom, M.J., A.H.N. Cillessen, and A. Eisenhower. "Children's Appraisal of Peer Rejection Experiences: Impact on Social and Emotional Adjustment." *Social Development* 12, no. 4 (2003): 530–0.

Story, M., D. Neumark-Sztainer, and S. French. "Individual and Environmental Influences on Adolescent Eating Behaviors." *Journal of the American Dietetic Association* 102, no. 3 (Supp) (2002): S40–S51.

Tompkins, T.L. et al. "A Closer Look at Co-rumination: Gender, Coping, Peer Functioning, and Internalizing/Externalizing Problems." *Journal of Adolescence* 34, no. 5 (2011): 801–11.

Underwood, M.K. *Social Aggression Among Girls.* Guilford Press, 2003.

Vaillancourt, T. et al. "Variation in Hypothalamic-pituitary-adrenal Axis Activity Among Bullied and Non-Bullied Children." *Aggressive Behavior* 34, no. 3 (2008): 294–305.

Vaillancourt, T. et al. "The Neurobiology of Peer Victimization and Rejection." In *International Handbook of Bullying*, ed. S.R. Jimerson, S.M. Swearer, and D.L. Espelage, 293–305. Taylor & Francis Publishers, 2010.

Chapter Five

Anderson, C., D. Keltner, and O.P. John. "Emotional Convergence Between People Over Time." *Journal of Personality and Social Psychology* 84, no. 5 (2003): 154–68.

Barchard, K.A. "Does Emotional Intelligence Assist in the Prediction of Academic Success?" *Educational and Psychological Measurement* 63, no. 5 (2003): 840–58.

Brackett, M.A. et al. "Enhancing Academic Performance and Social and Emotional Competence with the RULER Feeling Words Curriculum." *Learning and Individual Differences* 22, no. 2 (2010): 218–24.

Bryant, F.B., and J. Veroff. *Savoring: A New Model of Positive Experience*. Mahwah, N.J.: Lawrence Erlbaum Associates Publishers, 2007.

Cozolino, L. *The Neuroscience of Human Relationships: Attachment and the Developing Social Brain*. Norton Series on Interpersonal Neurobiology. W.W. Norton & Company, 2006.

Csikszentmihalyi, M. "If We Are So Rich, Why Aren't We Happy?" *American Psychologist* 54, no. 10 (1999): 821–27.

Denham, S.A. et al. "Preschool Emotional Competence: Pathway to Social Competence?" *Child Development* 74, no. 1 (2003): 238–56.

di Pellegrino, G. et al. "Understanding Motor Events: A Neurophysiological Study." Experimental Brain Research 91, no. 1 (1991): 176–80. Salovey, P., and J.D. Mayer. "Emotional Intelligence." *Imagination, Cognition, and Personality* 9, no. 3 (1990): 185–211.

Diener, E. "Subjective Well-being: The Science of Happiness and a Proposal for a National Index." *American Psychologist* 55, no. 1 (2000): 34–43.

Eisenberg, N. et al. "The Relations of Problem Behavior Status to Children's Negative Emotionality, Effortful Control, and Impulsivity: Concurrent Relations and Prediction of Change." *Developmental Psychology* 41, no. 1 (2005): 193–211.

Eisenberg, N., and M.J. Sulik. "Emotion-related Self-Regulation in Children." *Teaching of Psychology* 39, no. 1 (2012): 77-83.

Ekman, P., W. Friesen, and P. Ellsworth. *Emotion in the Human Face: Guidelines for Research and an Integration of Findings*. New York: Cambridge University Press, 1982.

Ekman, P., R.J. Davidson, and W.V. Friesen. "The Duchenne Smile: Emotional Expression and Brain Physiology II." *Journal of Personality and Social Psychology* 58 (1990): 342–53.

Evans, D.L. et al., eds. *Treating and Preventing Adolescent Mental Health Disorders: What We Know and What We Don't Know*. New York: Oxford University Press, 2005.

Frank, M.G., P. Ekman, and W.V. Friesen. "Behavioral Markers and Recognizability of the Smile of Enjoyment." *Journal of Personality and Social Psychology* 64, no. 1 (1993): 83–93.

Fredrickson, B.L. "What Good Are Positive Emotions?" *Review of General Psychology* 2, no. 3 (1998): 300–19.

Fredrickson, B.L., and C.A. Branigan "Positive Emotions Broaden the Scope of Attention and Thought-Action Repertoires." *Cognition and Emotion* 19, no. 3 (2005): 313-332.

Garner, A.S. et al. "Early Childhood Adversity, Toxic Stress, and the Role of the Pediatrician: Translating Developmental Science into Lifelong Health." *Pediatrics* 129, no. 1 (2012): 224–31.

Goleman, D. *Emotional Intelligence: Why It Can Matter More Than IQ*. New York: Bantam Books, 1995.

Goleman, D. *Social intelligence: The New Science of Human Relationships*. New York: Bantam, 2006.

Gottman, J.M. *What Predicts Divorce? The Relationship Between Marital Processes and Marital Outcomes*. Hillsdale, N.J.: Erlbaum, 1994.

Greenberg, M.T. et al. "Promoting Emotional Competence in School-aged Children: The Effects of the PATHS Curriculum." *Development and Psychopathology* 7 (1995): 117–36.

Harker, L., and D. Keltner. "Expressions of Positive Emotion in Women's College Yearbook Pictures and Their Relationship to Personality and Life Outcomes Across Adulthood." *Journal of Personality and Social Psychology* 80, no. 1 (2001): 112–24.

Izard, C.E. "Translating Emotion Theory and Research into Preventive Interventions." *Psychological Bulletin* 128, no. 5 (2002): 796–824.

Kahneman, D. "Objective Happiness." In *Well-being: The Foundations of Hedonic Psychology*, ed. D. Kahneman, E. Diener, and N. Schwarz, 3–25. New York: Russell Sage Foundation, 1999.

Kasser, T. et al. "The Relations of Maternal and Social Environments to Late Adolescents' Materialistic and Prosocial Values." *Developmental Psychology* 31, no. 6 (1995): 907–17.

Kessler, R.C., and P.S. Wang. "The Descriptive Epidemiology of Commonly Occurring Mental Disorders in the United States." *Annual Review of Public Health* 29 (2008): 115–29.

Keyes, C.L.M. "The Mental Health Continuum: From Languishing to Flourishing in Life." *Journal of Health and Social Behavior* 43, no. 2 (2002): 207–22.

———. "Mental Health in Adolescence: Is America's Youth Flourishing?" *American Journal of Orthopsychiatry* 76, no. 3 (2006): 395–402.

Konrath, S.H., E.H. O'Brien, and C. Hsing. "Changes in Dispositional Empathy in American College Students over Time: A Meta-analysis." *Personality and Social Psychology Review* 15, no. 2 (2011): 180–98.

Larson, R.W., D.M. Hansen, and G. Moneta. "Differing Profiles of Developmental Experiences Across Types of Organized Youth Activities." *Developmental Psychology* 42, no. 5 (2006): 849–63.

Lyubomirsky, S., L. King, and E. Diener. "The Benefits of Frequent Positive Affect: Does Happiness Lead to Success?" *Psychological Bulletin* 131, no. 6 (2005): 803–55.

Mayer, J.D., R.D. Roberts, and S.G. Barsade. "Human Abilities: Emotional Intelligence." *Annual Review of Psychology* 59 (2008): 507–36.

Norem, J.K. "Defensive Pessimism, Anxiety, and the Complexity of Evaluating Self-regulation." *Social and Personality Psychology Compass* 2, no. 1 (2008): 121–34.

Offer, D., and K.A. Schonert-Reichl. "Debunking the Myths of Adolescence: Findings from Recent Research." *Journal of the American Academy of Child and Adolescent Psychiatry* 31, no. 6 (1992): 1003–14.

Seligman, M.E.P., and M. Csikszentmihalyi, eds. "Positive Psychology: An Introduction." *American Psychologist* 55, no. 1 (2000): 5–14.

Seligman, M.E.P. et al. "Positive Psychology Progress: Empirical Validation of Interventions." *American Psychologist* 60, no. 5 (2005): 410–21.

———. "Positive Education: Positive Psychology and Classroom Interventions." *Oxford Review of Education* 35, no. 3 (2009): 293–311.

Todd, R.M. et al. "The Changing Face of Emotion: Age-related Patterns of Amygdala Activation to Salient Faces." *Social Cognitive and Affective Neuroscience* 6, no. 1 (2011): 12–23.

Twenge, J.M., and J.D. Foster. "Birth Cohort Increases in Narcissistic Personality Traits Among American College Students, 1982–2009." *Social Psychological and Personality Science* 1, no. 1 (2010): 99–106.

Center for Mental Health Services et al. "Mental Health: A Report of the Surgeon General." Rockville, Maryland: Center for Mental Health Services, U.S. Department of Health and Human Services, National Institute of Mental Health, 1999.

Wilson, T.D., and D.T. Gilbert. "Explaining Away: A Model of Affective Adaptation." *Perspectives on Psychological Science* 3, no. 5 (2008): 370–86.

Zins, J.E. et al. "The Scientific Base Linking Social and Emotional Learning to School Success." *Journal of Educational and Psychological Consultation* 17, nos. 2 & 3 (2004): 191–210.

Chapter Six

Bloom, B.S., ed. *Developing talent in young people.* N.Y.: Ballantine Books, 1985.

Coles, R. *The Moral Intelligence of Children: How to Raise a Moral Child.* N.Y.: Random House, 1997.

Corporation for National & Community Service. *The Health Benefits of Volunteering: A Review of Recent Research.* 2007. *nationalservice.gov/about/role_impact/performance_research.asp.*

Damon, W., ed. *Bringing in a New Era in Character Education.* Hoover Institution Press, 2002.

Danese, A., and B.X. McEwen. "Adverse Childhood Experiences, Allostasis, Allostatic Load, and Age-related Disease." *Physiology & Behavior* 106, no. 1 (2012): 29–39.

Duckworth, A.L. et al. "Grit: Perseverance and Passion for Long-term Goals." *Journal of Personality and Social Psychology* 92, no. 6 (2007): 1087–101.

Elias, M.J. et al. "Social and Emotional Learning, Moral Education, and Character Education: A Comparative Analysis and a View Toward Convergence." In *Handbook of Moral and Character Education,* ed. L.P. Nucci and D. Narvaez,. 248–66. Routledge Publishers, 2008.

Felitti, V.J. et al. "Relationship of Childhood Abuse and Household Dysfunction to Many of the Leading Causes of Death in Adults: The Adverse Childhood Experiences (ACE) Study." *American Journal of Preventive Medicine* 14, no. 4 (1998): 245–58.

Froh, J.J. et al. "The Benefits of Passion and Absorption in Activities: Engaged Living in Adolescents and Its Role in Psychological Well-being." *The Journal of Positive Psychology* 5, no. 4 (2010): 311–32.

Gillham, J. et al. "Character Strengths Predict Subjective Well-being During Adolescence." *The Journal of Positive Psychology* 6, no. 1 (2011): 31–44.

Gilligan, C. *In a Different Voice: Psychological Theory and Women's Development.* Harvard University Press, 1993.

Greenberger, E., and L. Steinberg. *When Teenagers Work: The Psychological and Social Costs of Adolescent Employment.* New York: Basic Books, 1986.

Hawkins, J.D. et al. "Effects of Social Development Intervention in Childhood Fifteen Years Later." *Archives of Pediatrics and Adolescent Medicine* 162, no. 12 (2008): 1133–41.

Kastner, L.S., and J. Wyatt. *The Launching Years: Strategies for Parenting from Senior Year to College Life.* Three Rivers Press, 2002.

Kohlberg, L. "The Development of Children's Orientations Toward a Moral Order." *Vita Humana,* University of Chicago (1063) 11-33.

Larson, R.W., D. M. Hansen, and G. Moneta. "Differing Profiles of Developmental Experiences Across Types of Organized Youth Activities." *Developmental Psychology* 42, no. 5 (2006): 849-863.

Leffert, N. et al. "Developmental Assets: Measurement and Prediction of Risk Behaviors Among Adolescents." *Applied Developmental Science* 2, no. 4 (1998): 209-230.

Luthar, S.S., and S.J. Latendresse. "Children of the Affluent: Challenges to Well-being." *Current Directions in Psychological Science* 14, no. 1 (2005): 49–53.

Masten, A.S. "Ordinary Magic: Resilience Processes in Development." *American Psychologist* 56, no. 3 (2001): 227–38.

Monahan, K.C., J.M. Lee, and L. Steinberg. "Revisiting the Impact of Part-time Work on Adolescent Adjustment: Distinguishing Between Selection and Socialization Using Propensity Score Matching." *Child Development* 82, no. 1 (2011): 96–112.

Park, N., and C. Peterson. "Moral Competence and Character Strengths Among Adolescents: The Development and Validation of the Values in Action Inventory of Strengths for Youth." *Journal of Adolescence* 29, no. 6 (2006): 891–909.

Peterson, C., and M.E.P. Seligman. *Character Strengths and Virtues: A Handbook and Classification.* New York, Washington, D.C.: American Psychological Association, Oxford University Press, 2004.

Ramey, H.L., and L. Rose-Krasnor. "Contexts of Structured Youth Activities and Positive Youth Development." *Child Development Perspectives* 6, no. 1 (2011): 85–91.

Roth, J.L., and J. Brooks-Gunn. "Youth Development Programs: Risk, Prevention, and Policy." *Journal of Adolescent Health* 32, no. 3 (2003): 170–82.

Schwartz, B. *The Paradox of Choice: Why More Is Less.* Ecco, 2004.

Toner, E. et al. "Character Strengths and Wellbeing in Adolescence: Structure and Correlates of the Values in Action Inventory of Strengths for Children." *Personality and Individual Differences* 52 (2012): 637–42.

Chapter Seven

Akers, A.Y., C.L. Holland, and J. Bost. "Interventions to Improve Parental Communication About Sex: A Systematic Review." *Pediatrics* 127, no. 3 (2011): 494–510.

Arnsten, A.F.T. "The Biology of Being Frazzled." *Science* 280, no. 5370 (1998): 1711–12.

Behringer, M. et al. "Effects of Resistance Training in Children and Adolescents: A Meta-analysis." *Pediatrics* 126, no. 5 (2010): 1199–210.

Berman, M.G., J. Jonides, and S. Kaplan. "The Cognitive Benefits of Interacting with Nature." *Psychological Science* 19, no. 12 (2008): 1207–12.

Born, J., and I. Wilhelm. "System Consolidation of Memory During Sleep." *Psychological Research* 76, no. 2 (2012): 192–203.

Brown, S., and C. Vaughan. *Play: How It Shapes the Brain, Opens the Imagination, and Invigorates the Soul.* Avery Publishers, 2009.

Centers for Disease Control, "Childhood Obesity." *cdc.gov/healthyyouth/obesity*

Cloninger, C.R. "Fostering Spirituality and Well-being in Clinical Practice." *Psychiatric Annals* 36, no. 3 (2006): 156–68.

Cotman, C.W., and N.C. Berchtold. "Exercise: A Behavioral Intervention to Enhance Brain Health and Plasticity." *Trends in Neurosciences* 25, no. 6 (2002): 295–301.

DeVore, E.R., and K.R. Ginsburg. "The Protective Effects of Good Parenting on Adolescents." *Current Opinion in Pediatrics* 17, no. 4 (2005): 460–65.

Duncan, L.G., J.D. Coatsworth, and M.T. Greenberg. "A Model of Mindful Parenting: Implications for Parent-Child Relationships and Prevention Research." *Clinical, Child and Family Psychology Review* 12, no. 3 (2009): 255–70.

Elkins, I.J. et al. "Personality Traits and the Development of Nicotine, Alcohol, and Illicit Drug Disorders: Prospective Links from Adolescence to Young Adulthood." *Journal of Abnormal Psychology* 115, no. 1 (2006): 26–39.

Fiese, B.H., and M. Schwartz. "Reclaiming the Family Table: Mealtimes and Child Health and Wellbeing." *Social Policy Report* 22, no. 4 (2008): 3–19.

Flook, L., and A.J. Fuligni. "Family and School Spillover in Adolescents' Daily Lives." *Child Development* 79, no. 3 (2008): 1017–29.

Fowler, J.H., and N.A. Christakis. "Cooperative Behavior Cascades in Human Social Networks." *Proceedings of the National Academy of Sciences* 107, no. 12 (2010): 5334-–8.

Hamer, M., and Y. Chida. "Physical Activity and Risk of Neurodegenerative Disease: A Systematic Review of Prospective Evidence." *Psychological Medicine* 39, no. 1 (2009): 3–11.

Hannley, P.P. "Back to the Future: Rethinking the Way We Eat." *The American Journal of Medicine* 125, no. 10 (2012): 947–8.

Jha, A.P., J. Krompinger, and M.J. Baime. "Mindfulness Training Modifies Subsystems of Attention." *Cognitive, Affective, & Behavioral Neuroscience* 7, no. 2 (2007): 109–19.

Johnston, L.D. et al. "Monitoring the Future: National Survey Results on Drug Use, 1975-2008." Volume I, Secondary School Students. *Publication No. 09-7402.* National Institutes of Health, 2009.

Kaiser Family Foundation. "Generation M2: Media in the Lives of 8- to 18-year-olds." 2010. *kff.org/entmedia/mh012010pkg.cfm.*

Kirkman, M., D.A. Rosenthal, and S. Feldman. "Talking to a Tiger: Fathers Reveal Their Difficulties in Communicating About Sexuality with Adolescents." *New Directions in Child and Adolescent Development* 97 (2002): 57–74.

Koenig, H.G., M.E. McCullough, and D.B. Larson. *Handbook of Religion and Health.* New York, N.Y.: Oxford University Press, 2001.

Kuo, F.E. "Parks and Other Green Environments: Essential Components of a Healthy Human Habitat." National Recreation and Park Association, 2010. *nrpa.org.*

Larun, L. et al. "Exercise in Prevention and Treatment of Anxiety and Depression Among Children and Young People." The Cochrane Library, 2009. *summaries.cochrane.org/cd004691.*

Lefcourt, H.M. "Humor." In *Handbook of Positive Psychology,* ed. C.R. Snyder and S. J. Lopez. New York, N.Y.: Oxford University Press, 2002.

Levi, J. et al. "F as in Fat: How Obesity Threatens America's Future 2012." Trust for America's Health/Robert Wood Johnson Foundation, 2012. *healthyamericans.org.*

Li, S., M.S. Treuth, and Y. Wang. "How Active Are American Adolescents and Have They Become Less Active?" *Obesity Reviews* 11, no. 12 (2010): 847–62.

Louv, R. *Last Child in the Woods: Saving Our Children from Nature-deficit Disorder.* Algonquin Books, 2008.

Mahoney, J.L., A.E. Schweder, and H. Stattin. "Structured After-school Activities as a Moderator of Depressed Mood for Adolescents with Detached Relations to Their Parents." *Journal of Community Psychology* 30, no. 1 (2002): 69–86.

Mahowald, M.W., and C.H. Schenck. "Insights from Studying Human Sleep Disorders." *Nature* 437 (2005): 1279–85.

Miller, B.C., B. Benson, and K.A. Galbraith. "Family Relationships and Adolescent Pregnancy Risk: A Research Synthesis." *Developmental Review* 21, No. 1 (2001): 1–38.

Munsey, C. "The Kids Aren't All Right: New Data from APA's Stress in America Survey Indicate Parents Don't Know What's Bothering Their Children." *Monitor on Psychology* 41, no. 1 (2010): 22–5.

Musick, K., and A. Meier. "Assessing Causality and Persistence in Associations Between Family Dinners and Adolescent Well-Being." *Journal of Marriage and Family* 74, no. 3 (2012): 476–93.

National Sleep Foundation, *sleepfoundation.org.*

Neumark-Sztainer, D.R. et al. "Shared Risk and Protective Factors for Overweight and Disordered Eating in Adolescents." *American Journal of Prevention Medicine* 33, no. 5 (2007): 359–69.

Nonnemaker, J.M., C.A. McNeely, and R.W. Blum. "Public and Private Domains of Religiosity and Adolescent Health Risk Behaviors: Evidence from the National Longitudinal Study of Adolescent Health." *Social Science & Medicine* 57, no. 11 (2003): 2049–54.

O'Donnell, L. et al. "Parenting Practices, Parents' Underestimation of Daughters' Risks, and Alcohol and Sexual Behaviors of Urban Girls." *Journal of Adolescent Health* 42, no. 5 (2008): 496–502.

Ortner, C.N.M., S.J. Kilner, and P.D. Zelazo. "Mindfulness meditation and reduced emotional interference on a cognitive task." *Motivation and Emotion* 31, no. 4 (2007): 241–83.

Owens, J.A., B.A. Belon, and P. Moss. "Impact of Delaying School Start Time on Adolescent Sleep, Mood, and Behavior." *Archives of Pediatrics and Adolescent Medicine* 164, no. 7 (2010): 608–14.

Preiss, R.W. et al., eds. *Mass Media Effects Research: Advances Through Meta-analysis.* New York, N.Y.: Routledge, 2006.

Pretty, J. et al. *Nature, Childhood, Health, and Life Pathways.* University of Essex, 2009.

Sadeh, A., R. Gruber, and A. Raviv. "The Effects of Sleep Restriction and Extension on School-age Children: What a Difference an Hour Makes." *Child Development* 74, no. 2 (2003): 444–55.

Santelli, J. et al. "Abstinence-only Education Policies and Programs: A Position Paper of the Society for Adolescent Medicine." *Journal of Adolescent Health* 38, no. 1 (2006): 83–7.

Satter, E. *Child of Mine: Feeding with Love and Good Sense.* Palo Alto: Bull Publishing, 2005.

———. *Your Child's Weight: Helping Without Harming (Birth Through Adolescence).* Kelcy Publishers, 2005.

Shapiro, S.L., and L.E. Carlson. *The Art and Science of Mindfulness: Integrating Mindfulness into Psychology and the Helping Professions.* Washington, D.C.: American Psychological Association, 2009.

Sheldrake, P. *A Brief History of Spirituality.* Wiley-Blackwell, 2007.

Singh, A. et al. "Physical Activity and Performance at School: A Systematic Review of the Literature Including a Methodological Quality Assessment." *Archives of Pediatrics and Adolescent Medicine* 166, no. 1 (2012): 49–55.

Small, G., and G. Vorgan. *iBrain: Surviving the Technological Alteration of the Modern Mind.* William Morrow, 2008.

Thompson, M., and J. Gauntlett-Gilbert. "Mindfulness with Children and Adolescents: Effective Clinical Application." *Clinical Child Psychology and Psychiatry* 13, no. 3 (2008): 395–407.

Townsend, M., and R. Weerasuriya. "Beyond Blue to Green: The Benefits of Contact with Nature for Mental Health and Well-being." Melbourne, Australia: Beyond Blue Limited, 2010.

Walsh, R. "Lifestyle and Mental Health." *American Psychologist* 66, no. 7 (2011): 579–92.

———. "Contemplative psychotherapies." In *Current psychotherapies*, ed. R.J. Corsini and D. Wedding, 9th ed., 454–501. Belmont, Calif.: Brooks/Cole, 2011.

Weis, R., and B.C. Cerankosky. "Effects of Video-game Ownership on Young Boys' Academic and Behavioral Functioning: A Randomized, Controlled Study." *Psychological Science* 21, no. 4 (2010): 463–70.

Wolfson, A.R., and M.A. Carskadon. "Sleep Schedules and Daytime Functioning in Adolescents." *Child Development* 69, no. 4 (1998): 875–87.

Zabriskie, R.B., and B.P. McCormick. "The Influences of Family Leisure Patterns on Perceptions of Family Functioning." *Family Relations* 50, no. 3 (2001): 281–9.

Index

About ParentMap

Northwest media company ParentMap (*parentmap.com*) inspires, supports, and connects a growing community of wise-minded parents by publishing intelligent, trusted and thought-leading content to equip them for their essential role as their child's first and most important teacher. ParentMap's unique social-venture business model drives its vision and day-to-day operations, ensuring that publication readers and website visitors are given the most current information related to early learning, child health and development, and parenting. In all of its work and through all of its resources and publishing channels, Parentmap is dedicated to providing outstanding editorial content, advocating for children and families, and contributing to community.

Visit us at *parentmap.com*.

Related ParentMap titles:

Getting to Calm: Cool-Headed Strategies for Parenting Tweens and Teens
By Laura S. Kastner, Ph.D., and Jennifer Wyatt

Beyond Smart: Boosting Your Child's Social, Emotional and Academic Potential
By Linda Morgan

ParentMap books are available at special discounts when purchased in bulk for premiums and sales promotions, as well as for fundraisers or educational use. Place book orders at *parentmap.com* or by calling 206-709-9026.

'cause parenting is a trip!

About the Authors

Laura S. Kastner, PH.D. is the co-author of a number of parenting books, including the acclaimed *Getting to Calm: Cool-Headed Strategies for Parenting Tweens and Teens*. She is a clinical associate professor of psychiatry and behavioral sciences at the University of Washington. Read more about Dr. Kastner at *laurakastnerphd.com*.

Kristen A. Russell is a Seattle-based journalist who has edited multiple books and publications, including *ParentMap* and *Seattle* magazine. She holds a master's degree in journalism from the University of California at Berkeley, and is certified in Montessori education.